Questions & Answers
Intellectual Property

Carolina Academic Press
Questions & Answers Series

Questions & Answers: Administrative Law,
Third Edition
Linda D. Jellum, Karen A. Jordan

Questions & Answers: Antitrust
Shubha Ghosh

Questions & Answers: Bankruptcy, Second Edition
Mary Jo Wiggins

Questions & Answers: Business Associations,
Second Edition
Douglas M. Branson

Questions & Answers: Civil Procedure,
Fourth Edition
William V. Dorsaneo, III, Elizabeth Thornburg

Questions & Answers: Constitutional Law,
Third Edition
Paul E. McGreal, Linda S. Eads, Charles W. Rhodes

Questions & Answers: Contracts, Second Edition
Scott J. Burnham

Questions & Answers: Copyright Law,
Second Edition
Dave Fagundes, Robert C. Lind

Questions & Answers: Criminal Law,
Fourth Edition
Emily Marcus Levine, Paul Marcus

Questions & Answers: Criminal Procedure—
Police Investigation, Third Edition
Neil P. Cohen, Michael J. Benza, Wayne A. Logan

Questions & Answers: Criminal Procedure—
Prosecution and Adjudication, Third Edition
Neil P. Cohen, Michael J. Benza, Wayne A. Logan

Questions & Answers: Environmental Law
Dru Stevenson

Questions & Answers: Evidence, Fourth Edition
Paul C. Giannelli

Questions & Answers: Family Law, Third Edition
Mark Strasser

Questions & Answers: Federal Estate & Gift
Taxation, Third Edition
James M. Delaney, Elaine Hightower Gagliardi

Questions & Answers: Federal Income Tax,
Second Edition
James M. Delaney

Questions & Answers: Intellectual Property,
Third Edition
Gary Myers, Lee Ann Wheelis Lockridge

Questions & Answers: International Law
Rebecca Bratspies

Questions & Answers: Patent Law
Cynthia M. Ho

Questions & Answers: Payment Systems,
Second Edition
Timothy R. Zinnecker

Questions & Answers: Professional Responsibility,
Fourth Edition
Patrick Emery Longan

Questions & Answers: Property, Second Edition
John Copeland Nagle

Questions & Answers: Remedies
Rachel M. Janutis, Tracy A. Thomas

Questions & Answers: Secured Transactions,
Third Edition
Bruce A. Markell, Timothy R. Zinnecker

Questions & Answers: Taxation
of Business Entities
Kristofer C. Neslund, Nancy G. Neslund

Questions & Answers: The First Amendment,
Third Edition
Russell L. Weaver, William D. Araiza

Questions & Answers: Torts, Fourth Edition
Anita Bernstein

Questions & Answers: Trademark and
Unfair Competition
Vince F. Chiappetta

Questions & Answers: Wills, Trusts, and Estates,
Third Edition
Thomas M. Featherston, Jr.

Questions & Answers
Intellectual Property

Multiple-Choice and Short-Answer
Questions and Answers

THIRD EDITION

Gary Myers

EARL F. NELSON PROFESSOR OF LAW
UNIVERSITY OF MISSOURI SCHOOL OF LAW

Lee Ann Wheelis Lockridge

DAVID WESTON ROBINSON PROFESSOR OF LAW AND THE
McGLINCHEY STAFFORD PROFESSOR OF LAW
LOUISIANA STATE UNIVERSITY PAUL M. HEBERT LAW CENTER

CAROLINA ACADEMIC PRESS
Durham, North Carolina

Names: Myers, Gary, author. | Lockridge, Lee Ann W., author.
Title: Questions & answers : intellectual property / by Gary Myers, Lee Ann
    W. Lockridge.
Description: Third edition. | Durham, North Carolina : Carolina Academic
    Press, LLC, [2020] | Series: The questions & answers series | Includes
    index.
Identifiers: LCCN 2019056176 | ISBN 9781531015985 (paperback) | ISBN
    9781531015992 (ebook)
Subjects: LCSH: Intellectual property--United States--Examinations,
    questions, etc. | Intellectual property--United States--Miscellanea. |
    LCGFT: Study guides.
Classification: LCC KF2980 .M94 2020 | DDC 346.7304/8--dc23
LC record available at https://lccn.loc.gov/2019056176

Carolina Academic Press
700 Kent Street
Durham, North Carolina 27701
Telephone (919) 489-7486
Fax (919) 493-5668
www.cap-press.com

Printed in the United States of America

Contents

Introduction

The questions and answers in this book cover the broad subject of "intellectual property" in a comprehensive way, targeted to an introductory or survey course. All of the major topics in this fascinating area of law are included—namely, trademark, the right of publicity, trade secret, patent, and copyright—and the coverage has been updated with major changes in the law through July 2019. The key aspects of trademark, patent, and copyright law are systematically addressed using the following organization—subject matter & validity, ownership & duration of rights, infringement & remedies, and defenses & limitations.

Aside from this legal framework, however, it is important to know that intellectual property covers an amazing array of varied creative endeavor. That is because intellectual property law has an impact on the most dynamic activities and enterprises in today's interconnected world—movies, music, the Internet, social media, inventive activity, business franchises, and entrepreneurship. If you can answer or at least understand the questions and answers in this book, you are ready to begin a journey into what we think is the most interesting area of law available to us today.

Each of the questions in this book has an answer that we believe—based on many years of study, practice, teaching, writing, and consulting work in the field—is superior to the other possible answers. We hope that our explanation of each question will shed some light on your understanding of this field. But keep in mind that intellectual property is one of the most debated areas of law that you will ever encounter; this means that strong opinions run deep in this field, and there is room for disagreement about some of the topics addressed. Nevertheless, we have endeavored to offer a clear statement of the law as it exists today.

The book begins with 161 multiple-choice and short answer questions divided by subject area, such as trademark or patent, and then for trademark, patent, and copyright, the questions are sub-divided by type of issue being addressed. These 161 questions are paired with detailed answers and explanations. The book also contains a 75-question practice "final examination," again followed by complete answers.

A few words about citations and editing: Many or most legal propositions in the "answer" portion of this book are supported by at least one or two citations to statutes, case law, books, or articles. We have attempted to provide these important citations without cluttering the book with long string citations. Most quotations have had internal citations and footnotes omitted without specific reference to these changes in the citations. Once again, the goal is to have a readable but authoritative introduction to the law of intellectual property.

As noted above, this third edition of this book is current as of July 2019. If you encounter any development after this date, please keep in mind that the law is ever changing. This disclaimer is more important in the field of intellectual property than it is in most areas of law because there are few fields in which changes are so dramatic and so frequent. It is this dynamic feature which convinces us that there is no more exciting area of law than intellectual property in which to study, write, or practice.

With our best wishes,

Gary Myers
Columbia, Missouri

Lee Ann W. Lockridge
Baton Rouge, Louisiana

About the Authors

Gary Myers is Earl F. Nelson Professor of Law at the University of Missouri School of Law. He served a term as the dean of the Law School from 2012–2016. Before joining the faculty at Missouri in 2012, he was a member of the faculty at the University of Mississippi School of Law for 23 years. He also practiced law in Atlanta and served as a law clerk to Judge Gerald Tjoflat of the United States Court of Appeals for the Eleventh Circuit.

Lee Ann Wheelis Lockridge is the David Weston Robinson Professor of Law and the McGlinchey Stafford Professor of Law at the Louisiana State University Paul M. Hebert Law Center, where she has been a faculty member since 2005. Before joining the LSU faculty, she taught for one year as a Visiting Assistant Professor at the University of Cincinnati College of Law and practiced intellectual property law for five years at Thompson & Knight in Dallas, Texas. She also served as a judicial clerk Judge Eugene E. Siler of the United States Court of Appeals for the Sixth Circuit.

Professors Myers and Lockridge, along with Professor Mary LaFrance (University of Nevada at Las Vegas) and Emeritus Professor David Lange (Duke University), are co-authors of an intellectual property case book, INTELLECTUAL PROPERTY, CASES AND MATERIALS (5th ed. West Academic 2018).

Questions

Trademark & Unfair Competition Law— Subject Matter & Validity

1. Which of the following statements most accurately describes the policy foundations of U.S. trademark law?

   (A) preventing consumer confusion as to source or affiliation in the marketplace while protecting the goodwill and reputation of trademark owners

   (B) preventing consumer confusion as to source or affiliation in the marketplace while promoting competition in the marketplace for goods and services

   (C) protecting the goodwill and reputation of trademark owners while promoting competition in the marketplace for goods and services

   (D) protecting goodwill and reputation of trademark owners by avoiding consumer confusion about source or affiliation while promoting competition in the marketplace

2. The source of Congress's authority to enact the Lanham Act (trademark law) and provide for federal trademark rights is:

   (A) the Commerce Clause

   (B) the Intellectual Property Clause

   (C) the Necessary and Proper Clause

   (D) the First Amendment

3. NBC, or the National Broadcasting Company, is a television network currently owned and broadcast by a subsidiary of Comcast. NBC primarily offers news and entertainment services in connection with the NBC name and logo, which is a stylized peacock in several colors. NBC also sells, however, a limited range of products bearing the marks in a few retail locations, such as the t-shirts, caps, and magnets it sells at stores near its facility in Rockefeller Center in New York and at the Universal Studios theme parks. Hundreds of products bearing the marks are given away daily to persons in the studio audience of certain shows, and to those waiting outside of other studios, such as the "Today Show" studio in New York.

   Which of the following most accurately describes NBC's position with respect to obtaining registered protection for its NBC name and logo mark?

    (A) NBC can seek trademark protection for the mark as used on the goods it sells, as well as service mark protection for the mark as used in connection with its news and entertainment business.

    (B) NBC can seek certification mark protection for the mark as used on the goods it sells, as well as service mark protection for the mark as used in connection with its news and entertainment business.

    (C) NBC can obtain either trademark protection for the mark as used on the goods or service mark protection for the mark as used in connection with its news and entertainment business, but it must elect between the two forms of protection.

    (D) NBC can obtain service mark protection for the mark as used in connection with its news and entertainment business, but it cannot obtain trademark protection for the mark as used on the goods because they are merely promotional.

4. The letters "NSF," in all capital letters and placed within a circle (where the letters originally stood for National Sanitation Foundation but now are simply used as part of the entity name "NSF International"), can be found on a variety of products, including manufacturing equipment, ingredients, and the like. The "NSF-in-a-circle" mark is used to distinguish a product that has been tested by and determined to meet the standards of NSF International, an independent product testing and inspection organization.

Given these facts, categorize this "NSF" mark under the Lanham Act. It is a:

    (A) certification mark

    (B) collective mark

    (C) service mark

    (D) trademark

5. What is a collective mark?

Answer:

6. What is the meaning and significance of a generic term in trademark law?

Answer:

7. Explain the meaning of an "arbitrary" trademark.

Answer:

8. Explain the meaning of a "fanciful" trademark.

Answer:

9. How is a trademark term that is a surname treated for distinctiveness and trademark protection purposes? Compare it to other marks on the spectrum of distinctiveness. For example, consider "Heinz" when used for ketchup or other condiment products.

   (A) Surnames are treated the same as generic terms, meaning they are never protected.

   (B) Surnames are treated the same as descriptive marks, meaning they require proof of acquired distinctiveness for protection.

   (C) Surnames are treated the same as arbitrary or suggestive marks, meaning they do not require proof of acquired distinctiveness for protection, but they might be reused by other persons in different contexts.

   (D) Surnames are treated the same as fanciful marks, meaning they do not require proof of acquired distinctiveness for protection, and it is highly unlikely that another person could reuse them in a different context.

10. The trademark term "Nikon" when used for cameras and related products is:

   (A) descriptive

   (B) suggestive

   (C) arbitrary

   (D) fanciful

11. The trademark term "Jaguar" when used for automobiles is:

   (A) descriptive

   (B) suggestive

   (C) arbitrary

   (D) fanciful

12. The trademark term "Penguin" for paperback books and a book publishing company is:

    (A) generic

    (B) descriptive

    (C) suggestive

    (D) arbitrary

13. The trademark term "Fresh Finds" for a chain of grocery stores featuring fresh produce, meats, fish, and deli products, but also selling packaged and frozen foods, is:

    (A) generic

    (B) descriptive

    (C) suggestive

    (D) arbitrary

14. In light of the governing statutory regime as well as case law through 2019, which of the following marks are precluded from federal registration on the Principal Register?

    (A) disparaging marks

    (B) immoral marks

    (C) scandalous marks

    (D) none of the above

15. Consider the ability to protect the color green as a trademark for chewable vitamins for adults (that is, the vitamin tablets are themselves are green in color). The vitamins have also been flavored with mint to make them more palatable.

    The application to protect the green color as a mark for chewable vitamins that are mint flavored would likely be considered:

    (A) descriptive, and protectable only upon a showing of secondary meaning

    (B) suggestive, and protectable without a showing of secondary meaning

    (C) arbitrary, and protectable without a showing of secondary meaning

    (D) unprotectable on grounds of functionality (i.e., aesthetically functional)

16. When is product packaging trade dress protectable under federal law? Consider the required trade dress strength or level of distinctiveness and complete the following sentence.

    Product packaging trade dress:

    (A) is always inherently distinctive and is protectable regardless of secondary meaning or acquired distinctiveness

(B) is never inherently distinctive; it is protectable only upon a showing of secondary meaning or acquired distinctiveness

(C) may be either non-inherently distinctive (and therefore protectable only upon a showing of secondary meaning or acquired distinctiveness) or inherently distinctive (protectable regardless of secondary meaning or acquired distinctiveness), depending on the circumstances, just like an ordinary word or design mark

(D) is protected only when it is famous because it is only protectable under a dilution theory

17. When is product configuration or product design trade dress protectable under federal law? Consider the required trade dress strength or level of distinctiveness and complete the following sentence.

Product configuration or product design trade dress:

(A) is always inherently distinctive and is protectable regardless of secondary meaning or acquired distinctiveness

(B) is never inherently distinctive; it is protectable only upon a showing of secondary meaning or acquired distinctiveness

(C) may be either non-inherently distinctive (and therefore protectable only upon a showing of secondary meaning or acquired distinctiveness) or inherently distinctive (protectable regardless of secondary meaning or acquired distinctiveness), depending on the circumstances, just like an ordinary word or design mark

(D) is protected only when it is famous because it is only protectable under a dilution theory

18. What is the connection between trademark incontestability and the concepts of genericism, descriptiveness, and acquired distinctiveness?

Answer:

Trademark & Unfair Competition Law— Ownership & Duration

19. After selecting a mark for a new product, what is the most secure way for a would-be trademark owner to establish protectable trademark rights under the common law?

    (A) register the claim of rights under state law, usually with the state trademark or secretary of state's office

    (B) successfully sue a competitor under the common law of unfair competition

    (C) use the mark in the marketplace on the goods, or on the packaging, labels, or tags

    (D) use the mark with a "TM" (or "tm") or similar designation in published advertisements for the goods, such as print advertisements

20. Under the Lanham Act, how can priority as to trademark ownership be attained over others? Select the best answer from those provided.

    (A) use of the mark in commerce only

    (B) use of the mark in commerce or filing a federal application with a bona fide intent to use (regardless of whether actual use in commerce ever takes place)

    (C) use of the mark in commerce or filing a federal application with bona fide intent to use (upon following the proper procedures to establish actual use in commerce)

    (D) use of the mark in commerce or obtaining a foreign trademark registration, if the United States and the foreign country are in the same international trademark treaty

21. Company A begins using a trademark in Illinois, Indiana, and Wisconsin in 2016. Company B begins using the same trademark to sell the same product state-wide in Texas in 2018. Company A files to federally register its trademark rights in 2019 and receives its registration in 2020. Neither company is aware of the other until 2025.

    Which of the following statements most accurately describes the situation?

    (A) Company A obtains exclusive rights to the trademark nationwide, by virtue of its first use followed by federal registration. Company B has no continuing rights.

(B) Company A obtains exclusive rights to the trademark in all states but Texas. Company B has exclusive rights in Texas.

(C) Company A obtains exclusive rights to the trademark in all states but Texas; its rights in Texas are nonexclusive. Company B may elect to continue using the mark in Texas, but it must share or overlap there with Company A.

(D) Company A obtains exclusive rights to the trademark only in Illinois, Indiana, and Wisconsin. Company B obtains exclusive rights in Texas. Company A's registration is invalidated by B's area of priority, making rights in other states available to the first of A or B to use the mark there.

22. Company A selects the mark CRICKET on March 15 to be used for handcrafted children's plush animal toys, test-markets it before a focus group on May 15, and begins on September 1 of that year to make use of the mark on its products in New York and the New England states. Company B, coincidentally and in good faith, also selects the mark CRICKET to be used for children's soft toys, such as those for babies. Company B selects the mark on June 1 and files a federal intent-to-use trademark application for the mark on July 1. Company B begins to make use of the mark on the goods in commerce on April 1 of the following year, after it receives USPTO approval of its application. B's use consists of selling the marked goods in retail stores in California, Oregon, Washington, and Nevada.

Who should own the rights to the CRICKET trademark under the Lanham Act?

(A) Company A, because it was the first to come up with the trademark.

(B) Company A, because it was the first to use the trademark in commerce.

(C) Company B, because it filed the intent-to-use application before Company A used the mark and ultimately received the notice of allowance.

(D) Both Company A and Company B. A court should equitably divide the rights based on the geographic market areas.

23. Which of the following statements most accurately describes the term of protection for trademarks under the Lanham Act?

(A) Trademarks are limited to a 10-year term.

(B) Trademarks can be perpetual as long as the registration is renewed.

(C) Trademarks can be perpetual as long as they have not become generic or lost secondary meaning.

(D) Trademarks can be perpetual as long as they have not been abandoned or become generic.

24. A trademark becomes "incontestable" under the Lanham Act when:

(A) it is continuously used in interstate commerce for five years and an affidavit of incontestability has been filed

(B)   it is continuously used in interstate commerce for ten years and an affidavit of incontestability has been filed

(C)   it has been registered under federal law for five years and continuously used in interstate commerce for five years

(D)   it has been registered under federal law for five years and continuously used in interstate commerce for five years, and an affidavit of incontestability has been filed

Trademark & Unfair Competition Law— Infringement & Remedies

25. What is the basic standard for infringement of a trademark, and what are the typical elements of the test that courts use to analyze whether a trademark owner has proven infringement?

Answer:

26. As explored by the question above, courts use a test for trademark infringement that applies a number of elements. According to the federal circuit courts, this multi-element analysis means that an issue of trademark infringement presents:

   (A) a question of fact

   (B) a question of law

   (C) a mixed question of law and fact

   (D) circuits are split, with some courts adopting (A) and others adopting (C)

27. Which of the following statements best describes the role of proof of actual confusion in trademark cases?

   (A) Actual confusion must be proven in order for the trademark owner to recover.

   (B) Actual confusion is not required, but if it is proven it is highly persuasive evidence of a likelihood of confusion and will carry great weight.

   (C) Actual confusion is easily shown and is given the same weight as other factors.

   (D) Actual confusion is one of the less important factors in a likelihood of confusion analysis since it is hard to prove.

28. How can a trademark plaintiff prove actual confusion?

Answer:

29. A trademark owner has not obtained federal registration for its trademark. Which of the following statements most accurately describes the trademark owner's ability to obtain relief under the Lanham Act?

    (A) The trademark owner has all the same potential claims and rights as owners who have registered a trademark.

    (B) The trademark owner can bring suit under section 43(a) of the Lanham Act, but is limited to injunctive relief (i.e., cannot recover monetary relief).

    (C) The trademark owner cannot bring suit under section 43(a) until it has registered the trademark, but can bring suit upon obtaining registration.

    (D) The trademark owner can bring suit for all relief available under section 43(a), but does not have other statutory rights that a registered trademark holder would have.

30. Federal trademark law contains various remedial provisions, including injunctive relief and monetary awards. The frequency varies, however, for awarding the two. Which of the following statements most accurately describes the approach taken by federal trademark law regarding the frequency of awarding injunctive relief and monetary awards?

    (A) The presumptive form of relief is injunctive, and monetary awards are rarely available.

    (B) The presumptive form of relief is monetary, and injunctions are rarely available.

    (C) Injunctive relief is frequently granted, and monetary awards are only available upon a showing of bad faith.

    (D) Injunctive relief is frequently granted, and monetary awards are usually available upon a showing of bad faith or actual harm.

31. What is corrective advertising, and what is its role in trademark law and litigation?

Answer:

32. In what circumstances can attorney's fees be obtained in trademark litigation?

Answer:

33. The strongest theory for infringement of a long-standing and widely recognized trademark such as the Nike "swoosh" design mark (below), when used by someone in a totally unrelated field of enterprise, such as a food truck selling tacos, is:

    (A) unfair competition under state law

(B) federal trademark infringement under section 32 or section 43(a)

(C) dilution by tarnishment

(D) dilution by blurring

34. Explain the standard for a famous mark under federal dilution law and how that standard relates to the statutory factors for fame.

Answer:

35. What is the difference between claims for trademark dilution by tarnishment and trademark dilution by blurring?

Answer:

Trademark & Unfair Competition Law— Defenses & Limitations

36. On which of the grounds listed below may the validity of an incontestable registration be challenged by an accused infringer?

    On the grounds that the mark in question is:

    (A) generic (only)

    (B) generic or descriptive (without secondary meaning)

    (C) generic or functional

    (D) generic, descriptive (without secondary meaning), or functional

37. Which of the following would be a basis for arguing that a trademark owner's mark is invalid because it has been abandoned?

    (A) assignment in gross

    (B) naked licensing

    (C) nonuse with intent not to resume use

    (D) all of the above

38. Company A is using the mark "Sweet" on athleticwear for women, and it owns an incontestable federal trademark registration for the mark. Company B begins selling decorated cell phone cases under the mark "Sweet." Company B argues that "Sweet" is a descriptive term that it is using fairly and in its descriptive sense—with the meaning of "sweet" being a more modern usage meaning "awesome," or perhaps "very good or appealing."

    Explain whether Company B can use the statutory fair use defense to an infringement claim brought by Company A.

Answer:

39. Company A wishes to refer to Company B's competing product in a television commercial wherein Company A is comparing the performance and desirability of its product to the performance and desirability of Company B's product.

Which of the following statements captures the best advice to give to Company A?

(A) Do not use Company B's name in the commercial as it will either constitute trademark dilution by blurring or by tarnishment, depending on the phrasing used.

(B) Do not use Company B's name in the commercial as it will constitute trademark infringement through likelihood of confusion.

(C) Company B's name can be used in the commercial as comparative advertising, even if the advertisement is misleading, as long as no false statements of fact are made.

(D) Company B's name can be used in the commercial as comparative advertising, but only if the advertisement is truthful and non-misleading.

40. A company purchases used tablet computers with broken or cracked touch screens, puts new screens into them, and sells them in mass quantities as used devices under the original brand names (e.g., Apple, Microsoft, Samsung, etc.).

Which of the following statements captures the best advice to give to the company?

(A) The tablets can be sold as used products under the original brand names with no additional markings, as this is a lawful repair of the products.

(B) The tablets can be sold under the original brand names as long as they are clearly marked as reconditioned and assuming that replacing the screens is not considered unlawful reconstruction.

(C) The tablets cannot be sold under the original brand names, because there is no label or marking that could be added to avoid likely consumer confusion.

(D) The tablets cannot be sold under the original brand names, even with added labels, due to the doctrine of reverse confusion; consumers would be confused about approval of the repairs by the original source.

Right of Publicity Law & Protection of Ideas

41. Which of the following would *not* be actionable under the right of publicity, if it were commercially used without the individual's consent?

    (A) a sound-alike performance closely imitating an individual's voice

    (B) a look-alike performance closely imitating an individual's appearance

    (C) a signature of an individual, who is a private citizen

    (D) personal information in a book written by a famous individual

42. Select the best characterization for how the right of publicity can be viewed:

    (A) as a commercial right only

    (B) as a personal privacy right only

    (C) as both a personal privacy right and a commercial right

    (D) as both a personal privacy right and a federal constitutional right

43. Does the right of publicity survive the death of the person whose name or likeness was used for commercial purposes?

Answer:

44. An ordinary citizen (i.e., not a celebrity) is photographed while walking down a public street. The person's image is then used in a cellular phone advertisement without the citizen's consent. What is the best intellectual property claim to assert in this situation?

    (A) copyright

    (B) false endorsement

    (C) right of publicity

    (D) trade secret

45. An artist specializing in sports-related subject matter depicts images of a famous professional basketball player in a series of paintings and limited-edition fine art prints. The paintings and prints include the athlete in his best-known "posture," which was flying toward the goal in the air with one arm up and his legs apart but relatively straight. This posture is well-known enough

that the player had licensed his rights to be used in silhouette by an athleticwear company as a trademark. The paintings and prints show him in a variety of settings in which the player won professional honors, such as the NBA Finals and the NCAA Final Four. The artwork therefore includes depictions of various arenas, other players and coaches in the background, and crowds of fans. The basketball player brings a right of publicity claim, and the artist argues that her artwork is exempt from the publicity tort, that the First Amendment freedom of expression protects her from liability, and that the basketball player waived his right of publicity by participating in the events depicted. Predict the likely outcome and reasoning.

The court will likely:

(A) find a clear violation of the right of publicity, because the First Amendment does not apply to right of publicity claims

(B) find that the right of publicity might be violated on these facts, but that First Amendment free expression considerations outweigh the tort claim, given the transformative and creative nature of the works, barring relief

(C) find no violation of the right of publicity because artworks are exempt from the scope of the tort claim

(D) find no violation of the right of publicity because professional athletes implicitly waive their right of publicity when they agree to participate in large, well-attended public events

46. Which of the following legal theories could not be used to protect an idea?

(A) quasi-contract or unjust enrichment

(B) express contract

(C) implied contract

(D) copyright law

47. A scriptwriter, D, with connections in the entertainment industry, decides to discuss a script and idea for a television series with another scriptwriter, C, who is a native of the city in which the series would be set. D's planned television series is about several deep-undercover police officers who are all in therapy to deal with the stress of their careers. The main characters of the series discover one another's identities while in a group therapy session — problems ensue. After some conversation, C suggests some locations, stories, and potential plot lines that are in the public domain or the public record, and she introduces D to some retired members of the municipal police force of the city in question. After C refuses payment for her time, D says she will "take care of" C if she gets the series produced. The series is produced and is highly acclaimed, but C is never compensated in any amount.

What result when C sues D for misappropriation of ideas?

(A) The misappropriation claim is successful because of the promise to "take care of" the plaintiff.

(B) The misappropriation claim is successful because D's script became a highly successful television series and the plaintiff is entitled to a share of the profit based on principles of equity.

(C) The misappropriation claim fails because any agreement to compensate for ideas must be in writing.

(D) The misappropriation claim fails because the plaintiff's contributions are not novel and therefore do not support such a claim.

Trade Secret Law

48. Can a customer list, consisting of names, addresses, telephone numbers, and the name and title of the primary sales contact, be protected as a trade secret under the Uniform Trade Secrets Act (UTSA) and federal civil Defend Trade Secrets Act (DTSA)? Why or why not?

Answer:

49. *Note: The next two questions use the same fact pattern:*

A restaurant that is a joint venture between an executive chef and her business partner adds to its menu a chile and fruit salsa with a surprising blend of spices mixed in with the chiles and fruit. After a year on the menu, the new salsa remains incredibly popular, and no other restaurant in the area has copied it yet. The key to the flavor is not simply the ingredient list but also the order and manner in which the spices are toasted and ground together. The executive chef decided from the start to keep the recipe a secret in order to avoid having her new dish leave the restaurant along with one of the restaurant's many short-term employees. She has written down the recipe only three times, and all three are marked "confidential." One copy is at her home, stored in the files she keeps for the restaurant. A second copy is in her business partner's files for the restaurant. The third copy stays at the restaurant, but only the sous chef (the second-in-command chef) is allowed to see it. He has been told it is a trade secret. The executive chef makes the spice blend at her house so that the other employees cannot see the spices used, the proportions used, or the method of preparation. The rest of the salsa-preparation process takes place at the restaurant because it requires fresh ingredients, but the sous chef is in charge of the entire process.

Could a court find the salsa recipe to be a trade secret of the restaurant within the meaning of the UTSA and DTSA?

(A) Yes, because the recipe is a type of formula, and the restaurant has kept it a complete secret from competitors up to this point in time, which means its efforts have been reasonable.

(B) Yes, because the recipe is kept relatively secret, and it is subject to reasonable efforts at secrecy even though there are no technological measures, locks, contracts, or other heightened protections.

(C) No, because although the recipe is kept relatively secret, the efforts being taken are not reasonable because there are no technological measures, locks, contracts, or other heightened protections.

(D) No, because a basic food recipe, as opposed to an industrial-scale manufacturing formula or process, is not the kind of formula or other business or technical information that is the proper subject matter for trade secret protection.

50. *Note: This question uses the fact pattern from the prior question.*

Assume for the purposes of this question (although not for purposes of the last question!) that (1) the salsa recipe in Question 49 was a trade secret of the restaurant and would be protected under the UTSA or DTSA, and (2) the sous chef moved out of the state to work as a chef at another restaurant, where he then began preparing the same chile and fruit salsa, which the second restaurant then placed on its menu and sold.

Using only these facts, would either the sous chef or the other restaurant be liable for misappropriation of the trade secret under the UTSA and DTSA? Why or why not?

(A) Both would be liable for misappropriation. The sous chef would be because he is using the secret for the benefit of the second restaurant in breach of a duty to the first restaurant to limit the use of the information, and the second restaurant would be because it is using the recipe after having derived it through a person who owed a duty of confidentiality and a duty to limit the use of the recipe.

(B) The sous chef would be liable, but the second restaurant would not be liable. The sous chef would be liable because he is using the secret for the benefit of the second restaurant in breach of a duty to the first restaurant to limit the use of the information, but the second restaurant would not be, and can use the recipe, because it has no reason to know it derived the recipe through a person who owed a duty of confidentiality or a duty to limit use of the recipe.

(C) The sous chef would not be liable, but the second restaurant would be liable. The sous chef would not be because he is not directly benefiting from the use of the recipe at the second restaurant, but the second restaurant would be because it is profiting from its use of the recipe and should have known that it was derived from the sous chef's work at the first restaurant.

(D) Neither would be liable for misappropriation. The sous chef would not be because he is not directly benefiting from the use of the recipe at the second restaurant, and the second restaurant would not be, and can use the recipe, because it has no reason to know it derived the recipe through a person who owed a duty of confidentiality or a duty to limit use of the recipe.

51. Green Co. is about to enter a bid for a construction project. The bidding is done by secret bid, with the contract going to the lowest bidder. If an employee of Green Co. "leaks" information about the amount of Green Co.'s bid to a competitor, who then undercuts Green Co.

and gets the contract, does Green Co. have any civil legal remedy in most states or under federal law?

(A) Probably yes, against both the employee and the competitor, because the bid is protected as a trade secret as providing an actual or potential advantage.

(B) Probably yes, but only against the employee, because the bid is protected as a trade secret; the competitor, however, can freely make use of this information.

(C) Probably no, because the bid is not protected as a trade secret; it violates the rule that "one time" pieces of information do not qualify as trade secrets.

(D) Almost definitely no, because the bid is almost certainly not protected as a trade secret, because trade secret information is almost always a formula or other technical information.

52. How long does trade secret protection last?

(A) indefinitely, as long as the requisite secrecy and competitive advantage exist

(B) perpetually, regardless of whether the information remains secret

(C) for 20 years from the date of first use

(D) for as long as it takes any one competitor to reverse engineer the subject matter of the trade secret

53. What is reverse engineering, and is it a violation of trade secret law? What about use of the information learned as a result of the reverse engineering—could such use misappropriate a trade secret?

Answer:

54. What are reasonable secrecy measures, and why are they relevant in trade secret law?

Answer:

55. What is a breach of confidence, and why is it relevant in trade secret law?

Answer:

56. Using a random password generator to identify an employee's confidential password in order to gain access to a competitor's computer system to obtain confidential information is likely to be actionable as:

(A) patent infringement

    (B) trade secret misappropriation based on breach of confidence

    (C) trade secret misappropriation based on improper means

    (D) none of the above

57. Garden hoses used for watering are made of several layers of different materials, including an outer layer that is tough enough for durability but thin enough for flexibility. A manufacturer of garden hoses spent about 10 months developing an innovative manufacturing technique for bonding the layers of various materials together. The new technique was faster than prior methods, and the manufacturer decided to keep it a secret, which it determined was realistic since the gardening supply business is not rife with economic espionage. The garden hose it made sold very well, particularly at large "big box" home supply stores. Unfortunately, an employee's departure about two years later disrupted the product's success. Just four months after the employee resigned, a competitor began selling a slightly less expensive garden hose that the original manufacturer suspected was produced using its "new" technique; the manufacturer also noticed that its sales at "big box" stores, where the products directly competed, began to slow down shortly thereafter. The manufacturer sued the competitor for misappropriation of its trade secret.

Given these facts, if the plaintiff manufacturer succeeds in proving misappropriation of its trade secret by the competitor, what remedies should be available to it under the UTSA or DTSA?

    (A) An injunction barring further use of this manufacturing information for at least six months because defendant obtained a head start on developing the technique of at least that long, and monetary damages for the lost sales during the head-start period because the defendant also caused lost sales that are compensable.

    (B) An injunction barring further use of this manufacturing information for at least six months because the defendant obtained a head start on developing the technique of at least that long, but no monetary damages for the lost sales because any diminished sales are not compensable.

    (C) No injunction barring further use of this manufacturing information because secrecy of the information cannot be reestablished after it is lost, but monetary damages for the lost sales during the head-start period of at least six months because the defendant caused lost sales that are compensable.

    (D) A strict injunction against similar behavior in the future, but no injunction barring use of this information because secrecy of the information cannot be reestablished after it is lost, and no monetary damages because any diminished sales are not compensable.

Patent Law—Subject Matter & Validity

58. What are three fundamental requirements for a valid utility patent?

    (A) novelty, usefulness, and distinctness

    (B) novelty, nonobviousness, and distinctness

    (C) novelty, nonobviousness, and usefulness

    (D) novelty, nonobviousness, and ornamentality

59. What are three fundamental requirements for a valid design patent?

    (A) novelty, usefulness, and distinctness

    (B) novelty, nonobviousness, and distinctness

    (C) novelty, nonobviousness, and usefulness

    (D) novelty, nonobviousness, and ornamentality

60. Review the following facts and consider the exclusions to patentability under the Supreme Court's section 101 caselaw.

    Maintaining nitrogen levels in the soil is well known to be important to the growth of all fruit and vegetable plants; research has also demonstrated that different plants or crops prefer different levels of nitrogen. Many farmers apply fertilizer, whether organic or inorganic in type, to boost nitrogen levels, and they add more when a crop is known to "want" or use more. Many farmers also know that instead of constantly adding fertilizer, it is possible to test the soil to measure the level of nitrogen, and they know that there are recommended amounts of fertilizer to add per square meter of soil to boost the nitrogen level by a specified amount—yet most farmers do not test and then adjust precisely. This practice is known to result in the overuse of fertilizer, which then runs off into the environment. This is a matter of priorities—fertilizer overuse and runoff is simply not a priority for many farmers in light of the various costs and benefits involved.

    An applicant for a patent operates a large organic strawberry farm. She decides that in order to minimize the environmental externalities of her farm (nitrogen runoff) and her fertilizer costs (organic fertilizer tends to cost more than inorganic), she will install a nitrogen monitoring probe. This probe provides daily readings to her, and she ultimately notices that her fertilizer use has indeed dropped off significantly, since she is adding only the amount needed (less than before) and she is adding it at fairly regular intervals (which predictably enough, has aided in absorption after watering and rainfall). She decides to share her process with others, but she thinks it might be worth sharing at a price. She therefore files a utility patent application for a method of optimizing use of organic fertilizer, comprising installing a soil probe capable of monitoring the nitrogen levels of the soil, and then repeatedly: (1) determining the level of nitrogen in the soil, (2) comparing the nitrogen level to the agricultural standard for the target crop, and (3) (a) if the level is at or above that agricultural standard, waiting three days before repeating steps (1)–(3), or (b) if the level is below that agricultural standard, then administering organic fertilizer to correct the deficiency and waiting three days after fertilizer administration before repeating steps (1)–(3).

The examining attorney at the USPTO is reading the application and studying the exclusions to patentability in the Supreme Court's section 101 caselaw. On these facts, could the examining attorney apply any of the exclusions to reject the application?

(A) yes, the exclusion of abstract ideas

(B) yes, the exclusion of laws of nature

(C) yes, the exclusion of products of nature

(D) no, none of the exclusions could apply

61. A toy developer has created a new toy for younger children that combines elements of known technologies to provide visual and audial entertainment; the toy has a small touch screen plus some other raised and lighted buttons that visually match the on-screen icons. The toy lights up and makes fun sounds and screen images when the child interacts with the colored icons and buttons in a matching pattern.

Could the examining attorney at the USPTO properly reject an application to patent the new toy for a lack of usefulness or lack of utility, relying on section 101 as it is currently interpreted and applied?

(A) yes, because the toy described has insufficient use or utility, given that it has no new "beneficial use" or function, and is just for fun, making it "frivolous and insignificant"

(B) yes, because the toy described has insufficient use or utility in that it does not "promote the progress of … useful arts," which broadly means advancing science or technology

(C) no, because the toy described has a sufficient use or utility in its means of entertaining children playing with the toy

(D) no, because the toy described has a sufficient use or utility in its capacity to help children learn basic shapes and colors

62. What is "prior art" in the context of a given invention? (If you need a hint, think about how you should define what is "prior" and what is the relevant "art" under patent law, both with respect to a specific inventor's given invention.)

Answer:

63. A mechanical engineering group working for an automotive parts supplier (P) determined that a new means of mounting a spare tire underneath the cars should be developed. The product development, patenting, and manufacturing process at company P consisted of, in this order: identifying the problem; researching existing (and historical) spare tire mounts; brainstorming possible new solutions; using pencil and paper to do some rough sketches of the preferred design; using computer-aided design to do technical drawings of that design; submitting the technical drawings and some specifications to the legal team for patenting assessment; making a model using alternate (non-realistic) materials; finalizing a complete, enabling patent application containing the drawings and claims describing the invention; sending the final specifications and drawings to a contract fabricator (company F) to obtain a physical sample of the item using real-world materials; receiving and testing the sample from the fabricator (F); filing the complete, enabling application with the USPTO; beginning mass production; and later receiving the granted patent (without amending the claims).

Later, an engineer from F, the fabrication company, claimed to be a joint inventor with the engineers from P, the parts supplier. This claim by the engineer arose only after P, the parts supplier, filed an infringement lawsuit against an accused infringer that was manufacturing infringing spare tire mounts. The fabrication engineer then attempted to license his ownership interest in the invention to that infringer, which would provide it with a defense to the infringement claim.

Determining the date of invention is vital to the court's inquiry into inventorship of the claimed spare-tire-mount invention. Identify the earliest date of invention for the final, patented design that is clearly supported by the facts above.

(A) the first rough sketches of the preferred design with pencil and paper

(B) finalizing a complete, enabling patent application containing the drawings and claims describing the invention

(C) receiving and testing the product sample that the fabricator produced using the claimed design, to actually reduce the invention to practice

(D) filing the complete, enabling application with the USPTO (containing the drawings and claims describing the invention)

64. Consider an application containing only claims effectively filed before March 16, 2013 and compare the following statements related to novelty of inventions.

Which statement below provides the most complete and accurate list of requirements for novelty of an invention in such an application? (*Note:* None of the statements below contains a comprehensive list of the requirements for novelty of an invention in such an application; you are simply asked to select the statement that, as among the choices, contains the most complete and accurate list.)

(A) The invention was not patented or described in a printed publication before the date the patent applicant invented it.

(B) The invention was not known or used, and it was not patented or described in a printed publication, in the United States before the date the patent applicant invented it.

(C) The invention was not known or used in the United States, and it was not patented or described in a printed publication anywhere in the world, before the date the patent applicant invented it.

(D) The invention was not known or used, and it was not patented or described in a printed publication, anywhere in the world before the date the patent applicant invented it.

65. Consider an application containing claims effectively filed after March 16, 2013 and compare the following statements related to novelty of inventions.

Which statement below provides the most complete and accurate list of requirements for novelty of an invention in such an application? (*Note:* None of the statements above contains a comprehensive list of the requirements for novelty of an invention in such an application; you are simply asked to select the statement that, as among the choices, contains the most complete and accurate list.)

(A) The invention was not patented or described in a printed publication before the date the patent applicant filed the patent application.

(B) The invention was not publicly used or sold, and it was not patented or described in a printed publication, in the United States before the date the patent applicant filed the patent application.

(C) The invention was not publicly used or sold in the United States, and it was not patented or described in a printed publication anywhere in the world, before the date the patent applicant filed the patent application.

(D) The invention was not publicly used or sold, and it was not patented or described in a printed publication, anywhere in the world before the date the patent applicant filed the patent application.

66. What form of patent protection is potentially available for a feature of a product that is primarily functional but is also ornamental, or pleasing to the eye?

(A) a utility patent only

(B) a design patent only

(C) both a design patent and a utility patent

(D) neither a design patent nor a utility patent

67. A plant researcher working to enhance yields of wheat crops without dependence on chemical fertilizer, has developed a new, higher-yield wheat by genetically modifying the plant. Wheat is a plant that sexually reproduces through seeds. This researcher's new plant is potentially eligible for protection through:

(A) plant patent

(B) utility patent

(C) both (A) and (B)

(D) neither (A) nor (B)

68. In summer 2008, Isabelle Inventor, working out of her home workshop, develops an innovative new tool that can be used open jars. In August 2011, Inventor begins selling her device through her online store. In December 2012, Inventor files a patent application on her device.

Choose one of the following as the most likely outcome for the application.

(A) Inventor can obtain a patent on her device because no facts indicate she is not the first to invent or the first to file.

(B) Inventor will be precluded from patenting her device because she abandoned the invention.

(C) Inventor will be precluded from patenting her device because of the prior sale.

(D) Inventor will be precluded from patenting her device because of the statute of limitations.

69. In summer 2015, Isabelle Inventor, working out of her home workshop, develops an innovative new tool that can be used open jars. In August 2018, Inventor begins selling her device through her online store. In December 2019, Inventor files a patent application on her device.

Choose one of the following as the most likely outcome for the application.

(A) Inventor can obtain a patent on her device because no facts indicate she is not the first to invent or the first to file.

(B) Inventor will be precluded from patenting her device because she abandoned the invention.

(C) Inventor will be precluded from patenting her device because of the prior sale.

(D) Inventor will be precluded from patenting her device because of the statute of limitations.

70. Do experimental uses of an invention affect an inventor's ability to later obtain patent protection for the invention? Explain.

Answer:

71. What is the test for nonobviousness?

Answer:

72. What are the Supreme Court's so-called "secondary considerations" and what role do they play in determining patent validity?

Answer:

73. What is the written description requirement?

Answer:

Patent Law—Ownership & Duration

74. Who is an "inventor," and how does inventorship affect patent prosecution?

Answer:

75. When an engineer or other researcher in a research and development (R&D) department creates an invention during the normal course of employment, to which of the following do the rights to the invention belong in the typical R&D employment situation?

    (A) the employee

    (B) the employer

    (C) the rights are shared under the "shop right" doctrine

    (D) ownership depends upon the specific terms of the employment contract

76. In the scenario set forth in the question above, explain in whose name the patent will be sought and then who will ultimately own the rights to that patent.

Answer:

77. Two competing inventors, A and B, independently develop an invention. Here is the timeline for the inventors' activities:

	Conceives of Invention	Reduces to Practice	Files Patent Application	Patent Issues
A	March 2010	March 2011	July 2011	n/a
B	January 2011	February 2011	April 2011	October 2013

On these facts alone, as between A and B, who should own the patent rights to the invention under applicable U.S. patent law?

    (A) B, because the first to reduce an invention to practice gets the rights, absent abandonment, suppression, or lack of diligence.

    (B) B, because the first to file a patent application gets the rights, as long as no statutory bar applies.

(C) B, because A's one-year delay in reducing the invention to practice is per se lack of diligence.

(D) A, because the first to conceive of an invention to practice gets the rights, absent abandonment, suppression, or lack of diligence.

78. On the facts set forth in the last question above, how would the parties' rights be affected if B published an article fully disclosing the invention in March 2011 in a widely distributed scientific journal? Select the statement below that most accurately describes the situation.

(A) The pre-AIA section 102 statutory bar would prevent A from obtaining the patent, but it would not affect other parties' ability to get the patent.

(B) The pre-AIA section 102 statutory bar would prevent B from obtaining the patent, but it would not prevent A from getting the patent.

(C) The pre-AIA section 102 statutory bar would prevent both inventors from obtaining the patent.

(D) The publication of an article in March 2011 would have no impact on anyone's rights, and the owner of the invention (as found in the question above) would still get all patent rights.

79. Two competing inventors, C and D, independently develop an invention. Here is the timeline for the inventors' activities:

	Conceives of Invention	Reduces to Practice	Files Patent Application	Patent Issues
C	February 2017	October 2017	June 2018	n/a
D	October 2017	November 2017	March 2018	January 2020

On these facts alone, as between C and D, who should own the patent rights to the invention under applicable U.S. patent law?

(A) C, because the first to reduce an invention to practice gets the rights, absent abandonment, suppression, or lack of diligence.

(B) D, because the first inventor to file a patent application gets the rights, as long as there has been no earlier disclosure or filing that destroys novelty.

(C) D, because D was the first to file and less than a year passed between C's reduction to practice and D's patent filing, which means the invention is still novel as of D's filing date.

(D) Neither, because while D was the first to file, C reduced the invention to practice before D's patent filing, which means the invention is not novel as of D's filing date.

80. On the facts set forth in the last question above (Question 79), how would the two inventors' rights be affected if Inventor C had published an article fully disclosing the invention in December 2017 in an electronically distributed scientific journal?

Answer:

81. Worldwide, what is the most common method for determining patent ownership between competing independent inventors? The proper owner of rights in an invention is:

(A) the first inventor to conceive of an invention

(B) the first inventor to reduce an invention to practice

(C) the first inventor to file a patent

(D) all competing independent inventors with co-pending patent applications, if more than one inventor has overlapping dates of conception, reduction to practice, and filing. They are treated as joint inventors and are required to share the rights.

82. What is the "shop rights" doctrine?

Answer:

83. How are joint inventors defined and recognized in U.S. patent law? Select the defining characteristic to become a joint inventor on a U.S. patent (containing several claims). Joint inventors must:

(A) work in the same location with one another

(B) make similar amounts or types of contributions to the invention claimed

(C) contribute in some way to every claim in the patent

(D) collaborate in some fashion and contribute to joint conception of at least one claim

84. What would be the basic term of protection for a utility patent that issued on an application filed today?

(A) 20 years from the date of patent filing

(B) 14 years from the date of patent issuance

(C) 15 years from the date of patent issuance

(D) 17 years from the date of patent issuance

85. What would be the basic term of protection for a design patent that issued on an application filed today?

    (A) 20 years from the date of patent filing

    (B) 14 years from the date of patent issuance

    (C) 15 years from the date of patent issuance

    (D) 17 years from the date of patent issuance

86. Which of the following statements most accurately describes Congress's ability to grant perpetual patents, or allow unlimited patent renewals, if it desires to do so?

    (A) The Intellectual Property Clause (Art. I, sec. 8, cl. 8) expressly precludes such a law.

    (B) The Intellectual Property Clause (Art. I, sec. 8, cl. 8) expressly precludes such a law, but Congress could easily avoid the problem by relying upon the Commerce Clause.

    (C) The Intellectual Property Clause (Art. I, sec. 8, cl. 8) expressly precludes such a law, yet, while the law is unclear, it is likely that the Commerce Clause would give Congress the power to circumvent the express limits of the Intellectual Property Clause.

    (D) Congress has already allowed for perpetual patents in the form of unlimited patent renewals in the utility patent field.

Patent Law—Infringement & Remedies

87. Which of the following accurately lists the activities that directly infringe U.S. patent rights in a product if done without authority of the patent owner?

   (A) making the invention, reconstructing the invention, offering to sell the invention, selling the invention (all in the United States); importing the invention into the United States.

   (B) making the invention, offering to sell the invention, selling the invention (all in the United States); importing the invention into the United States; exporting the invention from the United States.

   (C) making the invention, offering to sell the invention, selling the invention, using the invention (all in the United States); importing the invention into the United States.

   (D) making the invention, selling the invention, using the invention (all in the United States); importing the invention into the United States; exporting the invention from the United States.

88. How can the plaintiff owner of a utility patent prove that a product being made and sold by an accused infringer is, in fact, infringing on the patentee's rights in the patented invention?

   (A) proving that the patented invention and the defendant's product are, in light of the prior art, substantially the same to the ordinary observer, so as to deceive such an observer

   (B) proving that the patented invention and the defendant's product are, in light of the prior art, substantially the same to a person having ordinary skill in the art, so as to deceive such a person

   (C) proving that the patented invention and the defendant's product are the same, by comparing all elements of a claim to the product and showing each claim element to be individually present in the product, either literally or through an equivalent

   (D) proving that the patented invention and the defendant's product are the same, by comparing all elements of a claim to the product and showing that the defendant's product is either literally the same or is the overall equivalent of the patented invention as a whole

89. Which of the following is not an example of an infringement of a patent?

   (A) using a patented invention in university research laboratory experiments

   (B) selling an unpatented product that was manufactured using a patented process

(C) importing a product covered by a patent, without making it, offering it for sale, or selling it in the United States.

(D) none of the above

90. Does reverse engineering a patented product violate patent law? What about use of the information learned as a result of the reverse engineering—could such use infringe patent rights?

Answer:

91. What is the prosecution history estoppel (or file wrapper estoppel) doctrine, and which party invokes it in litigation—the patent owner or the accused infringer?

Answer:

92. Patentee owns a patent that claims a process for manufacturing a soft contact lens (for vision correction) that utilizes a specified plastic composition. The plastic composition is not itself patented, and it can be used in manufacturing other items. Seller makes and sells specifically sized and shaped pieces of this plastic composition, and the size of each little piece of the plastic composition contains precisely the right amount of material to make one contact lens. Unsurprisingly, Seller's customers, the Manufacturers, use these plastic pieces to make contact lenses—and it turns out that they do so using Patentee's patented process.

Assume that the Manufacturers' lens-making processes infringe the patent owned by Patentee and that the patent is valid. In a patent infringement lawsuit brought by Patentee against Seller, could Seller be found liable for infringement on the facts above? Select the best answer.

(A) No, because Seller is not using Patentee's patented process, and it is not selling products made using the patented process.

(B) No, because there is no evidence that Seller is encouraging or inducing the Manufacturers to use the pieces of plastic in the patented process.

(C) No, because there is no evidence that Seller has knowledge of the patent owned by Patentee and that the Manufacturers are not licensed to use the patented process.

(D) Yes, because Seller is selling a material, the little pieces of plastic, for use in practicing a patented process; the pieces are a material part of the process, especially adapted for use in infringement of the process, and not staple articles of commerce as sold by Seller, whose lack of knowledge does not matter because patent infringement is strict liability.

93. Which of the following statements most accurately describes appellate jurisdiction in patent cases under current law?

(A) Appeals go to the Federal Circuit, with certiorari review (discretionary) by the Supreme Court.

(B) Appeals go to the Federal Circuit, with no Supreme Court review possible (the Federal Circuit has the final say).

(C) Appeals go to the regional court of appeals (for example, the Fifth Circuit for cases filed in Louisiana), with certiorari review (discretionary) by the Supreme Court.

(D) Appeals go to the regional court of appeals (for example, the Fifth Circuit for cases filed in Louisiana), with en banc review (discretionary) by the Federal Circuit.

94. In patent cases, injunctive relief is:

(A) available upon a showing of a four-factor equitable test

(B) presumptively available to prevailing patent plaintiffs

(C) automatically available to prevailing patent plaintiffs

(D) only available in cases of bad faith on the part of the defendant (i.e., only in exceptional cases)

95. What evidence must be shown in order to receive lost profits in a patent case?

Answer:

96. What is the relevant standard for receiving attorney's fees and costs in a patent case?

Answer:

Patent Law—Defenses & Limitations

97. The following are, with the proper facts, valid defenses to a claim of patent infringement for making, using, or selling a patented device:

    (A) invalidity of the patent

    (B) lack of knowledge of the patent

    (C) expiration of the statute of limitations

    (D) all of the above

98. A medical practitioner makes use of a patented process in order to provide medical treatment. The physician is:

    (A) liable for patent infringement

    (B) liable for contributory infringement

    (C) not liable because the physician did not make the patented invention

    (D) not liable because of statutory immunity for medical providers

99. A process for separating the components of crude oil was patented in 2018 based on an application filed in 2016 by Company A. Company B began to use the same process in secret—and in good faith—in 2014, and B still continues to use the process in its facilities without knowledge of A's patent. B is an integrated processor and refiner that takes these separated components and further refines and processes them within the company's own various facilities, some of which are in Mexico, which requires export of the components by pipeline.

    Select the option that most likely applies to Company B if Company A sues B for infringement of the patent that issues to A in 2018 for the process. Company B is likely:

    (A) liable for patent infringement for using the process

    (B) liable for exporting a product made by a process patented in the United States

    (C) not liable because of the innocent infringer doctrine and defense

    (D) not liable because of the good faith prior commercial use defense

100. Company A, the owner of a patent on a new type of fastener for quickly but securely attaching automobile body parts to the automobile frame, licenses the patent to B, a manufacturer of automobile parts. B sells parts that include fasteners embodying the patent to C, an au-

tomobile manufacturer, who in turn attaches those automobile parts to its automobile frames and sells the resulting cars—including the fasteners—to consumers. Company A wishes to sue C for patent infringement for using the patent (by attaching the parts to the frames) and selling products embodying the patent (by selling the cars), both without a license from A.

Which of the following statements most accurately describes the result?

(A) Company A should succeed, because selling and using are both infringing activities, and only B has a license.

(B) Company A should succeed, because C is actively inducing B to make and to sell the fasteners.

(C) Company A should not succeed, because C is not making the fasteners, and C is also not inducing B to make them.

(D) Company A should not succeed, because the license to B to make the fasteners exhausts A's right to control the later sale and use of B's fasteners.

101. What is the patent misuse doctrine?

Answer:

Copyright Law—Subject Matter & Validity

102. Which of the following is *not* protected by copyright?

    (A) literary works

    (B) musical works

    (C) ideas

    (D) architectural works

103. A work is "fixed in a tangible medium of expression" for copyright law purposes when it is:

    (A) handwritten on paper, recorded on film, stored on a hard drive, or even stored in a computer's random access memory (RAM—i.e., memory that would be lost if the computer lost power)

    (B) handwritten on paper, recorded on film, stored on a hard drive, but not when stored on a computer's random access memory (RAM—i.e., memory that would be lost if the computer lost power)

    (C) recorded on film, stored on a hard drive, or even stored on a computer's random access memory (RAM—i.e., memory that would be lost if the computer lost power), but not merely handwritten on paper

    (D) recorded on film or stored on a hard drive, but not when it is merely on a computer's random access memory (RAM—i.e., memory that would be lost if the computer lost power) or handwritten on paper

104. The Great Food Guide (GFG) has assembled a great deal of information on New Orleans restaurants over the years. It has created two lists, both available via the GFG.com website: (1) a directory containing (in alphabetical order) the names, addresses, web address, and telephone numbers of all New Orleans restaurants (the "Directory"), and (2) a guide called "GFG's Guide to the 50 Best New Orleans Restaurants," which lists 50 restaurants selected based on GFG's assessment of quality, cuisine, and ambiance, with detailed explanations of the relative merits of each establishment (the "Guide").

    Consider the minimum standard of creativity for copyright protection as set forth in *Feist Publications, Inc. v. Rural Telephone Service Co.*, 499 U.S. 340 (1991). Under the Court's analysis in that case, which of the following statements is most accurate?

    (A) Both the Directory and the Guide are copyrightable.

    (B) Neither the Directory nor the Guide is copyrightable.

    (C) The Directory is not copyrightable, but the Guide is copyrightable.

    (D) The Directory is copyrightable if it is carefully maintained and updated on a regular basis, and the Guide is copyrightable in any event.

105. A law student takes photographs and videos during a vacation in Europe, making use of the camera/photo/video features of a smartphone. Which of the following statements is most accurate?

    (A) The law student has a valid copyright, as there is no minimum level of creativity required and courts do not assess the artistic merit of works.

    (B) The law student has a valid copyright on the images and video captured by the camera, assuming they are minimally creative or involve some judgment.

    (C) The law student does not have a valid copyright because the photographs and videos are not sufficiently creative to be copyrightable—the smartphone uses software to adjust settings, so it mechanically captured the content.

    (D) The law student does not have a valid copyright because only artistic and creative works of recognized stature are protected by copyright law.

106. A famous celebrity meets a friend for a casual lunch. Unbeknownst to the celebrity, the "friend" has surreptitiously audio-taped the conversation (the celebrity did most of the talking). What claim or claims can the celebrity bring to prevent publication of the conversation in the tabloids?

    (A) state law copyright only

    (B) federal copyright only

    (C) both federal and state law copyright claims

    (D) neither federal nor state law copyright claims

107. The first copyright law in the United States, enacted in 1790, did not protect which category of works?

    (A) books

    (B) charts

    (C) sculptures

    (D) maps

108. What is the "sweat of the brow" theory for copyright protection and what is its status under current law?

Answer:

109. Which of the following statements most accurately describes the current importance of a copyright notice for a work written and published in 1980?

    (A) Copyright notices are required and works published without the copyright notice fall into the public domain.

    (B) Copyright notices are required and works published without the copyright notice fall into the public domain unless "cured" under the Copyright Act of 1976.

    (C) Copyright notice is no longer required in light of the Berne Convention.

    (D) Copyright notice is no longer required under the Sonny Bono Copyright Term Extension Act.

110. How does the above—notice for works published in 1980—compare to the copyright notice requirement under the 1909 Act?

Answer:

111. How does the above—notice for works published in 1980—compare to the copyright notice requirement under present law?

Answer:

112. What is the so-called "poor man's copyright" and what is its significance under copyright law?

Answer:

113. The Visual Artists Rights Act of 1990 does not protect limited-edition or single copies of which of the following types of works?

    (A) sculptures

    (B) prints

    (C) architectural plans

    (D) photographs

114. Which of the following statements best characterizes the availability of copyright protection for the design of a utilitarian article, such as an attractive, original design for a picnic table and benches for use in public parks?

    (A) The design is protectable if the original, aesthetic features are physically separable from the utilitarian aspects of the picnic table and benches.

(B) The design is protectable if the original, aesthetic features are either physically or conceptually separable from the utilitarian aspects of the picnic table and benches.

(C) The design is protectable if the original, aesthetic features show a modicum of creativity and if the look and feel of the picnic table and benches is aesthetically pleasing as a whole.

(D) The design is not protectable because the article is useful, and copyright law does not protect functional articles.

115. What is the copyright doctrine of "scenes a faire"?

Answer:

116. What is the idea/expression distinction as it relates to copyright law?

Answer:

117. Consider the case of a cookbook written and created by a gourmet chef, such as Alice Waters or Giada De Laurentiis. What elements or content in the recipe book would consist of copyrightable material, and what parts of the book would not be eligible for copyright protection?

Answer:

Copyright Law—Ownership & Duration

118. The U.S. government can own which of the following types of copyrights?

    (A) works of U.S. government employees acting in the scope of their duties

    (B) rights to works assigned to it by non-governmental authors

    (C) copyrighted works by government employees that relate to the subject of national secrets

    (D) both (B) and (C) above

119. A student is hired to do research for a professor and provides 10 pages of material, which the professor copies verbatim into a 30-page article. Which of the following statements is most accurate?

    (A) The professor and student are joint authors under the Copyright Act, given that each has contributed copyrightable expression.

    (B) The professor and student are joint authors under the Copyright Act, because the professor stole the work from the student, who would share any proceeds and rights.

    (C) The professor is the sole author of the work under the Copyright Act, given that there was no intent to form a joint work.

    (D) The professor is the sole author of the work under the Copyright Act, given that the professor wrote more than 50 percent of the work.

120. If two coauthors specifically wish to have joint authorship of the copyright in their work, what do most courts require in order to reach such a conclusion?

Answer:

121. If (for whatever reason) one person is sole author of a work, but desires to allow a second person to have an equal ownership interest in that work, how can this result be accomplished under applicable law?

Answer:

122. Assume that a famous author writes a new novel in the year 2020. The novel is written in the author's own name (i.e., not anonymously or under a pseudonym) and is not a work made for hire. What is the current term of copyright protection for this work?

    (A) 95 years from the date of publication or 120 years from the date of creation, whichever comes first

    (B) 95 years from the date of creation or 120 years from the date of publication, whichever is longer

    (C) life of the author plus 50 years

    (D) life of the author plus 70 years

123. What is the current copyright duration for a joint work?

    (A) 95 years from the date of publication or 120 years from the date of creation, whichever comes first

    (B) 95 years from the date of creation or 120 years from the date of publication, whichever is longer

    (C) life of the last surviving author plus 50 years

    (D) life of the last surviving author plus 70 years

124. Assume that a movie is produced in the year 2020. The movie is a "work made for hire." What is the current term of copyright protection for this work?

    (A) 75 years from date of publication or 100 years from date of creation, whichever term is shorter

    (B) 95 years from date of publication or 120 years from date of creation, whichever term is longer

    (C) 95 years from date of publication or 120 years from date of creation, whichever term is shorter

    (D) life of the author plus 70 years

125. Your client runs across an old poem, originally written and published in Latin by an American author in the year 1915 and translated into English in 1935. Your client wishes to copy the poem, in its entirety, for a website containing poetry. The client has the original 1915 text and the 1935 translation in his library.

    Which of the following statements would most accurately summarize your advice to the client?

    (A) You can freely use either the Latin or the English version of the poem, as any copyright has necessarily expired and the poem is in the public domain.

    (B) You can freely use the Latin version, as the copyright has necessarily expired and the poem is in the public domain, but the English version may still be protected by copyright.

(C) You cannot use either version as the copyrights have not necessarily expired.

(D) You can freely use either version because of the fair use defense.

126. What is a "work made for hire" under copyright law?

Answer:

127. What test has the Supreme Court adopted for defining a "work made for hire" by an employee under copyright law?

(A) contractual right to control

(B) actual control

(C) common law agency

(D) formal, salaried employee

128. Which of the following is required to be in writing under the Copyright Act?

(A) an exclusive license

(B) a non-exclusive license

(C) an assignment of copyright

(D) both (A) and (C) above

129. What are terminations of transfers under the Copyright Act?

Answer:

130. A termination of transfer made under the Copyright Act for a work created, published, and transferred by license in the year 2000:

(A) can be effectuated (exercised/carried out) in the years 2030–2035

(B) can be effectuated (exercised/carried out) in the years 2035–2040

(C) can be effectuated (exercised/carried out) in the years 2040–2045

(D) can be effectuated (exercised/carried out) at any time during the renewal term of the copyright

131. What is the duration for rights under the Visual Artists Rights Act ("VARA") for a sculpture created in 1995?

(A) life of the author

(B) life of the author plus 50 years

(C) life of the author plus 70 years

(D) the rights are perpetual

Copyright Law—Infringement & Remedies

132. Your client wishes to record and sell 1000 copies of a cover version of a copyrighted song (like the Blackberry Smoke and Amanda Shires version of Tom Petty's song, "You Got Lucky").

The easiest way to record and sell these cover versions is to:

(A) obtain a public performance right from BMI, ASCAP, or SESAC

(B) obtain a mechanical (reproduction) license from the Harry Fox Agency

(C) obtain a distribution right from the songwriter

(D) obtain a public display right from the songwriter

133. Sally's Hair Salon wants to hook up a CD player to its telephone system so that people placed on hold can hear music being played on the CD player in the store. Which of the following statements is the most accurate?

(A) Sally has not engaged in an unlawful public performance under the Copyright Act as long as her store is small enough to fit within the "safe harbor" for small businesses.

(B) Sally has not engaged in an unlawful public performance under the Copyright Act as long as she purchased lawful copies of the CDs.

(C) Sally has not violated the Copyright Act because playing CDs does not constitute a public performance in any situation.

(D) Sally has violated the Copyright Act by publicly performing copyrighted works.

134. If Bob were to turn a published and copyrighted novel into a movie and release the movie on DVD, all without authorization, he would likely violate which right(s) of the author or other copyright owner of the novel?

(A) derivative works

(B) reproduction

(C) distribution

(D) all of the above

135. If Sally were to sell or rent a bootleg movie DVD (which she purchased from an anonymous seller who had the bootleg DVDs in the back of his van) she would likely violate which right of the copyright owner of the movie on the DVD?

    (A) derivative works

    (B) reproduction

    (C) distribution

    (D) all of the above

136. A public performance takes place when a copyrighted work is performed by:

    (A) being played on CD in a semipublic place

    (B) being played live in a place open to the public

    (C) being transmitted beyond the place it is located by electronic means

    (D) all of the above

137. What copyrighted work or works are embodied in the download or a stream of a file containing a song, such as the download or stream of a song like Taylor Swift's "We Are Never Ever Getting Back Together"? Select the best answer from the following:

    (A) a musical composition

    (B) a sound recording

    (C) both a musical composition and a sound recording

    (D) a sound recording and a work made for hire

138. Under present law, the owner of a copyright in a sound recording possesses which of the following rights:

    (A) reproduction and distribution, but not public performance or public display

    (B) reproduction, distribution, and public performance by digital transmission, but not general public performance or public display

    (C) reproduction, distribution, and full public performance rights, but not public display

    (D) reproduction, distribution, full public performance rights, and public display

139. The Music Modernization Act of 2018, which was recently signed into law by Congress, does which of the following things?

    (A) offers full public performance rights to sound recordings for the first time

    (B) streamlines the music licensing process to make it easier for rights holders to get paid when their music is streamed online and provides federal copyright protection for sound recordings made before 1972

    (C) provides federal copyright protection for sound recordings made before 1972 and creates a "small claims court" for any alleged copyright violations involving small amounts of money

(D) both (A) and (B) are correct

140. Identify the types of moral rights protected under the Visual Artists Rights Act ("VARA").

(A) attribution

(B) integrity

(C) divulgation

(D) both (A) and (B)

141. The Digital Millennium Copyright Act ("DMCA") provides copyright owners with rights regarding which of the following acts?

(A) circumventing access controls on a copyright-protected work

(B) selling products for circumventing access controls

(C) violating the moral rights of an author in a copyright-protected work

(D) both (A) and (B)

142. Copyright registration for U.S. authors is:

(A) required in order to recover any compensatory damages for copyright infringement (i.e., no compensatory damages for infringement occurring before registration)

(B) required in order to obtain injunctive relief (i.e., no injunctive relief for infringement occurring before registration)

(C) required as a condition precedent to filing suit

(D) entirely optional and has no consequence for copyright litigation

143. The Copyright Act preempts state law when that law is:

(A) equivalent to rights under copyright law

(B) within the general scope of copyrightable subject matter

(C) involving works of authorship fixed in a tangible medium of expression

(D) all of the above must be shown to establish preemption

144. Which of the following statements most accurately describes the approach taken by federal copyright law to questions of remedies?

(A) The presumptive form of relief is actual monetary damages and profits, and injunctions are rarely available.

(B) The presumptive form of relief is injunctive relief, and actual monetary damages and profits are rarely available.

(C) Injunctive relief is frequently granted, and actual monetary damages and profits are available only upon a showing of bad faith.

(D) Injunctive relief is frequently granted, and actual monetary damages and profits are available upon a showing of bad faith or actual harm.

145. A successful copyright plaintiff can recover which of the following types of damages?

(A) actual damages only

(B) statutory damages only

(C) either statutory or actual damages

(D) both statutory and actual damages

146. Statutory damages can be:

(A) increased or decreased based on the bad faith or good faith of the defendant

(B) increased based on the bad faith of the defendant but not decreased

(C) decreased based on the good faith of the defendant but not increased

(D) none of the above; they are specified by statute with no consideration of the good faith or bad faith of the defendant

147. Which statement most accurately describes the standard for recovering attorney's fees under the Copyright Act based on current law?

(A) Prevailing plaintiffs are automatically entitled to recover attorney's fees, and prevailing defendants can recover attorney's fees only upon a showing of bad faith or frivolous litigation.

(B) Prevailing plaintiffs are presumptively entitled to recover attorney's fees, and prevailing defendants can recover attorney's fees only upon a showing of bad faith or frivolous litigation.

(C) Both prevailing plaintiffs and prevailing defendants can recover attorney's fees, in the discretion of the district court, based on a variety of factors.

(D) Both prevailing plaintiffs and prevailing defendants are presumptively entitled to recover attorney's fees.

148. Unauthorized music file-sharing can be a violation of what aspect of copyright protection?

(A) public performance rights

(B) reproduction rights

(C) distribution rights

(D) either (B) or (C) or both depending on the circumstances

Copyright Law—Defenses & Limitations

149. Which of the following is *not* a complete defense to a copyright infringement action?

(A) independent creation

(B) common source

(C) innocent copying

(D) consent or license

150. Public performances of an audiovisual work in a classroom are permitted so long as:

(A) the copy of the work being performed is lawfully made

(B) the instructor provides notice to the copyright owner

(C) the educational institution registers with the copyright office

(D) both (A) and (B) above

151. In the course of making a movie about superheroes, a movie production company released a promotional poster of its lead actor kneeling and crouching in a red and gold mechanized and armored suit. Twelve years before, a comic book artist created a character for a comic book series as well as a picture depicting that character in a mechanized suit of armor; the armor was not red and gold, but the character was shown in a similar kneeling pose.

Which of the following statements describes a defense that may be asserted to a claim of copyright infringement on the facts presented?

(A) The movie production company did not have access to the comic book artist's picture and thus its poster does not infringe.

(B) The movie production company's poster is not substantially similar to the comic book artist's picture and thus its poster does not infringe.

(C) The idea of a comic book hero in a suit of armor in a kneeling pose is an uncopyrightable idea, and the merger doctrine prevents anyone from having an exclusive right on a depiction of this pose.

(D) All of the above are possible defenses.

152. The traditional "homestyle" exemption for public performances requires:

(A) receipt of a radio or television broadcast (or the equivalent cable/satellite)

(B) compliance with requirements regarding the number and type of receiving apparatus

(C) no direct charge for admission

(D) all of the above

153. Internet service providers are immune from copyright liability for user-generated material they store for their customers unless they:

(A) have actual knowledge of the infringement

(B) fail to take down infringing material after sufficient notice and opportunity

(C) have control of and receive substantial financial benefit from the infringement

(D) any of the above can extinguish the immunity

154. An undergraduate student buys one copy of a commercial outline. The student makes typical underlining, starring, and color-coded highlighting in the book, and then sells that book (otherwise still in its original form) to another student the next semester, who also makes similar marks in the book, and that second student resells the book (now, a second resale) the semester after that.

The second student:

(A) has violated the right of reproduction, and the "first sale" doctrine does not apply to create a defense

(B) has violated the right to create derivative works, and the "first sale" doctrine does not apply to create a defense

(C) has violated the right of distribution, and the "first sale" doctrine does not apply to create a defense because it only applies to the initial resale (and reseller) after the so-called "first sale"

(D) has not violated any copyright, because the "first sale" doctrine makes the subsequent resales of the copy non-infringing

155. Purchasing a lawfully made copy of a movie (DVD) manufactured in China and bringing the DVD into the United States is:

(A) lawful, as long as the DVD is not sold or otherwise transferred in the United States, because this action would violate the copyright owner's distribution right.

(B) lawful, and the DVD can be sold or otherwise transferred in the United States, because this action is protected by the first sale doctrine

(C) an unlawful use of the DVD in violation of the copyright owner's anti-circumvention rights under the Digital Millennium Copyright Act

(D) an unlawful importation in violation of the copyright owner's distribution right, because the work was not lawfully made in the United States

156. Assume that a professor at a state college copies an entire textbook and distributes the copies to the professor's class of 30 students. The professor charges the students only for the actual cost of making the copies. What is the college's best defense in a suit brought by the publisher of the textbook?

   (A) sovereign immunity under the Eleventh Amendment bars suits against the state college

   (B) there is no respondeat superior or vicarious liability under the Copyright Act

   (C) the fair use defense precludes recovery, given that educational uses are protected under the fair use provision

   (D) the copying did not violate the Copyright Act because no profit was made by the professor or the college

157. Which of the following statements most accurately describes the fair use defense under federal copyright law?

   (A) The scope of fair use is broader for factual works (i.e., fair use is more likely to be found when the taking is from a fact work), and the commercial purpose of the defendant's taking is but one factor in the analysis.

   (B) The scope of fair use is broader for factual works (i.e., fair use is more likely to be found when the taking is from a fact work), and if the defendant's taking is for a commercial purpose, the taking is presumed not to be a fair use.

   (C) The scope of fair use is broader for fictional works (i.e., fair use is more likely to be found when the taking is from a fictional work), and the commercial purpose of the defendant's taking is but one factor in the analysis.

   (D) The scope of fair use is broader for fictional works (i.e., fair use is more likely to be found when the taking is from a fictional work), and if the defendant's taking is for a commercial purpose, the taking is presumed not to be a fair use.

158. Which of the following statements most accurately describes the fair use defense under federal copyright law?

   (A) The qualitative and quantitative amount taken in relation to the plaintiff's copyrighted work is relevant, and good faith (or bad faith) is taken into account.

   (B) The qualitative and quantitative amount taken in relation to the defendant's alleged infringing work is relevant, and good faith (or bad faith) is taken into account.

   (C) The qualitative and quantitative amount taken in relation to the plaintiff's copyrighted work is relevant, and good faith (or bad faith) is irrelevant.

   (D) The qualitative and quantitative amount taken in relation to the defendant's alleged infringing work is relevant, and good faith (or bad faith) is irrelevant.

159. Which of the following statements most accurately describes the fair use defense under federal copyright law?

   (A) A legitimate parody is protected and is per se fair use.

   (B) A legitimate parody is presumed to be fair use, but this presumption can be rebutted using the factors on a case-by-case basis.

   (C) A legitimate parody is taken into account in analyzing the fair use factors on a case-by-case basis.

   (D) Whether a work is a legitimate parody does not affect the analysis of fair use, and courts simply analyze the fair use factors on a case-by-case basis.

160. Which of the following statements most accurately describes the fair use defense under federal copyright law?

   (A) Unpublished works are not protected under the copyright laws, so fair use is irrelevant.

   (B) Whether a work is published or unpublished is irrelevant under a fair use analysis.

   (C) Whether a work is published or unpublished is a factor in a fair use analysis, and fair use is more likely to be found if a work is published rather than unpublished.

   (D) Whether a work is published or unpublished is a factor in a fair use analysis, and fair use is more likely to be found if a work is unpublished rather than published.

161. Which of the following copyrighted works are not eligible for commercial rental under the first sale doctrine?

   (A) audiovisual works, e.g. DVD movies

   (B) computer programs, e.g. CD-ROMs containing software

   (C) sound recordings of musical works, e.g. music CDs

   (D) both (B) and (C)

Questions

Practice Final Examination

Exam Question 1. To what extent is "first to file" now the method for determining ownership of patents under U.S. law?

Answer:

Exam Question 2. Plaintiff operates a take-out restaurant and carefully guards the recipe for what it calls its "secret sauce." A competitor purchases an order of plaintiff's product, takes it to a chemical laboratory, and has its composition analyzed. Based on this chemical analysis, defendant begins selling the same sauce. Plaintiff sues the competitor under trade secret law.

What is the likely result?

(A) plaintiff will probably lose because the defendant's action constitutes lawful reverse engineering

(B) plaintiff will probably lose because recipes for food items cannot be protected as trade secrets

(C) plaintiff will probably prevail, because the defendant obtained the trade secret through improper means

(D) plaintiff will probably prevail, because the defendant knew or should have known that the recipe was a trade secret and intended to be held in confidence

Exam Question 3. A public library, which charges no fees and is completely supported by separately collected public tax dollars, can lend its patrons a lawfully purchased music CD based on which copyright law doctrine or defense?

(A) de minimis use

(B) fair use

(C) first sale

(D) noncommercial use

Exam Question 4. Which of the following is *not* protectable by copyright law?

(A) an accounting system

(B) the design of a building

(C) a recording of insect sounds

(D) the source code for a video game (aka computer code)

Exam Question 5. What is the minimum standard of originality for copyright protection, as announced in the Supreme Court's decision in *Feist Publications, Inc. v. Rural Telephone Service Co.*, 499 U.S. 340 (1991)?

Answer:

Exam Question 6. The Visual Artists Rights Act of 1990 does not protect limited-edition or single copies of:

(A) drawings

(B) films

(C) paintings

(D) photographs

Exam Question 7. What is a certification mark in federal trademark law?

Answer:

Exam Question 8. Which of the following *cannot* be protected as a utility patent under the Patent Act:

(A) a new genetically modified animal, such as a faster growing strain of Angus beef cattle

(B) a new mathematical algorithm that can be used to calculate flight times and airplane fuel use

(C) a new process for producing a known composition of motor oil

(D) a new type of paperclip

Exam Question 9. Which of the following is *not* an example of an infringement of a patent?

(A) importing a product covered by a patent, without making or selling it

(B) offering to make and sell a product covered by a patent, if no products are made or sold

(C) reselling a used product covered by a patent

(D) selling an unpatented product manufactured using a patented process

Exam Question 10. How long should injunctive relief last in most trade secret cases?

(A) indefinitely, as long as the requisite reasonable efforts to maintain secrecy and a competitive advantage exist

   (B) perpetually, as a sanction for the infringer's unlawful behavior and a deterrent to future infringers

   (C) until the end of 20 years from the date of the plaintiff's first use of the trade secret

   (D) for as long as it would take to reverse engineer the subject matter of the trade secret

Exam Question 11. Compare the level of knowledge and secrecy required in order for information to be protected as a trade secret with the standard of novelty required for an invention to be protected by patent law.

Answer:

Exam Question 12. What is the best way to protect the idea for a new video game?

   (A) contract law

   (B) copyright law

   (C) trademark law

   (D) none of the above; ideas are not protectable

Exam Question 13. Trade secret misappropriation can occur by:

   (A) encouraging an employee to disclose a computer password voluntarily

   (B) listening to sales employees while they discuss strategies in the boarding area of an airport

   (C) taking apart a product after buying it and examining components that are hidden at the point of sale and during normal use

   (D) all of the above

Exam Question 14. The overall appearance, presentation, and sales techniques of a retail store can be protected as:

   (A) a collective mark

   (B) a design patent

   (C) trade dress

   (D) a trade secret

Exam Question 15. What is the merger doctrine in copyright law?

Answer:

Exam Question 16. Which of the following would *not* be patentable subject matter under current law? Presume all are new.

(A) a business method that is useful for accountants because it quickly and repeatedly applies a mathematical algorithm to solve a complex accounting problem

(B) a complementary human DNA sequence useful in testing for certain forms of lung cancer

(C) a distinct, but not useful, plant that can be asexually reproduced

(D) an ornamental design for an automobile battery, which does not affect utility and is hidden once the battery is installed

Exam Question 17. Which of the following statements most accurately describes the approach taken by federal patent law to questions of remedies?

(A) The presumptive form of relief is injunctive relief, and money damages are rarely available.

(B) The presumptive form of relief is money damages, and injunctions are rarely available.

(C) Injunctive relief is frequently granted, and money damages are generally available.

(D) Injunctive relief is frequently granted, and money damages are generally available only upon a showing of bad faith or actual loss of profits.

Exam Question 18. Which of the following statements most accurately describes Congress's ability to grant perpetual copyrights, or allow unlimited copyright renewals, if it desires to do so?

(A) The Intellectual Property Clause (Art. I, sec. 8, cl. 8) permits such a law.

(B) The Intellectual Property Clause (Art. I, sec. 8, cl. 8) expressly precludes such a law, but Congress can and has already granted unlimited copyright renewals for foreign works based on its treaty powers.

(C) The Intellectual Property Clause (Art. I, sec. 8, cl. 8) expressly precludes such a law, yet while the law is unclear, it is likely that the Commerce Clause would give Congress the power to circumvent the express limits of the Intellectual Property Clause.

(D) The Intellectual Property Clause (Art. I, sec. 8, cl. 8) expressly precludes such a law, and Congress could not avoid the problem by relying on the Commerce Clause.

Exam Question 19. Assume that someone writes a new novel under a pseudonym in the year 2010. What is the current term of copyright protection for this work not published in the author's own name?

(A) life of the author plus 50 years

(B) life of the author plus 70 years

(C) 75 years from date of publication of 100 years from date of creation, whichever comes first

(D) 95 years from the date of publication or 120 years from the date of creation, whichever comes first

Exam Question 20. Your client wishes to use a copyrighted song and sound recording in a movie. What type of license would this require?

(A) a distribution right from the copyright owners

(B) a mechanical (reproduction) license from the Harry Fox Agency

(C) a public performance right from BMI, ASCAP, or SESAC

(D) synchronization and master use licenses from the copyright owners

Exam Question 21. Assume that the president of a private corporation sees an article published in an industry journal to which the company subscribes. She is reading the article within two days of the journal's publication, and she finds the article to be timely and relevant to a meeting taking place at the end of that same week among the executive management team. She therefore makes 5 copies of the article and distributes them to the members of the team to read in preparation for the meeting.

Does this action by the president give the copyright owner an action again the corporation under the Copyright Act? Choose the best response.

(A) Yes, because this action constitutes a reproduction for which the corporation is responsible.

(B) No, because while the action is a reproduction, the Copyright Act contains no contributory or vicarious liability provisions.

(C) No, because the fair use defense should eliminate copyright infringement liability in these circumstances.

(D) No, because the reproductions are noncommercial in nature while used within the corporation, and copies were not distributed outside the corporation.

Exam Question 22. A company hires a freelance professional website designer to create and design its website. Which of the following statements best describes the relative rights of the parties?

(A) The website designer most likely owns the copyright to the work, absent an agreement to the contrary.

(B) The hiring party (the company) most likely owns the copyright to the work, absent an agreement to the contrary.

(C) The website designer and the hiring party (the company) are most likely joint authors of the work.

(D) Copyright law does not address ownership in this circumstance, which is governed solely by contract law.

Exam Question 23. What is the general term of protection for a plant patent under the Plant Patent Act?

(A) 17 years from the date of patent filing

(B) 17 years from the date of patent issuance

(C) 20 years from the date of patent filing

(D) 20 years from the date of patent issuance

Exam Question 24. Which of the following statements most accurately describes the current importance of a copyright notice for a work first written and published in 2020?

(A) Copyright notices are required, and works published without the copyright notice fall into the public domain.

(B) Copyright notices are required, and works published without the copyright notice fall into the public domain unless "cured."

(C) Copyright notice is no longer required, and the notice is of informational value only.

(D) Copyright notice is no longer required, but the notice provides some amount of potential remedial benefit.

Exam Question 25. A law student prepares a written outline of a course based on the casebook readings and classroom discussion. Which of the following statements is the most accurate description of the existence or non-existence of copyright protection in the outline?

(A) The law student has a valid copyright on the outline because it is minimally creative and involves some judgment.

(B) The law student has a valid copyright, as there is no minimum level of creativity required and courts do not assess the artistic merit of works.

(C) The law student does not have a valid copyright, because the notes are based solely on the casebook and classroom discussion (i.e., are purely derivative).

(D) The law student does not have a valid copyright, because purely factual works are not protected by copyright law.

Exam Question 26. What form of protection is potentially available for an original and ornamental feature of a useful device?

(A) a copyright only

(B) a design patent only

(C) both a copyright and a design patent

(D) neither a copyright nor a design patent

Exam Question 27. Which of the following best describes the role of evidence as to the "sophistication of consumers" in trademark infringement cases?

(A) A low level of consumer sophistication must be shown in order for the trademark owner to succeed.

(B) A low level of consumer sophistication weighs in favor of the trademark owner's claim of infringement.

(C) A high level of consumer sophistication weighs in favor of the trademark owner's claim of infringement.

(D) A high level of consumer sophistication must be shown in order for the trademark owner to succeed.

Exam Question 28. When entering the market for slide presentation software, Prince Software Co. noticed that it might be advantageous to be able to name its software product "Prince PowerPoint" rather than "Prince Slide Software" or "Prince Presentations" or something else similar. Prince Software thinks that using "Prince PowerPoint" more quickly communicates to consumers exactly where its product "fits" in the software market. Assume that "PowerPoint" is currently registered to Microsoft Corp., another software and technology company, and that the trademark registration is incontestable.

Which of the following statements best captures Prince Software's ability to make noninfringing use of "Prince PowerPoint" in light of the facts and circumstances described above?

(A) Prince Software could use "Prince PowerPoint" under the doctrine of descriptive fair use.

(B) Prince Software could use "Prince PowerPoint" under the doctrine of nominative fair use.

(C) Prince Software could not use "Prince PowerPoint" unless it can demonstrate that "PowerPoint" is a generic term for slide presentation software.

(D) Prince Software could not use "Prince PowerPoint" under any theory, because the mark is incontestable.

Exam Question 29. The trademark term "Sun" for a bank is:

(A) descriptive

(B) suggestive

(C) arbitrary

(D) fanciful

Exam Question 30. The trademark term "Good Housekeeping Seal of Approval," used to denote approval of third parties' goods, is a:

(A) deceptive mark

(B) certification mark

(C) collective mark

(D) service mark

Exam Question 31. The trademark term "Roquefort" used for any cheese originating in Roquefort, France, that meets the production standard for that community's cured sheep's milk cheeses, is best characterized as a:

(A) primarily geographically descriptive mark

(B) certification mark

(C) collective mark

(D) service mark

Exam Question 32. The trademark term "Dallas Steak Company" for a steak restaurant in Dallas, Texas is:

(A) generic

(B) descriptive

(C) suggestive

(D) a certification mark

Exam Question 33. A candy maker produces a new candy product that is made with artificial chocolate flavoring and which it would like to call "Chocolaty Chompers." This mark is likely to be:

(A) generic

(B) descriptive

(C) suggestive

(D) deceptive

Exam Question 34. An automobile parts manufacturer develops a revolutionary new engine. The engine itself, as well as the process of manufacturing the engine, both involve significant improvements over existing automobile technology.

Review the following statements related to trade secret and patent law protection for the engine and the process. Select the statement that reflects the best legal advice for the situation, based on the limited facts available.

(A) The manufacturer should seek only patent protection for both the engine itself and for its new manufacturing process because it cannot maintain the process as a trade secret once it obtains patent protection for or begins to sell the engine.

(B) The manufacturer should seek only trade secret protection for both the engine itself and for its new manufacturing process because trade secret law offers longer potential exclusivity than patent law.

(C) The manufacturer should seek only patent protection for the engine itself and weigh its options on whether trade secret or patent law offers the best form of protection for its new manufacturing process.

(D) The manufacturer should seek only patent protection for its new manufacturing process and weigh its options on whether trade secret or patent law offers the best form of protection for the engine itself.

Exam Question 35. What is the significance of a transformative use in analysis of copyright infringement cases?

Answer:

Exam Question 36. The best form of intellectual property protection for a certain clothing design feature or fabric design for clothing is likely to be:

(A) copyright

(B) design patent

(C) trademark

(D) none of the above; clothing design features and fabric designs are not protectable

Exam Question 37. The trademark term "Lyft" for the service of providing temporary use of online non-downloadable software for locating transportation services, booking transportation services, providing transportation services, and dispatching motorized vehicles to customers, is:

(A) descriptive

(B) suggestive

(C) arbitrary

(D) fanciful

Exam Question 38. What is the minimum amount of damages recoverable for infringement of a utility patent under the language of the Patent Act?

(A) infringer's profits

(B) patentee's lost profits

(C) a reasonable royalty

(D) statutory damages

Exam Question 39. Nonobviousness can be best described as a showing that:

(A) the invention was not known by any other person prior to the date the patent applicant invents the device

(B) the invention was not publicly used or sold prior to the date the patent applicant files a patent application

(C) the invention involves an inventive step, i.e., a departure from the prior art that would not be apparent to a person having ordinary skill in the art (PHOSITA)

(D) the invention involves an inventive step, i.e., a departure from the prior art that would not be apparent to a reasonable inventor similar to the applicant

Exam Question 40. The changes to sections 102 and 103 of the Patent Act enacted as part of the America Invents Act (AIA) took effect on March 16, 2013. Select the answer that corresponds to how that effective date operates.

The changes in the AIA:

(A) affect the validity of all patents containing claims with an effective filing date on or after March 16, 2013

(B) affect the validity of all patents containing claims that are subject to a reexamination proceeding with an effective filing date on or after March 16, 2013

(C) affect the validity of all patents litigated in a patent infringement case with an effective filing date on or after March 16, 2013

(D) all of the above

Exam Question 41. A work is published in the United States without proper copyright notice in 1970. Under present law, what is the likely legal status of this work?

(A) Unprotected, because copyright notices were required under the 1909 Act for all published works.

(B) Unprotected, because copyright notices were required under the 1909 Act for all published works and the facts do not indicate that the lack of notice was "cured" under the provisions added in the Copyright Act of 1976.

(C) Protected, even though copyright notices were required under the 1909 Act, because copyright notice is no longer required after the 1989 implementation of the Berne Convention.

(D) Protected, even though copyright notices were required under the 1909 Act, because copyright notice is no longer required after the 1998 Sonny Bono Copyright Term Extension Act.

Exam Question 42. Misappropriation of a trade secret includes, for purposes of civil liability:

(A) obtaining the trade secret

(B) using the trade secret

(C) disclosing the trade secret to others

(D) all of the above

Exam Question 43. An ordinary citizen (who is not a famous celebrity) has her clearly visible and recognizable image used on a billboard advertisement for a restaurant without her consent. The image is from a photo that, from what she can tell, was taken without her consent.

The citizen's best claim against the restaurant would be under:

(A) copyright law

(B) false endorsement under the Lanham Act

(C) right of publicity or privacy under (applicable) state law

(D) none of the above, because the right of publicity protects only celebrity names and images

Exam Question 44. What is the minimum measure of damages recoverable for infringement of an unpublished novel under the language of the Copyright Act?

(A) harm to reputation

(B) lost profits

(C) statutory damages

(D) none of the above

Exam Question 45. Which of the following remedies are included in the plaintiff patent owner's monetary award in a typical utility patent infringement case where the infringement was unintentional and the defendant made a reasonable, but losing noninfringement or invalidity defense?

(A) the defendant's profits

(B) the plaintiff's attorney's fees

(C) the plaintiff's lost profits

(D) all of the above

Exam Question 46. Imagine that you represent the owner of a trademark that has been used from 2010 up to the present in Pennsylvania and New Jersey but never registered anywhere. You are advising that client in which courts in the United States—state or federal—you could file a civil suit for infringement without additional filings or registrations. Without diversity between the client and the infringer, you could file in:

(A) state court

(B) federal court

(C) either state or federal court

(D) neither state nor federal court

Exam Question 47. Imagine that you represent the owner of a trademark that has been used from 2010 up to the present in Pennsylvania and New Jersey and was registered in 2019 with the U.S. Patent & Trademark Office. You are advising that client in which courts in the United States—

state or federal—you could file a civil suit for infringement without additional filings or registrations. Without diversity between the client and the infringer, you could file in:

(A) state court

(B) federal court

(C) either state or federal court

(D) neither state nor federal court

Exam Question 48. Inventor A conceived of an invention and reduced it to practice in the year 2001, but A did not proceed to seek patent protection. Inventor B independently conceived of the same invention in December 2011. B reduced it to practice in March 2012. After learning of B's efforts at a scientific research conference, A applied for a patent in May 2012. B applied for a patent in June 2012. Litigation has arisen and priority is in dispute. Which of the following statements most accurately describes which of Inventors A and B is entitled to the patent rights?

(A) Inventor A is entitled to the patent, because A was the first to conceive of the invention.

(B) Inventor A is entitled to the patent, because A acted diligently in reducing the invention to practice.

(C) Inventor B is entitled to the patent, because Inventor A did not act diligently and was "spurred" by the actions of Inventor B to seek patent protection.

(D) Inventors A and B should be declared joint inventors; both will then share the patent rights.

Exam Question 49. The source of Congress's authority to protect semiconductors (i.e., computer chips or mask works) is:

(A) the Commerce Clause

(B) the Intellectual Property Clause

(C) the Necessary and Proper Clause

(D) the First Amendment

Exam Question 50. A consumer buys a copyrighted print and scans it to create a digital file and then posts a full-size image of the print on her personal blog. The consumer has:

(A) violated the right of reproduction only

(B) violated the right of public display only

(C) violated both the right of reproduction and the right of public display

(D) not violated any protected right, because of the first sale doctrine and the exception for private copies

Exam Question 51. A teenage computer hacker develops software code to enable anyone receiving streaming video, such as a movie watched via the Internet from Netflix, to be able to download a permanent copy onto a computer despite a streaming technology that disables such copying and storage. The hacker posts the code onto the Internet, with the announcement — "I am king of the world. Anyone can download movies for free now. Have at it, people!" The hacker most likely has:

   (A) directly violated reproduction and distribution rights of affected movie copyright owners

   (B) committed secondary copyright infringement by contributory infringement or inducement

   (C) violated the Digital Millennium Copyright Act ("DMCA")

   (D) violated rights under both (B) and (C)

Exam Question 52. How is "employee" status determined when analyzing whether a work is a "work made for hire" by an employee under copyright law (i.e., a work "prepared by an employee within the scope of ... employment")?

Answer:

Exam Question 53. Record Co. sells its copyrighted songs worldwide. It licenses a British company to make and sell CDs in the United Kingdom but not to import them into the United States. The British company makes CDs in a factory in England. One of its wholesale distributors sells them to a U.S. distributor, which sells them to buyers in the United States, resulting in a copyright suit by Record Co. against the U.S. distributor.

   Which of the following statements most accurately describes the result when Record Co. brings suit?

   (A) Record Co. will lose because of the first sale doctrine.

   (B) Record Co. will prevail because the first sale doctrine does not apply to musical recordings.

   (C) Record Co. will prevail because the first sale doctrine does not apply to works made abroad and imported into the United States.

   (D) Record Co. will lose because of the fair use doctrine.

Exam Question 54. Which of the following types of patentable subject matter has the shortest term?

   (A) design patents

   (B) plant patents

   (C) utility patents

   (D) both (A) and (B)

Exam Question 55. Which of the following statements most accurately describes the current importance of a copyright notice for a work first published in 1982?

   (A) Copyright notices are required and works initially published without the copyright notice fall into the public domain under the Copyright Act of 1976.

(B) Copyright notices are required and works initially published without the copyright notice fall into the public domain unless the failure was "cured" under the Copyright Act of 1976.

(C) Copyright notice is no longer required in light of the implementation of the Berne Convention.

(D) Copyright notice is no longer required under the Sonny Bono Copyright Term Extension Act.

Exam Question 56. Protection of intellectual property rights can be described as solving which type of economic problem?

(A) monopoly

(B) moral hazard

(C) public goods

(D) all of the above

Exam Question 57. Which intellectual property right offers its owner the greatest exclusivity during the term of protection, i.e., which intellectual property right offers third parties the fewest possibilities to enter the marketplace at the same time as the rights holder while using the same intellectual property?

(A) copyright

(B) patent

(C) trademark

(D) trade secret

Exam Question 58. A company's designers have developed a product with a design feature that is primarily functional, but the designers ensured that the way the design feature operates also makes the product aesthetically pleasing. The product has not yet been publicly used or sold, but the designers predict that consumers will respond well to it. They even think that the product design could become distinctive in the marketplace after a period of time.

Assume requirements related to the "newness" of the design feature could be met, such as novelty, originality, and the like. Which type of intellectual property would it be most advisable to use to protect the design feature?

(A) copyright law

(B) trademark law

(C) utility patent law

(D) all of the above

Exam Question 59. What form or forms of intellectual property protection are potentially available for computer software?

(A) copyright

(B) patent

(C) trade secret

(D) all of the above

Exam Question 60. Which subject matter within intellectual property requires its owner to prove that the subject matter has some kind of economic or market-based value before it can be protected?

(A) patent

(B) trademark

(C) trade secret

(D) none of the above

Exam Question 61. Under present U.S. copyright law, how long ago must a work have been published in order for it to be assuredly in the public domain?

Answer:

Exam Question 62. What are the four typical requirements for enforcement of an employees' covenants not to compete with their employers?

Answer:

Exam Question 63. Which form of intellectual property listed can best be used to protect the design shown below, which was created for use on the website of an online retailer as well as on its shipping boxes and labels?

(A) copyright law

(B) design patent law

(C) trademark law

(D) all of the above

Exam Question 64. What are the elements of a "hot news" claim of misappropriation under *INS v. AP* and its progeny?

Answer:

Exam Question 65. Which of the following receive *sui generis* protection under current federal law?

A "database," meaning an assembly of factual or other material

A "mask work," which are images or patterns related to semiconductor products

A "vessel hull design" (e.g., a boat hull), meaning the exterior design of the vessel hull

   (A)   databases and mask works

   (B)   databases and vessel hull designs

   (C)   mask works and vessel hull designs

   (D)   only databases

Exam Question 66. What is cybersquatting, what type of intellectual property right does it involve, and what remedies are available against this activity?

Answer:

Exam Question 67. At what point can the owner of a U.S. work (such as when the author is a U.S. national or the work was first published here) generally file suit in federal court in a case involving a typical copyrightable work, such as a book?

   (A)   as soon as it learns of copyright infringement, because copyright protection commences as soon as a work is fixed in a tangible medium of expression, and registration is optional

   (B)   as soon as it files an application for copyright registration with the United States Copyright Office, because the owner is required to register its copyright before filing a lawsuit

   (C)   as soon as it receives a decision on its application for copyright registration with the United States Copyright Office (i.e., a decision registering the copyright or declining to register it), because the owner is required to register its copyright before filing a lawsuit

   (D)   after it receives a favorable result—a copyright registration—from the United States Copyright Office (i.e., a decision registering the copyright), because the owner is required to register its copyright before filing a lawsuit

Exam Question 68. What is the test for determining whether a mark is deceptive under the Lanham Act? How does a finding of deceptiveness affect registrability?

Answer:

Exam Question 69. How important is the presence of the defendant's commercial or profit-making purpose in analysis of fair use in copyright cases? Select the statement below that best captures how courts will analyze or view such a purpose.

   (A)   A commercial or profit-making purpose weighs against fair use but is only one of the relevant factors.

   (B)   A commercial or profit-making purpose establishes a presumption against fair use.

(C) A commercial or profit-making purpose establishes a presumption of harm to the copyright owner, which weighs against fair use.

(D) A commercial or profit-making purpose is irrelevant to the fair use analysis.

Exam Question 70. A customer goes to a photography studio and has portraits made. The customer pays a sitting fee. The photographer sends a link to the customer to the photographer's website so that the customer can review the proofs of the portraits online. The proofs are "watermarked" with the photographer's name and a copyright notice. The customer buys an 8x10 print of one of the photos, which later arrives in the mail. The customer also downloads the watermarked version of the portrait to the customer's computer, then uses photo editing software to remove the copyright notice, and makes 2 extra 5x7 prints of the photo and 4 additional 2x3 (wallet-size) prints without the copyright "watermark" on them. The customer gives the 5x7 prints to family members for display in the family members' homes, and the 2x3 prints to family members for placement in their wallets or on their refrigerators.

In a copyright suit brought by the photographer, a court could find that:

(A) the customer violated the photographer's reproduction rights in the portrait, but no other rights

(B) the customer violated the photographer's reproduction rights in the portrait, as well as the Digital Millennium Copyright Act ("DMCA")

(C) the customer's acts violated or contributed to violations of the photographer's reproduction, distribution, and display rights in the portrait

(D) the customer did not violate the Copyright Act with any post-purchase activities because the customer purchased and therefore owns the portrait

Exam Question 71. Which of the following types of claims can only be brought in federal court (i.e., there is no concurrent state court jurisdiction)?

(A) federal copyright claims

(B) federal patent claims

(C) both (A) and (B)

(D) neither (A) nor (B)

Exam Question 72. A patent owner who imposes a tying arrangement on customers who purchase its patented product (requiring that they also purchase a second, unpatented product) is likely to:

(A) have waived its patent rights

(B) have committed patent misuse, if the patent owner has market power

(C) have committed patent misuse, regardless of whether the patent owner has market power

(D) be barred from recovery under the doctrine of prosecution history estoppel

Exam Question 73. If a home appliance manufacturer wished to obtain trademark protection for a particular shade of bright orange (standing alone) for use on the outer surface of all of its coffee makers, this bright orange trademark would most likely be found:

(A) protected once secondary meaning is shown, because it is not inherently distinctive

(B) protected even without a showing of secondary meaning, because it is inherently distinctive

(C) unprotected on grounds of functionality

(D) unprotected because a single color is not distinctive

Exam Question 74. Independent creation or development of the subject matter is a defense to the following causes of action:

(A) copyright infringement

(B) patent infringement

(C) trademark infringement

(D) none of the above

Exam Question 75. A video game fan created what he thought was a very solid concept for a new video game. He thought it would have the all the features to make it initially attractive to a variety of ages, genders, and types of gamers, and it would be sufficiently addictive to keep those gamers hooked. The gaming fan (now creator) wrote down this list of features and shared it with a couple of gaming friends he had sworn to secrecy, and they agreed it would be excellent. Not long thereafter, he happened to find himself seated next to a game designer from his favorite video game company on a 2-hour flight. Near the end of the flight, after he had already talked video games with her for a while and had become Facebook "friends" with her professional Facebook account, he decided to tell the designer about the game. He pitched the idea to her, saying: "I have this great idea for a game—and I've not known how to get it made—let me tell you about it and you can see what you think." The designer listened politely, and she asked a few questions. At the end, she said: "Sounds fun—I hope it gets made—I'll see what I can do to get you in touch with the right people. I have your contact info on Facebook now." A mobile game with very similar features was launched six months later by that video game company, although the video game fan had never been contacted.

The video game fan might have a claim against the designer or the company for:

(A) breach of contract

(B) trade secret misappropriation

(C) unjust enrichment or quasi contract

(D) none of the above; no violation

Answers

Trademark & Unfair Competition Law — Subject Matter & Validity

1. Answer (D) is correct. Trademark law has three major foundations that must be balanced and weighed: (1) preventing consumer confusion as to source or affiliation; (2) promoting competition in the marketplace; and (3) protecting the goodwill and reputation of trademark owners. This makes (D) the only good answer choice among the four offered, since it combines all three foundations.

> **Answer (A) is incorrect.** See above explanation.

> **Answer (B) is incorrect.** See above explanation.

> **Answer (C) is incorrect.** See above explanation.

2. Answer (A) is correct. The source of Congress's authority to enact the Lanham Act (trademark law) is the Commerce Clause, which gives Congress the power to regulate interstate and foreign commerce. The Intellectual Property Clause (Art. I, sec. 8, cl. 8) provides authority for the enactment of patents and copyrights for limited times but does not provide for protection of trademarks.

> **Answer (B) is incorrect.** As noted above, the Intellectual Property Clause provides authority for the enactment of patents and copyrights but does not provide for protection of trademarks.

> **Answer (C) is incorrect.** The Necessary and Proper Clause does not independently support Congress's authority to enact trademark law.

> **Answer (D) is incorrect.** The First Amendment is a limitation on the scope of Congress's power, not a grant of authority to it.

3. Answer (A) is correct. Under these facts, the owner offers both services and goods in connection with the same mark. Accordingly, the owner, NBC, can obtain trademark protection for the mark as used on the specified goods, as well as service mark protection for the mark as used in connection with the specified services. The company is offering bona fide products for sale in commerce, as well as services. There is no prohibition on obtaining both types of registrations for marks used both in goods markets and service markets. This scenario can be distinguished from that found in *In re Dr. Pepper Co.*, 836 F.2d 508 (Fed. Cir. 1987), in which the Federal Circuit held that trademark owners who use a mark for purely promotional purposes are ineligible for service mark protection for that mark because they have not made a bona fide use of the mark to sell a service.

> **Answer (B) is incorrect.** Neither the trademark nor the service mark qualifies as a "certification mark," a term that is discussed below in the answer to Question 4.

Answer (C) is incorrect. As noted above, there is no prohibition on obtaining both types of registrations for marks used to make bona fide sales in both goods markets and service markets.

Answer (D) is incorrect. The facts indicate that the mark is used to sell goods; the mark is not only placed on goods for promotional purposes. Even though some goods are given away (and are thus promotional in nature), on these facts, other goods are being sold for profit-making purposes.

4. Answer (A) is correct. The trademark term "NSF" used in a circle (by NSF International) is a certification mark. The Lanham Act defines a certification mark as a mark "used upon or in connection with the products or services of one or more persons other than the owner of the mark to certify regional or other origin, material, mode of manufacture, quality, accuracy or other characteristics of such goods or services." 15 U.S.C. § 1127. Here, the "NSF" mark serves to certify to purchasers that the products sold by third parties (i.e., not sold directly by NSF International) meet certain safety, quality, sustainability, or performance standards set by NSF. The Lanham Act provides that certification marks (as well as collective marks) may be registered:

> Subject to the provisions relating to the registration of trademarks, so far as they are applicable, collective and certification marks, including indications of regional origin, shall be registrable under this Act, in the same manner and with the same effect as are trademarks, by persons, and nations, States, municipalities, and the like, exercising legitimate control over the use of the marks sought to be registered, even though not possessing an industrial or commercial establishment, and when registered they shall be entitled to the protection provided herein in the case of trademarks, except in the case of certification marks when used so as to represent falsely that the owner or a user thereof makes or sells the goods or performs the services on or in connection with which such mark is used. Applications and procedure under this section shall conform as nearly as practicable to those prescribed for the registration of trademarks.

15 U.S.C. § 1054.

Answer (B) is incorrect. Collective marks and certification marks can seem somewhat similar, but NSF International is not a collective organization made up of members, as will become clearer in light of the answer to the next question below.

Answer (C) is incorrect. Under the facts provided, when the mark is being used on the products of others, NSF International is not using the mark to offer services for sale. The mark is being used in this context to denote that a given product bearing the mark meets NSF International's standards for certification.

Answer (D) is incorrect. A trademark use occurs when a mark is used to distinguish the goods of a given source, but here, the mark is used on a variety of different products from many different producers to denote that the goods have met the standards for safety, quality, sustainability, or performance set out by NSF International. The mark does not distinguish these goods as having a common source or control connected to NSF.

5. The Lanham Act states that a collective mark:

means a trademark or service mark—(1) used by the members of a cooperative, an association, or other collective group or organization, or (2) which such cooperative, association, or other collective group or organization has a bona fide intention to use in commerce and applies to register on the principal register established by this Act, and includes marks indicating membership in a union, an association, or other organization.

15 U.S.C. § 1127. An example of a collective mark is the Professional Golfers Association ("PGA"). A key distinction between a collective mark and a certification mark is that collective marks involve a membership organization whose members offer goods or services for sale (but where the mark simply denotes membership in the collective), whereas certification marks are not used on the goods or services of the owner and instead serve to show that a neutral third party certifies or vouches for the goods or services of others.

6. The treatment of generic terms in trademark law plays an important role in limiting the scope of trademark rights. In order for a brand name to serve as a trademark, it must be capable of identifying a particular producer or source of the goods in question. A generic term cannot qualify as a trademark, because it is the name of a product (or service) in the consuming public's mind, not an indication of the source of that product (or service). In other words, the term identifies the product (or service) itself, rather than serving as a brand name. A generic term thus fails to identify a particular source or producer.

A term can be generic because it has always been a product name or category, such as coffee, diapers, or deep-dish pizza. If trademark law allowed one producer to have exclusive trademark rights to such a generic term, it would place competitors at a considerable disadvantage. Competitors would have difficulty marketing a product such as a laser printer if they were precluded from using the term "laser printer" in advertisements, on product packaging, or on the Internet, where searches are often conducted using key words.

A term can also start out as a source-identifying brand name, but the brand can become so successful and dominant in consumer's minds that it eventually comes to be known to the consuming public as the product name itself. Historic examples of this phenomenon, known as "genericide," include aspirin—once "Aspirin"—as well as cellophane, thermos, and escalator. Each of these terms began as a brand name but eventually came to be used as a name for the product itself. Thus, even a well-established trademark, including a fanciful mark, can sometimes be challenged on the ground that it has become generic. To assess whether a term has become generic, courts generally consider consumer surveys, as well as trade publications, media reports, and other sources.

7. An arbitrary trademark involves the use of a common word applied in an unfamiliar way. In other words, the mark must have no connection to the underlying product, such as "Apple" when used for computer products or "Red Hat" when used for a computer software company.

8. A fanciful trademark is a word invented solely to be used as a trademark. In other words, fanciful marks are words that have been coined or made up to serve as a mark—not a word previously in existence but with an alternate meaning. An example of a fanciful mark would be "Kodak," which was coined for use in connection with photographic equipment. Another is "Clorox," a mark orig-

inally coined for use in connection with liquid bleach (merging portions of the sounds within "chlorine" and "sodium hydroxide," the two main ingredients).

9. Answer (B) is correct. A trademark term that is a surname (such as "Heinz," which is used for ketchup or other condiment products) is treated, for distinctiveness purposes, the same as a descriptive mark. *See* 15 U.S.C. § 1052(e)–(f) (excluding from registration marks that are "merely descriptive" and those that are "primarily merely a surname," but allowing registration of either type of mark if it "has become distinctive of the applicant's goods in commerce").

To see why, first consider the full range of the "spectrum of distinctiveness," which refers to the degree to which a mark is distinctive and can thereby serve a source-indicating trademark function. The spectrum extends from unprotectable generic words at one end of the spectrum to descriptive terms (which can serve as a trademark, but only upon a showing of secondary meaning) to suggestive, arbitrary, and finally fanciful marks at the other end of the spectrum (which are considered the strongest type of marks). Marks are thus classified in categories of generally increasing distinctiveness. As set forth by Judge Friendly in *Abercrombie & Fitch Co. v. Hunting World, Inc.*, 537 F.2d 4 (2d Cir. 1976), marks can be (1) generic; (2) descriptive; (3) suggestive; (4) arbitrary; or (5) fanciful. Descriptive marks generally make some reference to a characteristic of the product (or service) with which it is used, including a geographic location characteristic. A surname is the sort of term that a consumer would—at least initially—often perceive as being akin to a characteristic, meaning that a consumer would often perceive the surname to denote the name of an individual connected to the product or its source. A surname is therefore considered, like other terms describing a product characteristic, not to be inherently distinctive.

When marks are not inherently distinctive, they are protected as a trademark only upon a showing of secondary meaning (i.e., acquired distinctiveness). Because the Heinz trademark has been used for a very long period of time and is very well known as a source of condiment products, the Heinz mark has sufficient secondary meaning (i.e., acquired distinctiveness) to be protected under trademark law even though Heinz, as a recognizable surname, is deemed to be not inherently distinctive.

> **Answer (A) is incorrect.** To be generic, the mark must be a term that in the mind of the consuming public denotes or identifies the product or service itself, or its type, class, or category, or at least a key or dominant aspect of the product or service. As a general matter, surnames are not treated the same as generic terms because the consuming public will not typically consider a surname to denote the product or service itself, or to denote its type, class, or category.

> **Answer (C) is incorrect.** To be suggestive, the mark must indirectly suggest a connection to the trademark (involving a leap of imagination); a surname mark either makes a connection directly, or consumers would at least often presume that the connection exists or existed in the past. To be arbitrary, the word must be wholly unrelated or unconnected, and consumers must understand that the word and the goods or services are wholly unrelated. That is not true in the case of surnames. There are also good policy reasons not to treat a surname as inherently distinctive and easily capable of exclusive rights.

Answer (D) is incorrect. To be fanciful, the mark must be coined or "made up" for use as a trademark. That is not true in the case of surnames. Consumers will recognize the name as a surname; they will not merely connect the term to the product or service as a coined mark. In addition, for most surnames, multiple persons will have the same surname. As a result, there are strong policy reasons not to treat a surname like a fanciful mark.

10. **Answer (D) is correct.** The trademark term "Nikon" for cameras and related products is fanciful. It is a word that was coined specifically to be a trademark.

    Answer (A) is incorrect. "Nikon" does not describe a characteristic of the cameras and related products.

    Answer (B) is incorrect. The term "Nikon" does not have an indirect connection to camera products.

    Answer (C) is incorrect. Because "Nikon" is a coined term, it is not a preexisting word. To be arbitrary, a word must be both preexisting and without a connection to the products.

11. **Answer (B) is correct.** The term "Jaguar" for automobiles is suggestive. Suggestive marks have some association with the relevant goods or services, but some "imagination" or "perception" (or maybe an "aha, I get it!" moment) is required to see the connection or association between the mark and the goods or services. A jaguar is one of the "big cat" species. Although jaguar sizes vary, the cat's characteristics include having a sleek coat and being quite strong for its size. An automobile company would like for a consumer to connect characteristics like being sleek and strong to the automobiles branded with the "Jaguar" mark—in other words, the mark "Jaguar" suggests characteristics of the automobiles.

    Another (litigated) example: the mark "At-a-Glance" for calendars suggests quick visibility but requires a small imaginative step to discern that the calendar might enable the buyer to see a given time period, such as a month, "at a glance." *See Cullman Ventures, Inc. v. Columbian Art Works, Inc.*, 717 F. Supp. 96, 119–20 (S.D.N.Y. 1989). This one may be, however, closer to the descriptive line than is "Jaguar" when used for automobiles.

    Answer (A) is incorrect. As noted above, the term is suggestive. The term "Jaguar" does not itself describe an automobile or any of its features, attributes, or components to a consumer.

    Answer (C) is incorrect. The term "Jaguar" does create an indirect connection to characteristics of the automobiles, which excludes it from being arbitrary when used with automobiles.

    Answer (D) is incorrect. The term "Jaguar" is not a coined word, thus, it is not fanciful.

12. **Answer (D) is correct.** The trademark term "Penguin" used for paperback books and a book publishing company is arbitrary. To be arbitrary, the mark must have no connection to the underlying product, such as the commonly used example of "Apple" for computer products. There is no particular connection between penguins and books.

    Answer (A) is incorrect. The term "Penguin" does not, in the mind of the consuming public, denote or identify paperback books, or a book publishing company, or any type, class, or category of product or service related to books or book publishing.

Answer (B) is incorrect. The term "Penguin" does not describe a characteristic of paperback books or a book publishing company.

Answer (C) is incorrect. The term "Penguin" does not have an indirect connection to books or book publishing (as a general matter), even with a leap of the imagination.

13. Answer (B) is correct. The mark "Fresh Finds," for a chain of grocery stores featuring fresh produce, meats, fish, and deli products (plus other foods) is descriptive—a consumer can "find" "fresh" items there. This is true even though the stores do not sell only fresh foods, and consumers can expect more than "fresh finds." The mark nevertheless describes one characteristic of the stores.

Answer (A) is incorrect. The mark "Fresh Finds," while highly descriptive of one characteristic of the grocery store's services, is nevertheless not a term that denotes or identifies—to the general consuming public of the U.S.—either grocery stores themselves, or a type, class, or category of general grocery stores.

Answer (C) is incorrect. It does not take a leap of imagination to make the connection between the "Fresh Finds" mark and the services provided—the service of stocking and selling an array of fresh foods like those that one will find available in the store.

Answer (D) is incorrect. The term "Fresh Finds" does have a connection to a characteristic of the business, so it is not arbitrary.

14. Answer (D) is correct. Although the Lanham Act contains a provision barring the registration of immoral, scandalous, and disparaging marks, *see* 15 U.S.C. § 1052(a), two recent Supreme Court decisions struck down all of these prohibitions on the ground that they are content-based infringements of First Amendment free speech rights. In *Matal v. Tam*, 137 S. Ct. 1744 (2017), the Court struck down the disparagement clause as a content-based provision that violates the First Amendment. The case involved an Asian-American band that sought to register the name, "The Slants," as its service mark. In 2019, the Court in *Iancu v. Brunetti*, 139 S. Ct. 2294 (2019), held that the refusal to register the mark "FUCT" for a clothing line on grounds that it was immoral or scandalous also violated the First Amendment. Thus, in light of these decisions, there is no longer an enforceable prohibition on the registration of immoral, disparaging, and scandalous marks despite the fact that this language is still reflected on the face of the Lanham Act.

Answer (A) is incorrect. As explained above, in light of recent Supreme Court precedent, there is no longer an enforceable prohibition on the registration of immoral, scandalous, and disparaging marks.

Answer (B) is incorrect. As explained above, in light of recent Supreme Court precedent, there is no longer an enforceable prohibition on the registration of immoral, scandalous, and disparaging marks.

Answer (C) is incorrect. As explained above, in light of recent Supreme Court precedent, there is no longer an enforceable prohibition on the registration of immoral, scandalous, and disparaging marks.

15. Answer (D) is correct. The attempt to protect the color green for chewable vitamins that are also mint flavored presents a challenge in trademark law. This type of trademark application would most likely be unprotectable on grounds of functionality (i.e., aesthetically functional) because the green color can help consumers easily identify the flavor they can expect when they chew the vitamin tablets, given that in the United States, the consuming public often expects mint flavor and green color to correspond with one another. With the mint flavor itself remaining free for other producers to use under these facts, other producers should remain free to use the color green to communicate to consumers the flavor of the vitamin tablet in the non-reputation-related way that consumers have come to expect for vitamin products. In other words, barring the use of green to color a chewable mint-flavored vitamin would put the other producers at a significant non-reputation-related disadvantage in the vitamin marketplace. This is the essence of "functionality" in trademark, although here it is an appearance-based functionality rather than functionality based on whether the product works better or fulfills its intended purpose (as a vitamin product).

The prohibition on functional trademarks was only codified as to trade dress by amendment near the close of the 20th century, but it had long been recognized in the case law. The trademark statute now states that "[i]n a civil action for trade dress infringement ... for trade dress not registered on the principal register, the person who asserts trade dress protection has the burden of proving that the matter sought to be protected is not functional." 15 U.S.C. § 1125(a)(3).

As the Court noted in *Inwood Laboratories, Inc. v. Ives Laboratories, Inc.*, 456 U.S. 844, 850 (1982), a product feature is deemed functional and cannot serve as a trademark "if it is essential to the use or purpose of the article or if it affects the cost or quality of the article." In *Qualitex Co. v. Jacobson Products Co.*, 514 U.S. 159, 165 (1995), the Court added that a feature is functional if its exclusive use by one enterprise "would put competitors at a significant non-reputation-related disadvantage." In other words, a feature is functional, and thus unprotectable, if it is one of a limited number of efficient options available to competitors, and therefore free competition would be unduly hindered by giving the design or feature trademark protection. The functionality doctrine helps prevent the stifling of competition by the exhaustion of a limited number of options for product packing or design, or by preventing a competitor from replicating an important non-reputation-related product feature. As the Court noted in *Qualitex*, at 164–65:

> The functionality doctrine prevents trademark law, which seeks to promote competition by protecting a firm's reputation, from instead inhibiting legitimate competition by allowing a producer to control a useful product feature. It is the province of patent law, not trademark law, to encourage invention by granting inventors a monopoly over new product designs or functions for a limited time, after which competitors are free to use the innovation. If a product's functional features could be used as trademarks, however, a monopoly over such features could be obtained without regard to whether they qualify as patents and could be extended forever (because trademarks may be renewed in perpetuity).

Answer (A) is incorrect. As noted above, the color green is likely functional in this case. If it were non-functional, however, it would be analyzed in the same way that a descriptive mark is analyzed—requiring proof of secondary meaning—because color alone is deemed not to be inherently distinctive. (Color marks are still not technically or even theoretically "descriptive" in nature, however, since the Court's rule about color in *Qualitex* is mandatory without regard to any relationship between the goods and the color, or no relationship between the goods and the color. See the explanation for Answer (B) below.)

Answer (B) is incorrect. The color green, as discussed above, is likely functional for this product feature within the context of these facts and thus not protected under trademark law. Moreover, even if it were non-functional, a color standing alone has been deemed to be non-inherently distinctive for purposes of trademark analysis. In *Qualitex Co. v. Jacobson Products Co.*, 514 U.S. 159, 164–65 (1995), the Court found that a green-gold color for dry cleaning and laundry press pads could qualify for trademark protection but only if it possessed secondary meaning or acquired distinctiveness.

Answer (C) is incorrect. The color green, as discussed above, is likely functional on these facts and thus not protected under trademark law. Even if vitamins do not "need" to be green in color, and a given color like green does not have a "relationship" to vitamins, not all marks are analyzed in the same way that word marks are analyzed. There are other issues to consider in trademark law, as further explained above for correct Answer (D).

16. Answer (C) is correct. Product packaging trade dress may be either non-inherently distinctive (and therefore protectable only upon a showing of secondary meaning) or inherently distinctive (protectable regardless of secondary meaning), depending on the circumstances, just like an ordinary word mark. This rule is based on the Supreme Court's holdings in two cases. The first was *Two Pesos, Inc. v. Taco Cabana, Inc.*, 505 U.S. 763 (1992), which held that trade dress could be protected under section 43(a) of the Lanham Act if it is found either to be inherently distinctive or to have acquired distinctiveness (i.e., to have secondary meaning), rejecting an argument that secondary meaning was always required for the protection of unregistered trade dress (in that case, it was the trade dress of a restaurant). The second was *Wal-Mart Stores, Inc., v. Samara Bros., Inc.*, 529 U.S. 205 (2000), which held that although packaging and restaurant trade dress can be (but are not always) inherently distinctive, product design trade dress is deemed never to be inherently distinctive.

Answer (A) is incorrect. As noted above, the basic holding of *Two Pesos v. Taco Cabana* is that the larger category of trade dress is not so different from other trademarks—trade dress, generally speaking, can be either inherently distinctive or non-inherently distinctive, and if it is found to be inherently distinctive, then no additional proof of secondary meaning is required. The Court has never held, however, that all packaging is inherently distinctive.

Answer (B) is incorrect. As noted above, the basic holding of *Two Pesos v. Taco Cabana* is that the larger category of trade dress is not so different from other trademarks—trade dress, generally speaking, can be either inherently distinctive or non-inherently distinctive, and if it is found to be inherently distinctive, then no additional proof of secondary meaning is required. The Court has never held, however, that packaging is never inherently distinctive. It is true that the Court in *Qualitex*, discussed in the answers to Question 15 above, did find that a color mark, standing alone, is always to be considered non-inherently distinctive. Similarly, the

Court in *Wal-Mart Stores, Inc., v. Samara Bros., Inc.*, 529 U.S. 205 (2000), held that product design trade dress is never inherently distinctive.

Answer (D) is incorrect. It is clear from the Court's rulings that packaging trade dress can be protected under an ordinary trademark analysis. Thus, it is incorrect to state that only trade dress that has become famous can be protected (and then only under a dilution theory).

17. Answer (B) is correct. A product configuration or product design trade dress is never inherently distinctive; it is protectable only upon a showing of secondary meaning. This statement of the law is based on the Supreme Court's holding in *Wal-Mart Stores, Inc. v. Samara Bros., Inc.*, 529 U.S. 205 (2000). The Court specifically held that a product design (in this instance, children's dress designs) cannot be inherently distinctive. Product designs can be protected (whether registered or unregistered) only upon a showing of secondary meaning (i.e., acquired distinctiveness). The Court distinguished *Two Pesos v. Taco Cabana* based on the differences between product design and packaging trade dress:

> It seems to us that design, like color, is not inherently distinctive. The attribution of inherent distinctiveness to certain categories of word marks and product packaging derives from the fact that the very purpose of attaching a particular word to a product, or encasing it in a distinctive packaging, is most often to identify the source of the product. Although the words and packaging can serve subsidiary functions—a suggestive word mark (such as "Tide" for laundry detergent), for instance, may invoke positive connotations in the consumer's mind, and a garish form of packaging (such as Tide's squat, brightly decorated plastic bottles for its liquid laundry detergent) may attract an otherwise indifferent consumer's attention on a crowded store shelf—their predominant function remains source identification. Consumers are therefore predisposed to regard those symbols as indication of the producer, which is why such symbols "almost automatically tell a customer that they refer to a brand," and "immediately ... signal a brand or a product 'source.'" And where it is not reasonable to assume consumer predisposition to take an affixed word or packaging as indication of source—where, for example, the affixed word is descriptive of the product ("Tasty" bread) or of a geographic origin ("Georgia" peaches)—inherent distinctiveness will not be found. In the case of product design, as in the case of color, we think consumer predisposition to equate the feature with the source does not exist. Consumers are aware of the reality that, almost invariably, even the most unusual of product designs—such as a cocktail shaker shaped like a penguin—is intended not to identify the source, but to render the product itself more useful or more appealing. The fact that product design almost invariably serves purposes other than source identification not only renders inherent distinctiveness problematic; it also renders application of an inherent distinctiveness principle more harmful to other consumer interests. Consumers should not be deprived of the benefits of competition with regard to the utilitarian and esthetic purposes that product design ordinarily serves by a rule of law that facilitates plausible threats of suit against new entrants based upon alleged inherent distinctiveness.

Wal-Mart Stores v. Samara, 529 U.S. 205 (2000).

Answer (A) is incorrect. As discussed above, the Court's ruling in *Wal-Mart Stores v. Samara* directly contradicts the statement that product configurations are always inherently distinctive and are therefore protectable regardless of secondary meaning.

Answer (C) is incorrect. Although this statement is true as to product packaging trade dress cases, the Court's ruling in *Wal-Mart Stores v. Samara* specifically rejects this approach for product configurations or product design trade dress.

Answer (D) is incorrect. Although secondary meaning is required to protect a product configuration as a trademark, it is not necessary for it to achieve fame. The "fame" standard does apply to dilution cases, but product configurations are protectable on the ordinary showing of secondary meaning.

18. The trademark incontestability doctrine prevents challenges to the ownership and validity of trademarks (with certain exceptions), and it applies only to marks that have been registered and continuously used without successful challenge for five years, and for which an affidavit of incontestability has been filed. Careful examination of the relevant statutes reveals that "incontestability" cannot protect a registered mark from a challenge based on genericism (or, for that matter, abandonment, functionality, or fraudulent acquisition), but it can protect it from a challenge arguing that the mark is merely descriptive without evidence of acquired distinctiveness (i.e., secondary meaning). On the former point, see 15 U.S.C. §1065 and 15 U.S.C. §1115(b)(2) & 1127 (definition of "abandoned") and the explanation below. On the latter point, see *Park 'N Fly, Inc. v. Dollar Park and Fly, Inc.*, 469 U.S. 189 (1985) and the explanation below.

The statutory provision that provides in the first instance for incontestability states as follows:

> Except on a ground for which application to cancel may be filed at any time under paragraphs (3) and (5) of section 1064 of this title, and except to the extent, if any, to which the use of a mark registered on the principal register infringes a valid right acquired under the law of any State or Territory by use of a mark or trade name continuing from a date prior to the date of registration under this Act of such registered mark, the right of the registrant to use such registered mark in commerce for the goods or services on or in connection with which such registered mark has been in continuous use for five consecutive years subsequent to the date of such registration and is still in use in commerce, shall be incontestable.

15 U.S.C. §1065. Paragraphs (3) and (5) of section 1064, referred to above, include the cancellation grounds of genericism, abandonment, functionality, and uncontrolled certification marks, among others, but they do not include descriptiveness without acquired distinctiveness. *See* 15 U.S.C. §1064. Incontestability's relationship to genericism and descriptiveness can also be discerned—albeit not as expressly—by examining the preserved defenses to a claim of infringement of an incontestable mark, which are provided in Lanham Act section 33(b), or 15 U.S.C. §1115(b). Under that provision, the evidentiary power of incontestability is "conclusive" on certain points at issue in an infringement case, but the claim is still "subject to" certain listed "defenses or defects." The list does not include descriptiveness, *see also Park 'N Fly, Inc. v. Dollar Park and Fly, Inc.*, 469 U.S.

189 (1985), but does include situations when "the mark has been abandoned," §1115(b)(2). The Lanham Act definition of "abandoned," in turn, indicates that "A mark shall be deemed to be 'abandoned' if … any course of conduct of the owner, including acts of omission as well as commission, causes the mark to become the generic name for the goods or services on or in connection with which it is used or otherwise to lose its significance as a mark." *See* 15 U.S.C. §1127 (definition of "abandoned").

Trademark & Unfair Competition Law— Ownership & Duration

19. Answer (C) is correct. Under the common law, trademark rights are only established through bona fide public use of the mark in the marketplace on the goods, or on their packaging, labels, or tags. The essence of trademark ownership is use of the mark in connection with goods or services in a manner that builds consumer recognition in the marketplace. As Judge Easterbrook suggested in *Scandia Down Corp. v. Euroquilt, Inc.*, 772 F.2d 1423, 1429–30 (7th Cir. 1985), "[t]rademarks help consumers to select goods."

> **Answer (A) is incorrect.** Registration with the state trademark or secretary of state's office can serve to register a claim to trademark rights for a mark already in use, but the common law method of establishing ownership remains actual use in the marketplace.

> **Answer (B) is incorrect.** A successful suit for unfair competition against a competitor might be possible after establishing ownership rights in a mark, but it is not how trademark ownership is established as a preliminary matter.

> **Answer (D) is incorrect.** Use of "TM" or "tm" in an advertisement may bolster a consumer association that is being made through use of the mark on the goods, or it may help put a competitor on notice of a claim of trademark rights, but use of a mark in an advertisement does not constitute use of a mark on or in connection with goods under trademark law.

20. Answer (C) is correct. Priority over others as to trademark ownership under the Lanham Act can be attained through use in commerce or filing an application with bona fide intent to use (upon following the proper procedures to establish actual use in commerce). The amended language in the Lanham Act, codified at 15 U.S.C. § 1051(b) states as follows:

> (1) A person who has a bona fide intention, under circumstances showing the good faith of such person, to use a trademark in commerce may request registration of its trademark on the principal register hereby established by paying the prescribed fee and filing in the Patent and Trademark Office an application and a verified statement, in such form as may be prescribed by the Director.

> (2) The application shall include specification of the applicant's domicile and citizenship, the goods in connection with which the applicant has a bona fide intention to use the mark, and a drawing of the mark.

> (3) The statement shall be verified by the applicant and specify—

(A) that the person making the verification believes that he or she, or the juristic person in whose behalf he or she makes the verification, to be entitled to use the mark in commerce;

(B) the applicant's bona fide intention to use the mark in commerce;

(C) that, to the best of the verifier's knowledge and belief, the facts recited in the application are accurate; and

(D) that, to the best of the verifier's knowledge and belief, no other person has the right to use such mark in commerce either in the identical form thereof or in such near resemblance thereto as to be likely, when used on or in connection with the goods of such other person, to cause confusion, or to cause mistake, or to deceive.

Except for applications filed pursuant to section 1126 of this title, no mark shall be registered until the applicant has met the requirements of subsections (c) and (d) of this section.

(4) The applicant shall comply with such rules or regulations as may be prescribed by the Director. The Director shall promulgate rules prescribing the requirements for the application and for obtaining a filing date herein.

Answer (A) is incorrect. Traditionally, use in commerce was the only method of obtaining priority under federal trademark law, but this has been altered with the intent-to-use process.

Answer (B) is incorrect. Priority under the intent-to-use application is not fully established until actual use in commerce takes place, a statement of use is properly filed and accepted, and a registration issues.

Answer (D) is incorrect. Although filing a foreign trademark application can provide priority if it is followed within the requisite time period (six months under current treaties and federal law) by a federal application that requests priority based on the foreign application, and although holding a foreign registration provides the applicant with another basis for a U.S. application, obtaining or owning a foreign registration alone (as stated in this answer) does not provide priority under U.S. law.

21. Answer (B) is correct. Company A obtains all rights to the trademark nationwide, except that Company B has exclusive rights state-wide in Texas. These facts present an illustration of the limited-area exception under the Lanham Act. The critical facts in this case are that Company A was both first to use the mark and then file to federally register in 2019, at which point Company B had only state-wide operations in Texas, which it began in good faith without knowledge of A's mark. The Lanham Act gives Company A nationwide priority, except for geographic areas in which Company B already had ongoing operations at the time of the application for federal registration (as long as the application matures to a registration). Company B, therefore, enjoys the benefit of the limited-area exception, which allows it to continue doing business in the geographic areas where it had established goodwill — in this instance, the entire state of Texas. Company B is not permitted to expand its operations into other parts of the country and is effectively frozen into its present locations. (If Company B had only been actively doing business in a smaller area, such as the San Antonio, Texas, metropolitan area, then it would be limited to that smaller area.)

The governing provision of the Lanham Act, section 33(b), states:

> To the extent that the right to use the registered mark has become incontestable under section 1065 of this title [Lanham Act section 15], the registration shall be conclusive evidence of the validity of the registered mark and of the registration of the mark, of the registrant's ownership of the mark, and of the registrant's exclusive right to use the registered mark in commerce.... Such conclusive evidence of the right to use the registered mark shall be subject to proof of infringement as defined in section 1114 of this title [Lanham Act section 32], and shall be subject to the following defenses or defects:
>
> ....
>
> > (5) That the mark whose use by a party is charged as an infringement was adopted without knowledge of the registrant's prior use and has been continuously used by such party or those in privity with him from a date prior to (A) the date of constructive use of the mark established pursuant to section 1057(c) of this title [Lanham Act section 7(c)], (B) the registration of the mark under this Act if the application for registration is filed before the effective date of the Trademark Law Revision Act of 1988, or (C) publication of the registered mark under subsection (c) of section 1062 of this title [Lanham Act section 12]: Provided, however, That this defense or defect shall apply only for the area in which such continuous prior use is proved.

15 U.S.C. § 1115(b). Although Company A's mark is not noted to be incontestable, it will be subject to at least those defenses to which an incontestable mark is subject.

Answer (A) is incorrect. As discussed above, there is a carve-out based on the limited-area exception for Company B, which was doing business state-wide in one state before A's federal registration.

Answer (C) is incorrect. The limited-area exception gives Company B exclusive rights in its market area—to allow both companies to operate in the same geographic and product market would cause significant consumer confusion.

Answer (D) is incorrect. This answer ignores the nationwide rights that Company A obtains by virtue of its registration, except for areas within the limited-area exception. This answer would have been correct under the common law, without any federal filings.

22. Answer (C) is correct. Company B will own the rights to the mark because it filed the intent-to-use application before A used the mark and ultimately received the notice of allowance. This is true even though Company A developed the arbitrary trademark first and used the mark before Company B used it. The critical facts are that Company B filed an intent-to-use (or "ITU") application before any use in commerce by Company A. Given that Company B received a notice of allowance and proceeded to make its own use in commerce in timely fashion, it has perfected its rights under the ITU application process and will receive all rights to the mark under federal law. Moreover, there is no evidence that Company B acted in bad faith.

Answer (A) is incorrect. Neither the common law nor the Lanham Act gives priority for simply coming up with a mark, though a new user of a mark in a market is often given a window in which to develop trademark rights before others can appropriate it through subsequent common law use. Even this narrow window is limited in time and scope under the common law. *See generally Galt House, Inc. v. Home Supply Co.*, 483 S.W.2d 107 (Ky. Ct. App. 1972). The ITU provisions here would trump any common law claim on these facts.

Answer (B) is incorrect. Under the common law and traditional trademark principles, Company A would have obtained the rights, at least in New York and New England, because it was the first to make bona fide use of the trademark there. *See, e.g., Blue Bell, Inc. v. Farah Manufacturing Co.*, 508 F.2d 1260 (5th Cir. 1975). As discussed above, however, the ITU process changes this analysis when another party has properly and in good faith made use of its provisions, as in this case.

Answer (D) is incorrect. No division of rights would be available in this situation. In this situation, the ITU provision would definitively assign the rights across the United States to Company B.

23. Answer (D) is correct. The term of protection for trademarks under the Lanham Act can be perpetual as long as the trademark has not been abandoned and has not become generic. The Lanham Act protects both registered and unregistered marks; even as to a registered mark, there is no time limit on the ultimate duration of a trademark registration. Each registration period is 10 years, but the registration may be renewed for an unlimited number of additional 10-year periods. Renewals of registrations are subject to statutory requirements—many administrative—but with a primary substantive requirement of affirming and proving continued bona fide use in commerce in connection with the goods and services listed in the registration. *See* 15 U.S.C. §§ 1058–59. Despite this potential for perpetual protection, a trademark can always be challenged on grounds that it has been abandoned or has become generic. *See* 15 U.S.C. §§ 1059 (providing no limit on the number of times a registration may be renewed), 1064(3) (allowing a cancellation petition to be filed at any time if the mark has become generic or is abandoned), & 1115 (preserving abandonment and genericness as defenses to any action for infringement of a registered trademark).

Essentially, as long as a mark continues to function as a source indicator, it is eligible for continued protection under both federal and state law. Unlike patents and copyrights, which have a Constitutional restriction on their duration (the "limited times" provision of the Intellectual Property Clause), there is no similar limit on congressional authority under the Commerce Clause—the constitutional basis for trademark protection.

Answer (A) is incorrect. Each trademark registration is issued for 10 years, but the registration can be renewed an unlimited number of times if the requisites of renewal are met. *See* 15 U.S.C. §§ 1058–59. In addition, the Lanham Act protects both registered and unregistered marks. The term of protection for trademarks under the Lanham Act can be perpetual as long as the trademark has not been abandoned and has not become generic, as further explained above.

Answer (B) is incorrect. This statement overstates the potentially perpetual existence of trademarks and trademark registrations; a trademark can always be challenged on grounds that it has been abandoned or has become generic—even if the registration has been renewed.

Answer (C) is incorrect. This statement is the second-best answer, as it does provide one of the ways that a mark can lose its trademark status, but it ignores the potential challenge that can be made if a trademark has been abandoned. (While genericism is one form of abandonment within the Lanham Act's definition of "abandoned," it is not the *only* way in which a mark is "abandoned" or otherwise loses its significance as a mark.) This answer may also overstate the ability to challenge an incontestable descriptive mark that may have lost some secondary meaning yet has not become truly generic.

24. Answer (D) is correct. A trademark becomes incontestable under the Lanham Act when it is registered under federal law for five years and continuously used for five years and an affidavit of incontestability has been filed. These points are found in the plain language of the statute:

> The right of the owner to use such registered mark in commerce for the goods or services on or in connection with which such registered mark has been in continuous use for five consecutive years subsequent to the date of such registration and is still in use in commerce, shall be incontestable, provided that ... (3) an affidavit is filed within one year after the expiration of any such five-year period setting for the [certain required information related to use and lack of legal proceedings adverse to the claim of ownership].

15 U.S.C. § 1065.

Answer (A) is incorrect. The focus of incontestability is registration, not merely use.

Answer (B) is incorrect. As noted above, the focus of incontestability is registration, not merely a period of use.

Answer (C) is incorrect. By its terms, as noted above, the statute requires five years of registration and continuous use, as well as the filing of the required affidavit.

Trademark & Unfair Competition Law— Infringement & Remedies

25. In order to establish a case for trademark infringement or unfair competition, the trademark owner must ultimately show a likelihood that ordinary consumers will be confused regarding the source, sponsorship, or origin of the goods or services in question. This crucial "likelihood of confusion" standard applies to cases of infringement of registered trademarks (under section 32 of the Lanham Act, 15 U.S.C. § 1114) and of infringement of unregistered trademarks, which are protected under section 43(a) of the Lanham Act, 15 U.S.C. § 1125(a). The likelihood of confusion standard is also frequently applied in cases brought under state trademark and unfair competition law.

The typical elements of the likelihood of confusion test can be found in the Second Circuit's decision in *Polaroid Corp. v. Polarad Electronics Corp.*, 287 F.2d 492, 495 (2d Cir. 1961), which surveyed its own prior caselaw in a range of infringement cases before setting forth a multi-factor balancing test for determining the likelihood of confusion. It listed (1) the strength of the mark; (2) the degree of similarity between the two marks; (3) the marketplace proximity of the two marks; (4) the likelihood that the senior user of the mark will bridge the gap; (5) evidence of actual confusion; (6) the junior user's bad faith in adopting the mark; (7) the quality of the junior user's mark; and (8) the sophistication of the relevant consumer group. Other circuits apply varying formulations of the balancing test, with most of the same *Polaroid* factors included in the analysis, albeit sometimes with different wording. Additional factors considered by some circuits include the degree of purchaser care and the similarity of marketing channels.

26. Answer (D) is correct. Circuits are split on whether an issue of trademark infringement presents a question of fact or a "mixed question of law and fact." Trademark infringement, as discussed in the question above, uses the "likelihood of confusion" standard, and courts apply a multi-factor or multi-element balancing test to determine whether that "likelihood of confusion" standard has been met. If the "likelihood of confusion" is an issue of fact, then an assessment of the individual factors and the overall balancing of all factors is left to the factfinder, ordinarily a jury. If it is a mixed question of law and fact, then each of the individual confusion factors are fact issues, while the final weighing or balancing of the factors is an issue of law for the court. It is important to note that the standard of review for appeals of infringement determinations is also affected by this issue. If it is a fact issue, then district court determinations will only be overturned if clearly erroneous. On the other hand, if it is a mixed question of law and fact, then the appellate court would review the legal determination de novo, with no deference given to the lower court's judgment on the ultimate issue of law—the balancing of the factors.

Answer (A) is incorrect. As discussed above, courts are split on this issue.

Answer (B) is incorrect. No court has taken the view that the standard is purely a matter of law, given that the underlying confusion factors clearly involve factual determinations.

Answer (C) is incorrect. As discussed above, courts are split on this issue.

27. **Answer (B) is correct.** Proof of actual confusion in trademark cases is not required, but if it is proven it is persuasive evidence of a likelihood of confusion. Actual confusion can be shown directly by proof that consumers were in fact confused as to the source or sponsorship of the goods or services, or indirectly through the use of survey evidence. Thus, if the trademark owner (the senior user) can bring forward this type of evidence, it is a persuasive indicator of the likelihood of confusion. On the other hand, the owner/senior user is not required to prove actual confusion, as the ultimate question is whether there is a *likelihood of* confusion among ordinary consumers.

Answer (A) is incorrect. As discussed above, the plaintiff is not required to prove actual confusion, as the ultimate question is whether there is a likelihood of confusion among ordinary consumers.

Answer (C) is incorrect. In most cases, actual confusion is not easily shown. It requires either (1) rather precise testimony from consumers (which can only occur if the junior user, the accused infringer, has already begun selling or otherwise using the mark in the marketplace) or (2) quite expensive and intricately designed survey evidence. A single instance of actual confusion, a poorly constructed survey, or a survey showing very low percentages of confusion (such as 5 percent) would be insufficient to show actual confusion.

Answer (D) is incorrect. Actual confusion is not one of the less important factors in a likelihood of confusion analysis. It is true that it is difficult to prove (see explanation to incorrect Answer (C) above), but that does not make it one of the less important factors. As discussed above in connection with correct Answer (B), when an owner has such proof, it can be highly probative of a likelihood of confusion.

28. A trademark owner, typically the plaintiff in the action unless a declaratory judgment action has been filed by an accused infringer, can prove actual confusion either (1) directly by presenting evidence that consumers were in fact confused as to the source or sponsorship of the goods or services, via affidavit, deposition, or live testimony by those consumers, depending on the circumstances, or (2) indirectly through the use of survey evidence.

The central point is that if a substantial number of consumers were in fact confused, then there is a high likelihood of actual confusion. Thus, if the plaintiff trademark owner can show a meaningful number of instances in which consumers did in fact have confusion as to the source or sponsorship of the goods or services, actual confusion is established.

If affidavit, deposition, or live testimony by confused consumers is not available, as is often the case for a variety of reasons, the plaintiff can conduct a survey of ordinary and relevant potential purchasers. The survey must have a meaningful number of participants who are potential consumers of the relevant goods or services. Moreover, the survey must be written and conducted properly so as to elicit useful responses—for example, it should not have leading questions. It is unsettled whether any particular percentage of consumers in a survey must be shown to have been confused as to source or sponsorship to establish actual confusion. Valid surveys showing more than 25 percent confusion are given great weight. *See, e.g., Piper Aircraft Corp. v. WagAero, Inc.,* 741 F.2d 925 (7th Cir. 1984) (45 percent); *Union Carbide Corp. v. Ever-Ready, Inc.,* 531 F.2d 366 (7th Cir.) (over 50 percent), *cert. denied,* 429 U.S. 830 (1976); *A.T. Cross Co. v. TPM Distributing, Inc.,* 1985 U.S. Dist. LEXIS 18805 (D. Minn. June 18, 1985) (34–43 percent); *McDonald's Corp. v. McBagel's, Inc.,* 649 F. Supp. 1268 (S.D.N.Y. 1986) (25 percent). Some courts have found relatively low percentages to be sufficient to show confusion, including those as low as 11, 15, 16, and 20 percent. *See RJR Foods, Inc. v. White Rock Corp.,* 603 F.2d 1058 (2d Cir. 1979) (15 to 20 percent); *James Burrough, Ltd. v. Sign of Beefeater, Inc.,* 540 F.2d 266 (7th Cir. 1976) (15 percent); *Humble Oil & Refining Co. v. American Oil Co.,* 405 F.2d 803 (8th Cir.), *cert. denied,* 395 U.S. 905 (1969); *Quality Inns International, Inc. v. McDonald's Corp.,* 695 F. Supp. 198 (D. Md. 1988) (16 percent). Surveys showing less than 10 percent confusion have generally been deemed insufficient to show actual confusion (and are likely to be adduced by the defendant in order to negate actual confusion). *See, e.g., Henri's Food Products Co. v. Kraft, Inc.,* 717 F.2d 352 (7th Cir. 1983) (7.6 percent confusion found in defendant's survey; plaintiff did not present survey evidence); *Weight Watchers International, Inc. v. Stouffer Corp.,* 744 F. Supp. 1259 (S.D.N.Y. 1990) (9 percent confusion deemed insufficient); *G. Heileman Brewing Co. v. Anheuser-Busch, Inc.,* 676 F. Supp. 1436 (E.D. Wis. 1987) (survey showing 4.5 percent actual confusion weighs against finding likelihood of confusion), *aff'd,* 873 F.2d 985 (7th Cir. 1989); *Wuv's International, Inc. v. Love's Enterprises, Inc.,* 1980 U.S. Dist. LEXIS 16512 (D. Colo. Nov. 4, 1980) (9 percent insufficient). As noted above, if the trademark plaintiff can bring forward this type of evidence of actual confusion, it is a persuasive indication of the likelihood of confusion.

29. Answer (D) is correct. A trademark owner that has not obtained federal registration for its trademark can bring suit for all relief available under section 43(a) of the Lanham Act, 15 U.S.C. §1125, but does not have other statutory rights that a registered trademark holder would have. Claims for infringement of a registered trademark can be brought under section 32 of the Lanham Act, 15 U.S.C. §1114, but section 43(a) permits claims for both registered and unregistered trademarks. Section 43(a) states in relevant part:

> Any person who, on or in connection with any goods or services, or any container for goods, uses in commerce any word, term, name, symbol, or device, or any combination thereof, or any false designation of origin, false or misleading description of fact, or false or misleading representation of fact, which—
>
> (A) is likely to cause confusion, or to cause mistake, or to deceive as to the affiliation, connection, or association of such person with another person, or as to the origin, sponsorship, or approval of his or her goods, services, or commercial activities by another person, or
>
> (B) in commercial advertising or promotion, misrepresents the nature, characteristics, qualities, or geographic origin of his or her or another person's goods, serv-

ices, or commercial activities, shall be liable in a civil action by any person who believes that he or she is or is likely to be damaged by such act.

15 U.S.C. § 1125. A plaintiff suing under section 43(a) can recover monetary and injunctive relief. There are statutory benefits to federal registration of a trademark, including evidentiary benefits under section 33(a) of the Lanham Act, 15 U.S.C. § 1115(a); nationwide constructive use under section 7, 15 U.S.C. § 1057; and incontestability under section 15, 15 U.S.C. § 1065. A registration serves as prima facie evidence of the mark's validity, the registrant's ownership of the mark, and the registrant's exclusive right to use the mark in commerce in connection with the listed goods or services. The constructive use provision provides nationwide priority in the mark as of the filing date, and the constructive notice provision, 15 U.S.C. § 1072, means that the registration serves as notice to all junior (i.e., subsequent) users as of the registration date. The federal registrant secures rights to its mark throughout the country, enabling it to bar any later users, as well as to "freeze" any prior users in their then-existing markets under the limited-area exception. See the answer to Question 21 in Topic 2 regarding the limited-area exception. The benefits of incontestability are addressed in the answers to Question 18 in Topic 1 and Question 24 in Topic 2.

Answer (A) is incorrect. The trademark owner does not have the statutory benefits to federal registration, including constructive notice and incontestability.

Answer (B) is incorrect. The trademark owner is not limited to injunctive relief; monetary remedies are available as well.

Answer (C) is incorrect. Registration of the mark is not a condition precedent to suit in trademark litigation under section 43(a).

30. Answer (D) is correct. The following statement most accurately describes the approach taken by federal trademark law to questions of remedies—injunctive relief is frequently granted, and monetary awards are usually available upon a showing of bad faith or actual harm. There are varying standards for an award of profits around the country as noted below, and the Supreme Court granted certiorari on the issue in June 2019.

Injunctive relief is available under section 34 of the Lanham Act, which states:

> The several courts vested with jurisdiction of civil actions arising under this chapter *shall have power to grant injunctions, according to the principles of equity and upon such terms as the court may deem reasonable,* to prevent the violation of any right of the registrant of a mark registered in the Patent and Trademark Office or to prevent a violation under subsection (a), (c), or (d) of section 1125 of this title.

15 U.S.C. § 1116(a) (emphasis added). Courts are empowered to grant an injunction, and they frequently do so in order to protect the goodwill represented by a mark and to place that goodwill back within the control of the mark owner, protecting consumers from the likelihood of confusion arising from the infringing use.

The Lanham Act also provides for monetary relief in two primary forms, plaintiff's damages and infringer's profits (even aside from attorney's fees, which are separately addressed at the end of the provision quoted below):

> When a violation of any right of the registrant of a mark registered in the Patent and Trademark Office, or a violation under section 1125(a) of this title, shall have been established in any civil action arising under this chapter, the *plaintiff shall be entitled,* subject to the provisions of sections 1111 and 1114 of this title, *and subject to the principles of equity, to recover* (1) defendant's profits, (2) any damages sustained by the plaintiff, and (3) the costs of the action. The court shall assess such profits and damages or cause the same to be assessed under its direction. In assessing profits the plaintiff shall be required to prove defendant's sales only; defendant must prove all elements of cost or deduction claimed. In assessing damages the court may enter judgment, *according to the circumstances of the case, for any sum above the amount found as actual damages,* not exceeding three times such amount. If the court shall find that the *amount of the recovery based on profits is either inadequate or excessive the court may in its discretion enter judgment for such sum as the court shall find to be just, according to the circumstances of the case.* Such sum in either of the above circumstances shall constitute compensation and not a penalty. The court in exceptional cases may award reasonable attorney fees to the prevailing party.

15 U.S.C. § 1117(a) (emphasis added).

The basic principle of causation serves to limit "any damages sustained by the plaintiff" to require proof of actual harm to the plaintiff—and proof connecting the harm to the actions of the infringer. Courts have often interpreted "subject to the principles of equity" to mean that "defendant's profits" are obtainable when the trademark owner has shown either actual confusion (in which case it is reasonable to presume defendant's profits were the result of the confusion and should be paid to the plaintiff) or bad faith (which makes it appropriate to award the profits to the plaintiff owner of the mark). Some circuit courts have required proof of willful infringement for an award of an infringer's profits for a violation of section 43(a). The Supreme Court heard arguments on this issue in January 2020, in *Romag Fasteners Inc. v. Fossil Inc.* (Docket No. 18-1233).

Answer (A) is incorrect. There is no presumption in favor of injunctive relief, and monetary awards are granted when the evidence supports it—and not only in rare, unusual, or exceptional cases. Attorney's fees, on the other hand, are only available in "exceptional cases" under the language of the final sentence in the relevant provision (see the block quote above of 15 U.S.C. § 1117(a)).

Answer (B) is incorrect. There is no presumption in favor of monetary relief, and injunctions are frequently granted.

Answer (C) is incorrect. As noted above, monetary awards are available on principles of equity beyond "bad faith" alone. Many courts look to either bad faith or actual harm, and other circumstances can also be taken into account. See the more complete language of the statute and the explanation for correct Answer (D) above. More clarification may be available after the Supreme Court issues a decision in the pending case mentioned in that answer.

31. Corrective advertising is a form of damages recoverable by plaintiffs in order to correct any false and misleading impression created by the defendant's false or confusingly similar advertising. For example, in *U-Haul International, Inc. v. Jartran, Inc.*, 793 F.2d 1034 (9th Cir. 1986), the plaintiff recovered $13.6 million in corrective advertising, which easily exceeded the original $6 million expended by the defendant in its alleged false advertising campaign. The court concluded that the role of the expensive advertising campaign was needed to correct harm that had been done to the U-Haul trademark. In *ALPO Petfoods, Inc. v. Ralston Purina Co.*, 997 F.2d 949 (D.C. Cir. 1993), the court upheld a $3.6 million award for corrective advertising to compensate for the cost of reasonably responding to the defendant's advertisements.

32. Under the Lanham Act, attorney's fees can be obtained in trademark litigation as follows: "The court in exceptional cases may award reasonable attorney fees to the prevailing party." 15 U.S.C. §1117(a). The Lanham Act leaves the matter of fees to the district court's discretion, following the lead of the same "exceptional case" language in the Patent Act and the Supreme Court's interpretation of that language. Under the Supreme Court's interpretation, an "exceptional" case is simply one that "stands out from others with respect to the substantive strength of a party's litigating position (considering both the governing law and the facts of the case) or the unreasonable manner in which the case was litigated." *Octane Fitness, LLC v. Icon Health & Fitness, Inc.*, 134 S. Ct. 1749, 1756 (2014). "District courts may determine whether a case is 'exceptional' in the case-by-case exercise of their discretion, considering the totality of the circumstances." The Court in *Octane* also referred back to an earlier copyright case on attorney's fees where it noted: "there is no precise rule or formula" for exercising discretion, which is to be exercised "in light of the considerations we have identified," which were simply a "nonexclusive list" of "factors," such as "frivolousness, motivation, objective unreasonableness [factual and legal] and the need in particular circumstances to advance considerations of compensation and deterrence," confined only by fidelity to the purposes of the Act in question (citing to *Fogerty v. Fantasy, Inc.*, 510 U.S. 517 (1994)).

33. Answer (D) is correct. The strongest theory for infringement of a long-standing and widely known trademark such as the Nike "swoosh" design mark when used by someone in a totally unrelated field or enterprise, such as a food truck selling tacos, is dilution by blurring. Because of the wide disparity in the product markets in this situation, proving a likelihood of confusion is difficult. A theory of dilution resulting from blurring the selling power of the famous Nike swoosh mark is therefore a stronger claim than the theory that there was confusion as to source or sponsorship of the defendant's taco truck. Even if the ordinary consumer would not be confused, the distinctive quality of the plaintiff's famous design mark is damaged when the name is used to market unrelated products or services. *See* 15 U.S.C. §1125(c)(2)(B) (defining "dilution by blurring" as an "association arising from the similarity between a mark or trade name and a famous mark that impairs the distinctiveness of the famous mark"). Over time, if these uses were allowed to proceed unabated, the swoosh design, when seen being used as a mark, would no longer automatically bring to mind the maker of athletic shoes and accessories.

To address the potential loss of selling power of marks in situations similar to the one described, some states enacted trademark dilution statutes beginning in the middle of the 20th century, allowing relief when a distinctive or famous trademark was blurred or tarnished by the use of a substantially similar or identical mark, even in the absence of a showing of consumer confusion or direct competition in the plaintiff's market. In 1995, Congress enacted the Federal Trademark Dilution Act, which made dilution doctrine a matter of federal trademark law. The federal act, now revised by the Trademark Dilution Revision Act of 2006, requires that a mark be "famous" across the United States in order to receive protection from dilution. Some states also require fame, but only within the state, while others do not include "famous" mark status in the statute (although judges typically still view unusual mark strength as a requirement. *See, e.g., Sally Gee, Inc. v. Myra Hogan, Inc.*, 699 F.2d 621, 625 (2d Cir. 1983) (stating that New York antidilution law protected "only extremely strong marks"). The federal dilution law, as amended in 2006, states:

> Subject to the principles of equity, the owner of a famous mark that is distinctive, inherently or through acquired distinctiveness, shall be entitled to an injunction against another person who, at any time after the owner's mark has become famous, commences use of a mark or trade name in commerce that is likely to cause dilution by blurring or dilution by tarnishment of the famous mark, regardless of the presence or absence of actual or likely confusion, of competition, or of actual economic injury.

15 U.S.C. § 1125(c)(1). Additional portions of the statute provide a standard for the level of fame required for a mark to be found "famous" and provide more detail on blurring and tarnishment, among other issues.

Answer (A) is incorrect. A state law unfair competition claim is not the strongest claim on these facts — it generally requires a showing of a likelihood of confusion and may offer less satisfactory remedies than a federal claim (depending on applicable state law). Given the wide disparity in the product markets at issue here, proving a likelihood of confusion would be difficult, even though the marks would be identical.

Answer (B) is incorrect. A federal trademark infringement claim, whether under section 32 or section 43(a), is not the strongest claim on these facts — it requires a showing of a likelihood of confusion, which would be quite difficult in light of the wide disparity in the product markets in this situation.

Answer (C) is incorrect. A claim of dilution by tarnishment requires a negative association with the famous mark, *see* 15 U.S.C. § 1125(c)(2(C) (defining "dilution by tarnishment" as an "association arising from the similarity between a mark or trade name and a famous mark that harms the reputation of the famous mark"), which is unlikely to be shown on these facts.

34. Section 43(c)(1) of the Lanham Act, of course, requires that a mark have become "famous" before the allegedly diluting use begins in order for a dilution action to be viable. Section 43(c)(2)(A) of the Act, in turn, provides for a standard of fame: "For purposes of paragraph (1), a mark is famous if it is widely recognized by the general consuming public of the United States as a designation of source of the goods or services of the mark's owner." This standard was a key change introduced by the 2006 TDRA (Trademark Dilution Revision Act); the original dilution provision did not contain a standard for just how famous a mark needed to be. Now, a mark must be "widely recognized by the general consuming public of the United States," and it cannot be a mark known only within a niche group of consumers or a small area of the country. *See, e.g., Cosi, Inc. v. WK*

Holdings, L.L.C., No. 05-2770, 2007 WL 1288028, 2007 U.S. Dist. LEXIS 31990 (D. Minn. May 1, 2007) (D. Minn. May 1, 2007) ("Cosi" restaurant mark not sufficiently famous); *Milbank Tweed Hadley & McCoy LLP v. Milbank Holding Corp.*, 82 U.S.P.Q.2d 1583 (C.D. Cal. 2007) (Milbank Tweed law firm's "Milbank" mark not sufficiently famous).

The Lanham Act proceeds, after having provided the standard for a famous mark, to list factors that may be considered in reaching a determination as to whether a mark is, in fact, "widely recognized by the general consuming public."

> In determining whether a mark possesses the requisite degree of recognition, the court may consider all relevant factors, including the following:
>
> (i) The duration, extent, and geographic reach of advertising and publicity of the mark, whether advertised or publicized by the owner or third parties.
>
> (ii) The amount, volume, and geographic extent of sales of goods or services offered under the mark.
>
> (iii) The extent of actual recognition of the mark.
>
> (iv) Whether the mark was registered under the Act of March 3, 1881, or the Act of February 20, 1905, or on the principal register.

15 U.S.C. § 1125(c)(2)(A). Factors (i)–(ii) gather circumstantial evidence of consumer understanding, and they should focus a court on whether the "general consuming public of the United States" has had the opportunity to encounter the mark at a level that would lead to wide recognition. Factor (iii) appears to invite direct evidence of consumer understanding, such as survey evidence that a trademark owner might have gathered. One issue with that factor would be timing, however, since the evidence of "actual recognition" should be from a time before the allegedly diluting use began.

35. Claims of dilution by tarnishment and dilution by blurring are distinct, although both are actionable under the federal Trademark Dilution Revision Act (TDRA), at 15 U.S.C. § 1125(c), and under most state dilution statutes. A dilution-by-blurring theory simply involves damage to the distinctive quality of the plaintiff's famous brand name when the name is used to market unrelated products or services. The association is neutral, but over time, if these uses were allowed to proceed unabated, rather than being restrained, the famous mark would no longer automatically bring to mind the plaintiff as source or sponsor, with a resulting loss of selling power for the famous mark. The TDRA delineates the factors relevant to a blurring claim:

> For purposes of paragraph (1), "dilution by blurring" is association arising from the similarity between a mark or trade name and a famous mark that impairs the distinctiveness of the famous mark. In determining whether a mark or trade name is likely to cause dilution by blurring, the court may consider all relevant factors, including the following:
>
> (i) The degree of similarity between the mark or trade name and the famous mark.
>
> (ii) The degree of inherent or acquired distinctiveness of the famous mark.

(iii) The extent to which the owner of the famous mark is engaging in substantially exclusive use of the mark.

(iv) The degree of recognition of the famous mark.

(v) Whether the user of the mark or trade name intended to create an association with the famous mark.

(vi) Any actual association between the mark or trade name and the famous mark.

15 U.S.C. § 1125(c)(2)(B).

A claim of dilution by tarnishment, on the other hand, requires a harmful negative association with the famous mark. As stated in the Lanham Act: "'[D]ilution by tarnishment' is association arising from the similarity between a mark or trade name and a famous mark that harms the reputation of the famous mark." 15 U.S.C. § 1125(c)(2)(C). Tarnishment cases can involve use of the famous mark in settings involving illegal drugs, pornography, and other unsavory material. *See generally Coca-Cola Co. v. Gemini Rising, Inc.*, 346 F. Supp. 1183 (E.D.N.Y. 1972) (state law dilution claim involving "Enjoy Cocaine" poster, which elicited the Coca-Cola brand and color scheme). The tarnishment claim can involve other types of unfavorable or negative associations. For example, even though gambling was not characterized by the court as unsavory, the Second Circuit in *New York Stock Exchange, Inc., v. New York, New York Hotel, LLC*, 293 F.3d 550 (2d Cir. 2002), reversed a grant of summary judgment for the defendant casino on the stock exchange's tarnishment claim, noting that tarnishment was not limited to "seamy" conduct and that the plaintiff, a stock exchange, might be able to demonstrate that its reputation for integrity might be harmed by a connection to casino gambling, which many consumers believe as a general matter involves odds that are stacked in favor of the casino.

Trademark & Unfair Competition Law— Defenses & Limitations

36. Answer (C) is correct. The validity of an incontestable registration can be challenged by an accused infringer on the ground that the mark is either generic or functional, but no challenge based on descriptiveness can be mounted. As discussed previously (see Question 18 in Topic 1 and Question 24 in Topic 2), the trademark incontestability doctrine prevents challenges to the ownership and validity of trademarks (with certain exceptions) that have been registered and continuously used without successful challenge for five years if an affidavit of incontestability is filed. The incontestability provision carves out certain bases for challenge, which means some "contestability" remains: "Except on a ground for which application to cancel may be filed at any time under paragraphs (3) and (5) of section 14 of this Act, … the right of the registrant to use such registered mark … shall be incontestable." 15 U.S.C. § 1065. Paragraph (3) of section 14 of the Lanham Act (which governs cancellations) provides for challenges:

> [a]t any time if the registered mark becomes the generic name for goods or services, or a portion thereof, for which it is registered, or is functional, or has been abandoned, or its registration was obtained fraudulently or contrary to Section 4 [certification and collective marks] or of subsection (a), (b), or (c) of section 2 [trademark and service marks] for a registration under this Act.

15 U.S.C. § 1064 (3) (emphasis added). Challenges based on descriptiveness or lack of secondary meaning are not included within the carved-out bases, so those challenges by accused infringers are precluded after a mark becomes incontestable. Challenges based on generic status or functionality (as well as other marks precluded from registration in 15 U.S.C. § 1064(3), as shown above), can still be made at any time. In addition, as for challenges based on genericness, the Lanham Act specifically states that "no incontestable right shall be acquired in a mark which is the generic name for the goods or services or a portion thereof, for which it is registered." 15 U.S.C. § 1065.

Answer (A) is incorrect. The trademark incontestability doctrine does allow challenges based on the mark's being generic, but it also allows challenges for being functional. See the explanation above.

Answer (B) is incorrect. As discussed above, the trademark incontestability doctrine prevents challenges based on descriptiveness or lack of secondary meaning.

Answer (D) is incorrect. As discussed previously, the trademark incontestability doctrine prevents challenges based on descriptiveness or lack of secondary meaning.

37. Answer (D) is correct. Any of the following would be a basis for a trademark abandonment defense: assignment in gross, naked licensing, and nonuse with no intent to resume use. Trademark owners can involuntarily lose or voluntarily abandon their trademark rights in several ways. Under the Lanham Act, a mark is deemed to be "abandoned" in the following circumstances:

> (1) When its use has been discontinued with intent not to resume such use. Intent not to resume may be inferred from circumstances. Nonuse for 3 consecutive years shall be prima facie evidence of abandonment. "Use" of a mark means the bona fide use of such mark made in the ordinary course of trade, and not made merely to reserve a right in a mark.

> (2) When any course of conduct of the owner, including acts of omission as well as commission, causes the mark to become the generic name for the goods or services on or in connection with which it is used or otherwise to lose its significance as a mark. Purchaser motivation shall not be a test for determining abandonment under this paragraph.

15 U.S.C. § 1127. A firm might simply abandon its mark voluntarily because it decides to change its name or to liquidate its business. It might also abandon the mark by sheer inactivity or nonuse. Another basis for abandonment is naked licensing—the failure to exercise control over the licensing of a mark, resulting in uncontrolled or indiscriminate use of the mark in a manner that can deceive consumers. Uncontrolled use of a mark causes it to lose its source significance or "otherwise to lose its significance as a mark." Abandonment can thus result involuntarily through naked licensing, although such instances are rare. *See TMT North America, Inc. v. Magic Touch GmbH*, 124 F.3d 876, 885–86 (7th Cir. 1997); *Exxon Corp. v. Oxxford Clothes, Inc.*, 109 F.3d 1070 (5th Cir. 1997) (no abandonment). *See generally* McCarthy on Trademarks §§ 18:42, 18:48 (1995). Finally, a trademark can only be assigned with the goodwill associated with the mark. The assignment of a mark without its associated goodwill is prohibited as an "assignment in gross." *See Sugar Busters LLC v. Brennan*, 177 F.3d 258 (5th Cir. 1999). Like naked licensing, separation of a mark from its goodwill by assignment in gross causes the mark "otherwise to lose its significance as a mark."

Answer (A) is incorrect. As discussed above, any of the grounds can establish abandonment.

Answer (B) is incorrect. As discussed above, any of the grounds can establish abandonment.

Answer (C) is incorrect. As discussed above, any of the grounds can establish abandonment.

38. The Lanham Act describes the trademark fair use defense as follows:

> That the use of the name, term, or device charged to be an infringement is a use, otherwise than as a mark, of the party's individual name in his own business, or of the individual name of anyone in privity with such party, or of a term or device which is descriptive of and used fairly and in good faith only to describe the goods or services of such party, or their geographic origin.

15 U.S.C. § 1115(b)(4). As a result, for a descriptive term, the basic elements of the trademark fair use defense are (1) use of the term other than as a mark, (2) in good faith, and (3) use of the term descriptively.

Company B, because it is using the term "Sweet" as its trademark, will fail to make out a statutory fair use defense on a key point—"other than as a mark." Depending on the circumstances, the finder of fact might even have some trouble with "descriptive use" (unless this more modern or slang use of "sweet" is considered to be descriptive in this instance, which might or might not work). In any event, it is Company B's use of "Sweet" as its own trademark that definitively dooms a descriptive fair use defense, regardless of its good faith and the potential for the average consumer to understand the term "sweet" in this context (cell phone cases) in a descriptive sense—as meaning "awesome."

On the other hand, just by way of example, under the statutory descriptive fair use defense, a producer of canned vegetables would be permitted to describe its goods as being "green" in color or "giant" in size without infringing on the "Green Giant" trademark, as long as the elements of the fair use test are otherwise satisfied. In *KP Permanent Make-Up, Inc. v. Lasting Impression I, Inc.*, 543 U.S. 111 (2004), the Supreme Court addressed the fair use defense in a case involving two producers of permanent makeup, both using the term "micro color" in the marketing and sale of their products. The Court held that a defendant asserting trademark fair use defense is not required to negate or disprove that its actions cause a likelihood of confusion. Thus, even if some likelihood of confusion might take place, the defendant can prevail if it has proven the requisite elements of the fair use defense.

39. Answer (D) is correct. In this scenario, Company A wishes to make reference to Company B's competing product in a television commercial. Company B's name can be used in the commercial as comparative advertising, but only if the advertisement is truthful and non-misleading. Thus, although many companies avoid directly identifying competitor brands as a matter of policy or for pragmatic reasons, the comparative advertising defense does permit such references in limited circumstances. *See R.G. Smith v. Chanel, Inc.*, 402 F.2d 562 (9th Cir. 1968).

> **Answer (A) is incorrect.** As long as the comparative advertising is truthful and non-misleading, it is not actionable as either trademark infringement or dilution.

> **Answer (B) is incorrect.** As long as the comparative advertising is truthful and non-misleading, it is not actionable as either trademark infringement or dilution.

> **Answer (C) is incorrect.** If the attempt at comparative advertising is either false or misleading, it is actionable and is not shielded by this defense.

40. Answer (B) is correct. In this scenario, the company purchases products with a broken part, inserts a new part to replace the broken one, and leaves the brand name in place upon resale of the used items. In general, the products, here, tablet computers, can be sold under the original brand name as long as they are clearly marked as reconditioned and assuming that replacing the screen is not considered unlawful reconstruction. In the landmark case of *Champion Spark Plug Co. v. Sanders*, 331 U.S. 125 (1947), the Supreme Court held that repaired or reconditioned products can continue to be sold under the trademark of the original seller, as long as the following provisos are met: (1) the identity of the repairer must be clear; (2) the product must be clearly marked as repaired, used, or reconditioned; and (3) the repair must not be so extensive as to make any reference to the original manufacturer misleading (i.e., it cannot constitute a complete reconstruction of the product). The Lanham Act provides no relief to the original manufacturer if these conditions are met.

Answer (A) is incorrect. As discussed above, repaired or reconditioned products can be lawfully sold, but the identity of the repairer must be clearly marked and the product must be clearly labeled as repaired, used, or reconditioned—as applicable to the facts of the situation. Here, the goods are not merely used; they have been reconditioned or repaired. Because they are not merely used, they need some additional markings.

Answer (C) is incorrect. As discussed above, repaired or reconditioned products can be sold as long as the conditions set forth in *Champion Spark Plug Co. v. Sanders* are met. Used goods provide a valuable form of competition in the marketplace for new trademarked goods, which is beneficial to consumers and which increases the amount of competition in the marketplace.

Answer (D) is incorrect. See the explanation for correct Answer (B) above. The doctrine of reverse confusion does exist, but it has no bearing on this fact scenario. Reverse confusion is a name given to situations where a junior trademark user becomes better known than the senior user, and consumer confusion runs in the reverse direction compared to a typical infringement situation (i.e., the junior user overwhelms the marketplace, which means that the average consumer ends up being more likely to think that the junior user is the owner of the mark, since the senior user is less well known).

Right of Publicity Law & Protection of Ideas

41. Answer (D) is correct. The use of personal information in a book written by a famous individual would not be protected under the right of publicity. The expression in the book would be the subject of copyright protection, although the facts therein would not be. On the other hand, a sound-alike performance, a look-alike performance, and most clearly a signature can give rise to liability for a violation of the right of publicity, depending upon applicable state law. Signatures are commonly protected under standard formulations of the right of publicity, and some courts have expanded the right to cover sound-alike performance and look-alike performances. *See, e.g., Midler v. Ford Motor Co.*, 849 F.2d 460 (9th Cir. 1988) (sound-alike Bette Midler commercial for Ford automobiles); *Wendt v. Host International, Inc.*, 125 F.3d 806 (9th Cir. 1997) (animatronic, life-size figures resembling Cliff and Norm from television series *Cheers*, and therefore also resembling the individuals who played those roles). *See also White v. Samsung Electronics America, Inc.*, 989 F.2d 1512 (9th Cir. 1993) (robot evoking Vanna White found potentially actionable).

> **Answer (A) is incorrect.** As discussed above, the right of publicity can encompass this claim, depending on state law.

> **Answer (B) is incorrect.** As discussed above, the right of publicity can encompass this claim, depending on state law. *See also Onassis v. Christian Dior-New York, Inc.*, 122 Misc. 2d 603 (N.Y. Sup. Ct. 1984) (Jacqueline Kennedy Onassis look-alike in advertisement).

> **Answer (C) is incorrect.** As discussed above, the right of publicity is very likely to encompass this claim, depending on state law.

42. Answer (C) is correct. The right of publicity can be viewed as both a personal privacy right and a commercial right. With regard to personal privacy foundations, Warren and Brandeis in their 1890 article identified the right of publicity as one of the four privacy torts. *See* Samuel D. Warren & Louis D. Brandeis, *The Right To Privacy*, 4 Harv. L. Rev. 193 (1890). Thus, the right of publicity originated as a personal right, akin to defamation, but it has developed in more recent years into a significant commercial right. The Restatement (Third) of Unfair Competition § 46 focused on the commercial aspects of this tort: "One who appropriates the commercial value of a person's identity by using without consent the person's name, likeness, or other indicia of identity for purposes of trade is subject to liability for the relief appropriate under the rules stated in §§ 48 and 49."

> **Answer (A) is incorrect.** As discussed above, the right of publicity can be viewed as either a personal privacy right or a commercial right.

> **Answer (B) is incorrect.** As discussed above, the right of publicity can be viewed as either a personal privacy right or a commercial right.

Answer (D) is incorrect. The right of publicity is not constitutionally protected. Although it is a form of privacy protected under state tort law, this type of privacy claim is analytically distinct from the line of United States Supreme Court cases addressing a "constitutional right of privacy."

43. Whether the right of publicity survives the death of the person whose name or likeness was used for commercial purposes in that state depends upon state law and on the primary policy underpinnings of the right of publicity claim. States are split on this issue, and a small number of states address this issue by statute. States that view the right of publicity as primarily a commercial right deem it to survive death, whereas states that view the claim as primarily a personal tort (akin to a defamation or invasion of privacy claim) often hold that the claim does not survive death. In some states, the posthumous right of publicity is only available if the person's identity has commercial value at or after death. For representative cases finding the right of publicity to survive death, see *State ex rel. Elvis Presley International Memorial Foundation v. Crowell*, 733 S.W.2d 89 (Tenn. Ct. App. 1987) (Tennessee law); *McFarland v. Miller*, 14 F.3d 912 (3d Cir. 1994) (New Jersey law); *Martin Luther King, Jr. Center for Social Change, Inc. v. American Heritage Products, Inc.*, 694 F.2d 674 (11th Cir. 1983) (Georgia law); *Joplin Enterprises v. Allen*, 795 F. Supp. 349 (W.D. Wash. 1992) (California law). For cases holding that the right of publicity does not survive death, see *Pirone v. MacMillan, Inc.*, 894 F.2d 579 (2d Cir. 1990) (New York law); *Southeast Bank, N.A. v. Lawrence*, 489 N.E.2d 744 (N.Y. 1985) (Florida law); *Reeves v. United Artists Corp.*, 765 F.2d 79 (6th Cir. 1985) (Ohio law).

44. **Answer (C) is correct.** An ordinary citizen (i.e., not a celebrity) is photographed while walking down a public street. The person's image is then used in a cellular phone advertisement without the citizen's consent. The best intellectual property claim to assert in this situation is the right of publicity. It might appear to be counterintuitive that any claim can be asserted on these facts because the individual photographed was not a celebrity and was photographed on a public street. Neither of these considerations, standing alone, would vitiate a right of publicity claim. First, ordinary persons who are not public figures or celebrities are entitled to protection under the right of publicity, as are celebrities and other public figures. In some states, the posthumous right of publicity is only available if the person's identity has commercial value at or after death. Most right of publicity cases happen to involve well-known persons because their images are often used in advertising and because they will have much higher potential recoveries for compensatory damages than ordinary persons. Second, the presence of a person on a public street does not serve as implied consent to the use of their image for advertising or commercial purposes.

Answer (A) is incorrect. Copyright law would not provide a right of action for this situation; the photographer did not take any creative expression owned by another.

Answer (B) is incorrect. False endorsement under the Lanham Act would require proof of a likelihood of confusion as to the person's endorsement of the product being advertised (not mere confusion as to whether the person was a paid model). This generally restricts false endorsement claims to famous persons. *See, e.g., Albert v. Apex Fitness, Inc.*, 1997 U.S. Dist. LEXIS 8535 (S.D.N.Y. June 12, 1997).

Answer (D) is incorrect. Trade secret law would not provide a right of action for this type of photography in a public setting and use of those images for commercial purposes.

45. Answer (B) is correct. This question is based on the facts and holding in the case of *ETW Corp. v. Jireh Publishing, Inc.*, 332 F.3d 915 (6th Cir. 2003), which involved paintings and prints depicting golfer Tiger Woods. The majority opinion concluded:

> Rush's work consists of a collage of images in addition to Woods's image which are combined to describe, in artistic form, a historic event in sports history and to convey a message about the significance of Woods's achievement in that event. Because Rush's work has substantial transformative elements, it is entitled to the full protection of the First Amendment. In this case, we find that Woods's right of publicity must yield to the First Amendment.

Id. at 938. Courts are split on how to approach situations like this one, and the Sixth Circuit panel was divided on the facts of this particular cases. As discussed below, however, none of the other possible answers is correct.

Answer (A) is incorrect. This blanket statement is incorrect because the First Amendment can apply to bar a right of publicity claim; the issue is how to analyze the competing considerations and strike a balance between tort and speech concerns.

Answer (C) is incorrect. There is no blanket exemption for artworks from the right of publicity. Each claim would need to be assessed on the facts.

Answer (D) is incorrect. This overstates any possible waiver argument. Merely because professional athletes participate in a sporting event or tournament does not mean that they implicitly waive their right of publicity.

46. Answer (D) is correct. A copyright law theory of recovery will not provide relief for the unauthorized use of an idea. Section 102(b) of the Copyright Act of 1976 expressly precludes copyright protection for an idea: "In no case does copyright protection for an original work of authorship extend to any idea, procedure, process, system, method of operation, concept, principle, or discovery, regardless of the form in which it is described, explained, illustrated, or embodied in such work." 17 U.S.C. § 102(b). On the other hand, state law claims for breach of express or implied contract or for quasi-contract or unjust enrichment can protect ideas in certain circumstances, depending upon applicable state law.

Answer (A) is incorrect. A quasi-contract claim or unjust enrichment claim can be asserted. In *Matarese v. Moore-McCormack Lines, Inc.*, 158 F.2d 631 (2d Cir. 1946), where the defendant sought the disclosure by the plaintiff, defendant promised compensation, the idea disclosed was specific and novel (and in the case, patentable), and the defendant subsequently used the idea without compensating the plaintiff, the court ruled for the plaintiff on his claim for the defendant's unjust enrichment. Some states also provide for a claim of misappropriation of an idea, while others do not. Where such a claim exists, it will generally require proof of the idea's novelty, disclosure of the idea in confidence, and defendant's use of the idea, and novelty will be fairly strictly judged. *See, e.g., Baer v. Chase*, 392 F.3d 609 (3d Cir. 2004); *Nadel v. Play-by-Play Toys & Novelties, Inc.*, 208 F.3d 368 (2d Cir. 2000).

Answer (B) is incorrect. An express contract can protect the disclosure of an idea in some circumstances, *see Nadel v. Play-by-Play Toys & Novelties, Inc.*, 208 F.3d 368 (2d Cir. 2000) (exploring the level of novelty of an idea that will support a claim of breach of contract), but a court will generally not waive any of the usual requirements for the formation of a contract, including mutual intent to contract, an exchange of promises, and definiteness. *See Smith v. Recrion Corp.*, 541 P.2d 663 (Nev. 1975) (explaining that even when related to the disclosure of an idea, a contract requires an exchange of promises (whether implied via conduct or expressly in words) and mutual intent to enter into a contract). *See also Baer v. Chase*, 392 F.3d 609 (3d Cir. 2004) (rejecting, for lack of definiteness, a contract-based claim related to disclosure of ideas to the producer and writer of *The Sopranos*).

Answer (C) is incorrect. As discussed above, an implied contract can protect the disclosure of an idea in some circumstances, if the idea purveyor can prove the usual requirements for the creation of a contract.

47. Answer (D) is correct. To uphold a misappropriation claim, courts will generally require proof of the idea's novelty, disclosure of the idea in confidence, and defendant's use of the idea, and novelty will be fairly strictly judged. *See, e.g., Baer v. Chase*, 392 F.3d 609 (3d Cir. 2004); *Nadel v. Play-by-Play Toys & Novelties, Inc.*, 208 F.3d 368 (2d Cir. 2000). (This question is based on the facts of *Baer v. Chase*, where the court rejected a misappropriation claim related to disclosure of ideas to the producer and writer of "The Sopranos.")

Answer (A) is incorrect. The mere promise to "take care of" the plaintiff is an insufficient basis on which to assert a misappropriation claim, the elements of which are stated above. (And in *Baer v. Chase*, that type of promise was also insufficiently certain for a claim based in contract.)

Answer (B) is incorrect. The fact that the defendant's script is successful is an insufficient basis on which to assert a misappropriation claim. It would be relevant to damages if the elements of a claim were met.

Answer (C) is incorrect. Although a written agreement might be more easily enforced under contract law because its terms would be express, the question asks about a claim made for misappropriation of ideas rather than a claim based in contract. The tort of misappropriation does not depend on agreements or promises of compensation, either made orally or in writing.

Trade Secret Law

48. Yes, a customer list, consisting of names, addresses, telephone numbers, and the name and title of the primary sales contact, can be protected as a trade secret, but it will depend on additional facts and circumstances. In particular, the party claiming ownership of the list as a trade secret needs to show that the information is not readily ascertainable by proper means, such as by observing the front door of the business or by simply researching all of the relevant businesses in the area who need the goods or services offered by that party. For some businesses, a customer list might well not be readily ascertainable or generally known, particularly where it also includes—as it does here—the name of the primary sales contact for each customer. Knowing the person at the customer entity who makes purchasing decisions would also enhance the economic value of the list compared to other information known by or readily available to a competitor. The person claiming that the list is a trade secret must also be able to demonstrate that it uses efforts reasonable under the circumstances to maintain the list's secrecy. *See* Uniform Trade Secrets Act § 1(4) (defining a trade secret); 18 U.S.C. § 1839(3) (same, DTSA).

49. Answer (B) is correct. The measures required for secrecy under the Uniform Trade Secrets Act (UTSA) and federal civil Defend Trade Secrets Act (DTSA) are "reasonable" efforts or measures at secrecy, given the particular circumstances; what is reasonable will vary based on the value of the information and the context. Here, with a restaurant's salsa recipe, keeping a highly limited number of physical copies rigorously separated by location and tightly restricting individual access would seem reasonable. Technology is not required. All measures to maintain secrecy will involve some cost or inconvenience, and thus a balancing of the benefits of a particular measure against its cost is necessary. *See, e.g., E.I. du Pont de Nemours & Co. v. Christopher*, 431 F.2d 1012 (5th Cir. 1970).

> **Answer (A) is incorrect.** Trade secret law does not ask simply whether a secret has in fact been kept; it asks whether, in the words of the statutes, "the owner thereof has taken reasonable measures to keep such information secret" (DTSA) or the information "is the subject of efforts that are reasonable under the circumstances to maintain its secrecy" (UTSA). Success in secrecy can affect a court's assessment of the measures, but success alone is not *the* measure of reasonableness.

> **Answer (C) is incorrect.** No particular measures or efforts are required for all types of trade secrets. See the explanation for correct Answer (B).

> **Answer (D) is incorrect.** The definition of a trade secret under both the UTSA and the DTSA is capable of encompassing the "formula" for or recipe for food. Such a trade secret might be relatively short-lived—someone with a good sense of taste and a lot of culinary experience might be able to recreate the recipe after enough attempts at experimentation—but that does not keep the recipe from being a trade secret for so long as it can otherwise be maintained as one. The "type" of information is not what controls trade secrecy. It is how widely known the

information is, how ascertainable it is, whether the information derives value from secrecy, and whether it is subject of reasonable efforts to maintain secrecy.

50. Answer (B) is correct. Under these facts, which include those in the previous question, the sous chef has acquired the recipe under circumstances giving rise to a duty to maintain its secrecy and to limit its use to use for the benefit of the first restaurant. He therefore cannot use the recipe after leaving for a new employer. The executive chef's measures to maintain secrecy were obvious and made clear to the sous chef; she segregated the different aspects of the process and made clear that she purposely restricted access to the recipe. Once the sous chef uses the recipe at the second restaurant, he is liable for trade secret misappropriation because he is using it while knowing or having reason to know that he had acquired it under a duty of confidentiality.

But as to the restaurant, the "knew or had reason to know" aspect of misappropriation is missing at the time of the use of the trade secret. Under the given facts, there is no indication that the salsa's "fame" had spread far and wide enough to be known "out of the state," and one cannot assume that the sous chef voluntarily disclosed the provenance of the recipe to his new employer or that the new employer would otherwise have had reason to know that it was not a recipe concocted by the sous chef himself. This means that the second restaurant does not have reason to know that the recipe was a trade secret taken by the sous chef from a former employer. As such, the second restaurant can use it (under these facts) because it has no reason to know it is deriving this information through someone who owes a duty of confidentiality or a duty to limit use of the information.

>   **Answer (A) is incorrect.** This answer correctly notes that the sous chef would be liable, but it misstates the liability of the restaurant. See the explanation for correct Answer (B) above for why the sous chef is liable as stated in this answer, but why the restaurant would not be.

>   **Answer (C) is incorrect.** This answer is wrong on both counts. See the explanation for correct Answer (B) above for why the sous chef would, in fact, be liable. There is no requirement of a direct benefit accruing from trade secret misappropriation. Simply disclosing or using a trade secret of another without consent is enough, if the rest of the requirements are met—which they are for the sous chef, as explained above. The explanation for correct Answer (B) also explains why the restaurant would not be liable on these facts.

>   **Answer (D) is incorrect.** This answer correctly notes that the second restaurant would not be liable, and why. See the explanation for correct Answer (B) above for why the sous chef would, in fact, be liable. There is no requirement of a direct benefit accruing from trade secret misappropriation. Simply disclosing or using a trade secret of another without consent is enough, if the rest of the requirements are met—which they are for the sous chef, as explained above.

51. Answer (A) is correct. Green Co. probably has a legal remedy against both the employee and the competitor, because the bid is protected as a trade secret, as providing an actual or potential advantage, under the Uniform Trade Secrets Act ("UTSA") as well as federal law (commonly called the DTSA, for the Defend Trade Secrets Act of 2016). The employee is liable for divulging the trade secret (which is at least implicitly confidential), and the competitor is liable because it knew or should have known that it was receiving trade secret information. Even though the bid is a one-time piece of information, it is protected under the UTSA and the DTSA as long as it provides a business advantage

Answer (B) is incorrect. As noted above, under the UTSA and DTSA the competitor is liable because it knew or should have known that it was receiving trade secret information.

Answer (C) is incorrect. As noted above, the UTSA and DTSA both cover a wide array of information. Even though the bid is a one-time piece of information, it is protected as long as it provides a business advantage. Thus, if the information is secret and sufficient secrecy measures have been taken, trade secret protection can encompass almost any kind of information. The law in most states does not require that information be continuously used in a business (i.e., of long-term value) to be protectable as a trade secret, although until a state adopts the UTSA it may still follow the prior Restatement rule (which only protected information that is regularly used in a business). For example, in *Inflight Newspapers, Inc. v. Magazines In-Flight, LLC*, 990 F. Supp. 119 (E.D.N.Y. 1997), the court held that an airline magazine distributor's secret bids were protectable trade secrets because information would permit underbidding. Similarly, in *Martin Marietta Corp. v. Dalton*, 974 F. Supp. 37 (D.D.C. 1997), a government contractor's Navy bid was trade secret because it contained confidential cost, pricing, and strategy information and thus bids could not be revealed under the trade secret exemption to the Freedom of Information Act.

Answer (D) is incorrect. Trade secret law can protect formulas, but it also covers almost any kind of proprietary information that has value to a firm, that is maintained making use of reasonable secrecy measures, and that is not common knowledge. In other words, the subject matter of trade secrets is extremely broad. Thus, a trade secret can involve any type of information, such as technical or non-technical data, a formula, a pattern, a compilation (a collection of data or information), a computer program, a device or product, a method or technique, a drawing, a process (such as a manufacturing or fabrication process), financial data, or a list of actual or potential customers, prospects, or suppliers.

52. Answer (A) is correct. Trade secret protection can extend indefinitely, as long as the requisite secrecy and competitive advantage exist. A classic example of a trade secret that has been maintained for many years is the formula for Coca-Cola.

Answer (B) is incorrect. If the information no longer remains sufficiently secret so as to offer a competitive advantage, then the trade secret ceases to satisfy the requirements of any state's trade secret law.

Answer (C) is incorrect. There is no express term for trade secrets, unlike the term for patents.

Answer (D) is incorrect. Even if one competitor were to reverse engineer a trade secret, the original trade secret owner might still have a competitive advantage over other competitors.

53. Reverse engineering means, generally speaking, inspecting and analyzing a product in order to learn what it contains, how it is made, how it functions, and the like. Reverse engineering a publicly available product does not violate trade secret law, and it serves as a defense or limitation on the scope of trade secret rights. Reverse engineering is a lawful means of competition and is not within "improper means" in trade secret law. Thus, a competitor is free to purchase a sample of a product and use a wide variety of analytical techniques to attempt to determine its composition, structure, chemical makeup, etc. Similarly, independent development is a lawful method of competition. In either case, the owner of the original trade secret has no cognizable claim under trade secret law, for either the reverse engineering or independent development itself or for the use of the information learned in manufacturing or selling a new product.

54. Reasonable secrecy measures are essential for purposes of maintaining information as a trade secret. *See* UTSA § 1(4) (defining a trade secret, in part, as information that is "the subject of efforts that are reasonable under the circumstances to maintain its secrecy"); 18 U.S.C. § 1839(3) (defining a trade secret, in part, as depending on whether "the owner thereof has taken reasonable measure to keep [the] information secret"). A company seeking to protect its trade secrets should consider a variety of secrecy measures. Both federal and state law require only reasonable secrecy measures, which recognizes that secrecy measures will involve some cost or inconvenience, and thus a balancing of the benefits of a particular measure against its cost is necessary. *See, e.g., E.I. du Pont de Nemours & Co. v. Christopher*, 431 F.2d 1012 (5th Cir. 1970).

A firm might consider adoption of some or all of the following measures: (1) external physical security measures to protect the plant from intrusion; (2) internal physical security measures to prevent employees and visitors from gaining access to areas in which proprietary information is kept; (3) confidentiality agreements or clauses for all employees, customers, suppliers, and other third parties who have access to any trade secret information; (4) prohibiting persons who are not bound by these agreement from gaining access to trade secret information; (5) requiring employees with access to proprietary information to sign reasonable covenants not to compete; (6) keeping trade secret information "under lock and key," including securing all documents and ensuring that computers have password protection; (7) identifying and labeling all confidential information; and (8) maintaining a policy of informing all incoming and departing employees of the firm's trade secret policies and of the particular types of information considered to be trade secrets (and to which the employee has had or will have access).

Whether adequate action has been taken to protect a trade secret is ordinarily a fact question.

55. A breach of confidence for purposes of trade secret law is key to one of two basic methods for establishing that the trade secret information has been misappropriated, whether under the UTSA (most state civil actions) or the DTSA (federal civil actions). The other method hinges on showing that improper means were used to obtain the trade secret. A breach of confidence, which can lead to misappropriation, occurs after a person violates or breaches a duty owed to another to keep or maintain the secrecy of a trade secret. *See* UTSA § 2(2)(ii)(B) (within definition of misappropriation, references to persons owing a duty to maintain the secrecy of a trade secret or limit its use, and circumstances giving rise to such a duty to maintain secrecy or limit use); 18 U.S.C. § 1839(5)(B)(ii) (same).

Section 41 of the Restatement (Third) of Unfair Competition describes the typical situations in which a duty of confidence can be found:

> A person to whom a trade secret has been disclosed owes a duty of confidence to the owner of the trade secret for purposes of the rule stated in § 40 [misappropriation] if:

(a) the person made an express promise of confidentiality prior to the disclosure of the trade secret; or

(b) the trade secret was disclosed to the person under circumstances in which the relationship between the parties to the disclosure or the other facts surrounding the disclosure justify the conclusions that, at the time of the disclosure,

> (1) the person knew or had reason to know that the disclosure was intended to be in confidence, and

> (2) the other party to the disclosure was reasonable in inferring that the person consented to an obligation of confidentiality.

56. Answer (C) is correct. Gaining unauthorized access (sometimes known as "hacking") into a competitor's computer system to obtain confidential information—in this case by using a random password generator to identify an employee's confidential password—is likely to be actionable as trade secret misappropriation based on improper means. Under section 43 of the Restatement (Third) of Unfair Competition,

> [i]mproper means of acquiring another's trade secret ... include theft, fraud, unauthorized interception of communications, inducement of or knowing participation in a breach of confidence, and other means either wrongful in themselves or wrongful under the circumstances of the case. Independent discovery and analysis of publicly available products or information are not improper means of acquisition.

Some methods are clearly improper because they violate existing laws, such as discovery of information through fraud, trespass, or wiretapping. Hacking a computer might fall into this category. But even if a competitor uses methods having ambiguous legitimacy, courts will focus on whether the means used fall below the generally accepted standards of commercial morality and reasonable conduct. This standard dovetails with the extent of reasonable secrecy measures that a firm can be expected to take. If the defendant engages in a method of discovering information that would breach the wall of reasonable secrecy measures, it is more likely that the means used will be deemed improper.

Answer (A) is incorrect. There is no indication that a patent is in effect on these facts.

Answer (B) is incorrect. Absent unusual circumstances, there is no reason to assume that one competitor would have an obligation of confidentiality toward another.

Answer (D) is incorrect. As discussed above, unauthorized access to competitor computers—sometimes called "hacking"—is likely to be an improper means of discovering trade secret information, and thus a violation is likely to have occurred.

57. Answer (A) is correct. This answer correctly states that an injunction can be used to remedy a head start that a competitor gains by not using a lawful means of ascertaining information, such as independent development or reverse engineering, and by instead using either improper means or breach of confidence for gaining trade secret information. Here, there was a head start, and an injunction should issue to delay the competitor for at least that long. *See* UTSA §2; 18 U.S.C. 1836(b)(3)(A); *Lamb-Weston, Inc. v. McCain Foods, Ltd.*, 941 F.2d 970 (9th Cir. 1991) (affirming an 8-month injunction that a district court had issued to remedy a "head start" gained by misappropriation). The answer also correctly states that damages for lost sales are compensable under the UTSA or the DTSA with proof that the loss was caused by the misappropriation. *See* UTSA § 3; 18 U.S.C. § 1836(b)(3)(B)(i)(I).

Answer (B) is incorrect. This answer inaccurately states that diminished sales are not compensable. Monetary damages for lost sales are compensable under the UTSA or the DTSA with proof that the loss was caused by the misappropriation. *See* UTSA § 3; 18 U.S.C. § 1836(b)(3)(B)(i)(I).

Answer (C) is incorrect. See the explanation for correct Answer (A) above. This answer inaccurately states the capacity of an injunction to remedy misuse of trade secret information. Under these facts, where only one competitor appears to have had access to the trade secret, an injunction remains an appropriate remedy, as it would stop further disclosure by this competitor and thereby contain the damage. Not barring disclosure and not restraining use for least for some period of time, with only damages for the six-month period, would be insufficient to remedy the situation.

Answer (D) is incorrect. See the explanation for correct Answer (A) above. This answer inaccurately states the capacity of an injunction to remedy misuse of trade secret information. Under these facts, where only one competitor appears to have had access to the trade secret, an injunction remains an appropriate remedy, as it would stop further disclosure by this competitor and thereby contain the damage to the secret. This answer inaccurately states that diminished sales are not compensable. Monetary damages for lost sales are compensable under the UTSA or the DTSA with proof that the loss was caused by the misappropriation. *See* UTSA § 3; 18 U.S.C. § 1836(b)(3)(B)(i)(I).

Patent Law—Subject Matter & Validity

58. Answer (C) is correct. The three fundamental requirements for a utility patent are novelty, nonobviousness, and usefulness. Section 101 of the Patent Act requires usefulness by its very terms: "Whoever invents or discovers any new and *useful* process, machine, manufacture, or composition of matter, or any new and *useful* improvement thereof, may obtain a patent therefor, subject to the conditions and requirements of this title." *See* 35 U.S.C. § 101. Section 102 sets out the content of the novelty requirement, which examines whether the invention—in full—was available to the public ("the claimed invention was patented, described in a printed publication, or in public use, on sale, or otherwise available to the public") or described in a prior-filed patent application before the filing date of the application containing the claimed invention. *See* 35 U.S.C. § 102(a). Certain exceptions to the general novelty rule are set forth in section 102(b). Then, section 103 of the Patent Act requires nonobviousness by barring a patent

> if the differences between the claimed invention and the prior art are such that the claimed invention as a whole would have been obvious before the effective filing date of the claimed invention to a person having ordinary skill in the art to which the claimed invention pertains. Patentability shall not be negated by the manner in which the invention was made.

35 U.S.C. § 103.

> **Answer (A) is incorrect.** These are not the three fundamental requirements for any one of the types of patents, although it does include requirements that are applicable to different types of patents (i.e., usefulness for a utility patent, and distinctness for a plant patent).

> **Answer (B) is incorrect.** These are actually the requirements for a plant patent—novelty, nonobviousness, and distinctness. *See* 35 U.S.C. § 161 (emphasis added below):

> Whoever invents or discovers and asexually reproduces any *distinct* and *new* variety of plant, including cultivated sports, mutants, hybrids, and newly found seedlings, other than a tuber propagated plant or a plant found in an uncultivated state, may obtain a patent therefor, *subject to the conditions and requirements of this title. The provisions of this title relating to patents for inventions shall apply to patents for plants, except as otherwise provided.*

> **Answer (D) is incorrect.** See the explanation for Answer (C) above.

59. Answer (D) is correct. Three fundamental requirements for a design patent are novelty, nonobviousness, and ornamentality. Section 171 of the Patent Act provides for a patent as follows: "Whoever invents any new, original and ornamental design for an article of manufacture may obtain a patent therefor, subject to the conditions and requirements of this title." 35 U.S.C. 171(a). Ornamentality is thus one fundamental requirement for patenting a design. Section 171(a) refers also to the fact that design patents are "subject to the conditions and requirements of this title," and it is followed by § 171(b), which emphasizes that, "The provisions of this title relating to patents for inventions shall apply to patents for designs, except as otherwise provided." No provision of the Patent Act excepts design patents from the demands of sections 102 and 103, which require novelty and nonobviousness of an invention, respectively. As a result, three fundamental requirements for a design patent are those set forth in option (D) above: novelty, nonobviousness, and ornamentality.

Answer (A) is incorrect. These are not the three fundamental requirements for any one of the types of patents, although it does include requirements that are applicable to different types of patents (i.e., usefulness for a utility patent, and distinctness for a plant patent).

Answer (B) is incorrect. These are actually the requirements for a plant patent—novelty, nonobviousness, and distinctness. *See* 35 U.S.C. § 161 (emphasis added below):

> Whoever invents or discovers and asexually reproduces any *distinct* and *new* variety of plant, including cultivated sports, mutants, hybrids, and newly found seedlings, other than a tuber propagated plant or a plant found in an uncultivated state, may obtain a patent therefor, *subject to the conditions and requirements of this title. The provisions of this title relating to patents for inventions shall apply to patents for plants, except as otherwise provided.*

Answer (C) is incorrect. See the explanation for Answer (D) above.

60. Answer (B) is correct. The claim described above is sufficiently comparable to the claims discussed in *Mayo Collaborative Servs.* that it would justify the same treatment. *See Mayo Collaborative Servs. v. Prometheus Labs., Inc.*, 566 U.S. 66 (2012). The Court ruled those claims to be unpatentable under the "natural laws" or "laws of nature" exclusion, explaining that while the claims nominally recited elements of a process beyond the "law of nature," the other elements, even when combined, did not present an "inventive concept" that was "sufficient to ensure that the patent in practice amount[ed] to significantly more than a patent upon the natural law itself." *Id.* at 72. As the Court characterized the situation in *Mayo v. Prometheus*:

> Beyond picking out the relevant audience, namely those who administer doses of thiopurine drugs, the claim simply tells doctors to: (1) measure (somehow) the current level of the relevant metabolite, (2) use particular (unpatentable) laws of nature (which the claim sets forth [appropriate concentration range for the metabolite in the blood]) to calculate the current toxicity/inefficacy limits, and (3) reconsider the drug dosage in light of the law. These instructions add nothing specific to the laws of nature other than what is well-understood, routine, conventional activity, previously engaged in by those in the field. And since they are steps that must be taken in order to apply the laws in question, the effect is simply to tell doctors to apply the law somehow when treating their patients.

Id. at 82. As such, it decided that upholding the patents would "risk disproportionately tying up the use of the underlying natural laws, inhibiting their use in the making of further discoveries." *Id.* at 73.

Answer (A) is incorrect. While the line between an abstract idea and a law of nature might sometimes become a bit blurry, depending on the particular idea or law of nature in question, here, the claim is sufficiently comparable to that in *Mayo v. Prometheus* that the best answer would be (B), since the focus of the Court's decision in that case was quite clearly laws of nature and not abstract ideas, and this claim also focuses on the natural world and how nitrogen, soil, and plants interact with one another. The Court has focused more on "abstract ideas" in cases where financial transactions have been involved, such as *Alice Corp. Pty. Ltd. v. CLS Bank Int'l*, 134 S. Ct. 2347 (2014) (which in turn relied on *Mayo v. Prometheus*), and *Bilski v. Kappos*, 561 U.S. 593 (2010).

Answer (C) is incorrect. The products of nature exclusion will not apply to a method or process claim.

Answer (D) is incorrect. While in this case, it may well be that sections 102 and 103 could also play a role, and an examiner might also reject an application on those bases, a section 101 exclusion can be applied under currently applicable Supreme Court caselaw.

61. Answer (C) is correct. Under current U.S. law, the usefulness or utility requirement is fairly minimal, and it simply requires the invention to be operable (as opposed to being widely known not to work, such as with a perpetual motion machine) and capable of providing an identifiable benefit or use. Entertainment is such an identifiable benefit or use, and a variety of new toys have been patented over the years (having met the remaining requirements of patentability, of course). These facts describe a "toy" that provides "visual and audial entertainment" in a particular way: a "matching" activity that then triggers the toy to "light[] up and make[] fun sounds and screen images."

Answer (A) is incorrect. See the explanation in Answer (C) above. The turn of phrase "frivolous and insignificant," used with respect to the requirement of usefulness in contrast with an invention with "beneficial use" comes from 19th-century decisions authored by Justice Story. In *Brenner v. Manson*, 383 U.S. 519 (1966), the Supreme Court explained that it did not find those contrasting characterizations to be helpful in defining a "useful" invention. In *Brenner v. Manson*, the Court emphasized that the applicant must identify an existing use (versus a potential future one), and it rejected an applicant's arguments of utility in a new chemical, a steroid, based on (a) the chemical invention's similarity to a steroid known to have a useful effect and (b) the fact that the chemical fell within a class of compounds being investigated by others (but without a claim that the new chemical was itself the subject of current testing or research for any particular purpose).

Answer (B) is incorrect. Although Article I, sec. 8, cl. 8 does base Congress's power to create the patent system in the United States on a theory of promoting "progress of ... useful arts," there is no restraint within the *usefulness* or *utility* requirement related to "advancing" technology or making "progress." Sections 102 (novelty) and 103 (nonobviousness) do most of the work within the Patent Act related to advancing the state of knowledge and promoting progress. The Court has also embraced the exclusions from statutory subject matter (abstract ideas, laws of nature, products of nature) in recent years as vital to promoting scientific and technological exploration and progress, although these decisions are not without controversy. In any event, the subject-matter decision are also not directly part of the Court's interpretation of the usefulness or utility requirement within section 101.

Answer (D) is incorrect. See the explanation in Answer (C) above. If the facts described a toy that definitely had a use of teaching shapes and colors, this might be a good answer, but the facts do not so state. The facts only describe a "matching" activity that then triggers the toy to "light[] up and make[] fun sounds and screen images." It is possible the child learns, and it is possible the child does not, but the facts do describe a "toy" that provides "visual and audial entertainment" in a particular way. With this use set forth, the correct answer is (C).

62. "Prior art" is a term of art in patent law that regularly appears in judicial opinions and all other discussions of the novelty or nonobviousness of an invention in a claim. It refers to the level of available information and innovation relevant to a particular invention. Prior art is relevant to determinations of novelty and nonobviousness, as the claimed invention must not be part of the prior art defined in section 102 (novelty) and must involve an inventive step beyond that prior art in order to establish nonobviousness under section 103.

Under current law, the defining line for what is "prior" is the effective filing date of the application (with some exceptions in section 102(b) to provide a grace period for the inventor to publicly disclose the invention and then file an application within a year). As to the relevant "art," section 102(a) first defines the basic prior art categories of inventions that have already been "patented, described in a printed publication, or in public use, on sale, or otherwise available to the public." Then section 102(b) adds another category of "art": inventions in most prior-filed applications (applications that are ultimately published, deemed published, or issued as patents). Specifically, this additional category of prior art includes inventions "described in a patent issued under section 151, or in an application for patent published or deemed published under section 122(b), in which the patent or application, as the case may be, names another inventor and was effectively filed before the effective filing date of the claimed invention."

63. **Answer (B) is correct.** While one possible date of invention for the invention as filed is always the filing date of that application, which is also the date of "constructive reduction to practice," a party needing to prove an earlier date can use other evidence to do so. An earlier date of invention that P could prove here comes from the evidence that it had earlier finalized a complete, enabling patent application containing the drawings and claims describing the invention just as it was later claimed in the filed patent application—which is the situation in the factual scenario above.

This problem is based in large part on *Burroughs Wellcome Co. v. Barr Laboratories, Inc.*, 40 F.3d 1223 (Fed. Cir. 1994). In that case, a complete, enabling patent application containing particular claims had been prepared for filing by Burroughs Wellcome no later than February 6, before additional testing for effectiveness of a pharmaceutical was done in the middle of the month by scientists with the National Institutes of Health. The company filed its first patent application in March, after learning of good test results on February 20. In a subsequent inventorship dispute raised by an accused infringer (not by the NIH scientists), where the accused infringer was arguing that the list of inventors on the application had been incomplete, the Federal Circuit found that the draft application sufficed "to confirm that [as of the draft's date of completion] the inventors had concluded the mental part of the inventive process—that they had arrived at the final, definite idea of their inventions, leaving only the task of reduction to practice to bring the inventions to fruition." The court later noted that "We do not know precisely when the inventors conceived their inventions, but the record shows that they had done so by the time they prepared the draft patent application that thoroughly and particularly set out the inventions as they would be later used." This proved to the court that the only joint inventors were those persons participating in the project up to the date of the complete draft application containing the relevant claims—persons who had participated in testing activity after that date, whose participation was being raised by the accused infringer, were not joint inventors for those claims.

Answer (A) is incorrect. Although the engineers at P might have conceived of the full invention at the time they made the first sketches or drawings on paper that contained the final design, a court is unlikely to use that date as the first date of invention, even though there is some corroborating evidence in the form of the sketches. Sketches without additional technical details will not assure a court—using the language from *Burroughs Wellcome* quoted above in connection with correct Answer (B)—that the inventors "had arrived at the final, definite idea of their inventions, leaving only the task of reduction to practice." See more above.

Answer (C) is incorrect. There is no indication in the facts that the testing resulted in any change to the design of the tire mount invention, so there is no reason to use this date within the analysis, under the reasoning of cases like *Burroughs Wellcome*, cited in connection with the explanation of correct Answer (B) above.

Answer (D) is incorrect. This is the latest date in the facts recited above that the court would use as the date of invention. An earlier date is available under the facts provided, as explained in connection with correct Answer (B) above.

64. Answer (C) is correct. Under pre-AIA law, novelty requires assessment of knowledge and use of the invention in the United States, as well as patents and printed publications anywhere in the world, all prior to the date of invention by the applicant. This standard for novelty is set forth in pre-AIA section 102(a) of the Patent Act, which states: "A person shall be entitled to a patent unless … the invention was known or used by others in this country, or patented or described in a printed publication in this or a foreign country, before the invention thereof by the applicant for patent." In pre-AIA section 102, Congress expressly drew a distinction between knowledge or use of an invention in the United States—which would preclude patentability—and knowledge or use abroad, which would not. On the other hand, Congress did not draw that geographic distinction for patents and printed publications; it deemed information published or patented anywhere in the world to be sufficiently available to preclude a U.S. patent.

There are, of course, other barriers to patentability in pre-AIA section 102, including, but not limited to, the novelty bar created by a prior-filed U.S. patent application, which is the subject of pre-AIA section 102(e) (barring a patent when "the invention was described in (1) an application for patent, published under section 122(b), by another filed in the United States before the invention by the applicant for patent or (2) a patent granted on an application for patent by another filed in the United States before the invention by the applicant for patent [with an exception related to the PCT]"). There are also the so-called "statutory bars," which are barriers based on the applicant's failure to file a patent application within a year of certain activities or occurrences, including a domestic public use or sale or a patent or printed publication anywhere (in pre-AIA section 102(b)).

Answer (A) is incorrect. This statement ignores the effect of knowledge or use in the United States, which would preclude a pre-AIA finding of novelty, even if the knowledge or use had not been reduced to "printed publication" form (much less a patent) before the applicant's date of invention.

Answer (B) is incorrect. This statement ignores the relevance of foreign publications and foreign patents, both of which also preclude a pre-AIA finding of novelty.

Answer (D) is incorrect. This statement goes "too far" under pre-AIA law. If, before the date of the patent applicant's invention, an invention is known or used *outside* the United States without being subject to a patent or printed publication, and without being known or used *within* the United States, it is still eligible for patent protection under pre-AIA law (i.e., it can still be found to be novel).

65. Answer (D) is correct. Under the post-AIA law of novelty, lack of novelty precludes patentability of an invention when the device is publicly used, sold, patented, or described in a printed publication—and any of these takes place anywhere in the world before the date the patent applicant files the patent application. This standard for novelty is set forth in post-AIA section 102(a) of the Patent Act, which states: "A person shall be entitled to a patent unless—(1) the claimed invention was patented, described in a printed publication, or in public use, on sale, or otherwise available to the public before the effective filing date of the claimed invention." 35 U.S.C. § 102(a).

As noted in the question, not all barriers to patentability in post-AIA section 102 are addressed by the statements above. The "otherwise available to the public" language in section 102(a) is new in post-AIA section 102 compared to the prior statute and will be interpreted over time. The AIA novelty provision also implements a first-to-file rule, in part, by adding a novelty bar when the claimed invention was described in another inventor's patent application "effectively filed before the effective filing date of the claimed invention." *Id.*

Section 102(b) provides the applicant with a one-year grace period by excluding from the prior art the inventor's own disclosures within the year before filing. *See* 35 U.S.C. § 102 (b). It also excludes third-party disclosures within the year before filing, but only if the third-party disclosure was preceded by a public disclosure by the inventor. *See id.*

Answer (A) is incorrect. This statement ignores pre-filing-date sales and public use, which would preclude a post-AIA finding of novelty.

Answer (B) is incorrect. To state that the post-AIA novelty standard is not met when certain events occur "in the U.S." is incomplete in that it excludes those events when they occur in other countries; this statement ignores the relevance of foreign prior art, which will also preclude a post-AIA finding of novelty.

Answer (C) is incorrect. Although under pre-AIA law Congress expressly drew a distinction between sales or use of an invention in the United States, which would preclude patentability, and sales or use abroad, which would not, the AIA eliminates geographic distinctions in prior art.

66. Answer (A) is correct. A feature of a product that is primarily functional, but is also ornamental and aesthetically pleasing, can potentially be protected under utility patent law, which protects useful inventions. The fact that the functional feature also happens to be aesthetically pleasing or original will not disqualify it from being protected by a utility patent. Section 101 of the Patent Act states: "Whoever invents or discovers any new and useful process, machine, manufacture, or composition of matter, or any new and useful improvement thereof, may obtain a patent therefor, subject to the conditions and requirements of this title." This provision grants utility patent protection to three types of inventions: (1) products (i.e., a machine, manufacture, or composition of matter); (2) processes (such as a new chemical manufacturing process); and (3) improvements on existing products or processes. The fact that a useful feature is also attractive will not disqualify it from protection as an "invention" under the Patent Act, so long as all of the requirements are met. Historical examples of utility patents include the Wright Brothers' airplane, Alexander Graham Bell's telephone, and Thomas Edison's light bulb.

Answer (B) is incorrect. Design patent law does not offer protection for primarily functional or useful features of an article of manufacture, but only for features that are original and primarily ornamental. *See, e.g., Avia Group, Int'l, Inc. v. L.A. Gear California, Inc.*, 853 F.2d 1557 (Fed. Cir. 1988) (abrogated on other grounds by *Egyptian Goddess, Inc. v. Swisa, Inc.*, 543 F.3d 665, (Fed. Cir. 2008) (explaining that "if a patented design [protected under design patent law] is 'primarily functional,' rather than 'primarily ornamental,' the patent is invalid. When function dictates a design, protection [through design patent] would not promote the decorative arts, a purpose of the design patent statute.").

Answer (C) is incorrect. The same features of a product cannot be protected under both a design patent and a utility patent since, as explained above in connection with incorrect Answer (B), a design patent cannot protect subject matter that is primarily functional, while a utility patent requires usefulness (or functionality). It is possible for the functional features of a product to be covered by a utility patent while distinctly different ornamental aspects of the same product are protected by a design patent.

Answer (D) is incorrect. As noted above, utility patent protection is potentially available for functional features of a product.

67. Answer (B) is correct. A genetically modified, sexually reproduced plant with utility, such as a higher-yield wheat, is eligible for protection through a traditional utility patent. This result may seem counterintuitive, particularly since there are also "plant patents" under section 161 of the Patent Act, but "plant patents" protect only asexually reproduced plants (other than edible tubers). The Supreme Court expressly resolved the question of whether utility patent protection can extend to plants—in light of the separate category of plant patents—in *J.E.M. Ag Supply, Inc. v. Pioneer Hi-Bred International, Inc.*, 534 U.S. 124 (2001). The Court held that plants can qualify as patentable subject matter under section 101 of the Patent Act if they meet the ordinary requirements of novelty, nonobviousness, and usefulness. This holding confirmed the Patent Office's practice of granting utility patents on plants that satisfy the ordinary utility patent standard. Utility patent protection is only available if the plant characteristic is the product of human ingenuity— which would be the case if the higher-yield trait resulted from genetic modifications introduced by the human researcher. The concept of utility patent protection for genetically modified plants logically follows from the Supreme Court's biotechnology ruling in *Diamond v. Chakrabarty*. Just as a genetically modified bacterium can receive utility patent protection, so too might a genetically modified strain of corn, soybeans, or wheat.

Answer (A) is incorrect. Plant patents protect distinct plant varieties that are *asexually* reproduced. These plant varieties receive protection under the Plant Patent Act of 1930 ("PPA"). Section 161 of the Plant Patent Act, the "subject matter" provision, does not contain a utility requirement, instead requiring distinctness — that is, that the plant be a distinct and new variety:

> Whoever invents or discovers and asexually reproduces any distinct and new variety of plant, including cultivated sports, mutants, hybrids, and newly found seedlings, other than a tuber propagated plant or a plant found in an uncultivated state, may obtain a patent therefor, subject to the conditions and requirements of this title.

35 U.S.C. § 161.

Answer (C) is incorrect. As noted above, although the plant described could potentially be protected with a utility patent, it could not be protected with a plant patent.

Answer (D) is incorrect. As noted above, the plant described could potentially be protected with a utility patent.

68. Answer (C) is correct. In summer 2008, Isabelle Inventor, working out of her home workshop, develops an innovative new tool that can be used open jars. In August 2011, Inventor begins selling her device through her online store. In December 2012, Inventor files a patent application on her device. Inventor will be precluded from patenting her device because of the prior sale beginning in August 2011, which triggers the on-sale bar in pre-AIA section 102(b). That section sets forth ways in which there can be a loss of rights to an otherwise valid patent, including an on-sale bar and a public use bar:

> A person shall be entitled to a patent unless — the invention was patented or described in a printed publication in this or a foreign country or in public use or on sale in this country, more than one year prior to the date of the application for patent in the United States.

See pre-AIA § 102(b). This rule essentially placed a one-year time limit for filing a patent application once there had been a public use of the invention or the invention had been sold or offered for sale in the United States. The inventor in this case failed to file the patent application within the one-year period. Although this rule may seem harsh, it encouraged the prompt filing of patents and was more lenient than the patent law rules in many foreign countries, which did not and still do not provide the one-year grace period.

Answer (A) is incorrect. As noted above, Inventor would be precluded from patenting her device because of the prior sale.

Answer (B) is incorrect. The 16-month delay in filing the patent application following the start of sales of the device does trigger the on-sale bar, but even a four-year delay between initial invention and the filing of an application is highly unlikely to have been long enough to constitute abandonment under the meaning of either subsection (c) or (g) of pre-AIA section 102. *See* pre-AIA § 102(c) (abandonment of invention) & § 102(g) (abandonment, suppression, or concealment in connection with priority contest with competing inventor vying for the rights in an interference).

Answer (D) is incorrect. As noted above, Inventor would be precluded from patenting her device because of the prior sale. A statute of limitations places a time limit on when a plaintiff can bring suit once a cause of action has accrued. *Cf.* 35 U.S.C. § 286 (not providing a statute of limitations but limiting damage recovery in patent suits to infringement occurring within six years of filing of suit).

69. Answer (C) is correct. In summer 2015, Isabelle Inventor, working out of her home workshop, develops an innovative new tool that can be used open jars. In August 2018, Inventor begins selling her device through her online store. In December 2019, Inventor files a patent application on her device. Inventor will be precluded from patenting her device because of the prior sales beginning in August 2018. Post-AIA rules of novelty and priority still allow an inventor a one-year grace period, but only as to the inventor's own disclosures, by excluding from the prior art the inventor's own disclosures occurring within the year before filing. This rule is thought to encourage the prompt filing of patents. Although it is more restrictive than the pre-AIA section 102(b) grace period, which covered third-party disclosures as well, the U.S. rule remains more lenient than the patent law rules in many foreign countries, which do not provide a one-year grace period.

Answer (A) is incorrect. As noted above, Inventor would be precluded from patenting her device because of the prior sale.

Answer (B) is incorrect. Post-AIA section 102 does not include a specific bar to patentability for an inventor who has "abandoned" the invention. There is no priority provided for inventors with early dates of conception, and the priority value of being the first inventor to file should provide sufficient incentive not to "abandon" an invention after it is conceived and before an application is filed.

Answer (D) is incorrect. As noted above, Inventor would be precluded from patenting her device because of the prior sale. A statute of limitations places a time limit on when a plaintiff can bring suit once a cause of action has accrued. *Cf.* 35 U.S.C. § 286 (not providing a statute of limitations but limiting damage recovery in patent suits to infringement occurring within six years of filing of suit).

70. Experimental uses, if recognized as such by a court, do not affect the inquiry into novelty, which means they cannot destroy the novelty required for patent protection or become part of the prior art used in determining obviousness. The experimental use exception, which excludes experimental uses from becoming prior art that is "in public use" under section 102, recognizes the common-sense idea that an inventor often seeks to test the invention to assure that it works properly. This type of experimentation is entirely proper and should not lead to forfeiture of rights to the invention. The scope of the experimental use exception requires a careful analysis.

In *Baxter International, Inc. v. Cobe Laboratories, Inc.*, 88 F.3d 1054, 1060 (Fed. Cir. 1996), the Federal Circuit identified a series of factors for assessing whether a use is experimental:

An analysis of experimental use, which is also a question of law, requires consideration of the totality of the circumstances and the policies underlying the public use bar. Evidentiary factors in determining if a use is experimental include the length of the test period, whether the inventor received payment for the testing, any agreement by the user to maintain the use confidential, any records of testing, whether persons other than the inventor performed the testing, the number of tests, and the length of the test period in relation to tests of similar devices.

On the facts of the case, the court found that the use in question was *not* experimental. Tests were conducted on the inventor's device (a blood-processing centrifuge) by a third party to determine if the centrifuge would have additional uses, and the court concluded that these tests would not fall within the experimental use exception. The court focused on the fact that the additional applications for the centrifuge were not recited in the patent application and that the inventor did not have any direction or control over the third-party testing:

> The experimental use doctrine operates in the inventor's favor to allow the inventor to refine his invention or to assess its value relative to the time and expense of prosecuting a patent application. If it is not the inventor or someone under his control or 'surveillance' who does these things, there appears to us no reason why he should be entitled to rely upon them to avoid the statute.

Id. The court therefore held that the public testing by the third party for its own purposes was an invalidating public use, not an experimental use. All case law through the date of this study guide interpreting the "experimental use exception" to prior art is under pre-AIA section 102, but there is no reason to think that it will differ under post-AIA section 102, as it is an exception from "in public use," a type of prior art reference carried forward in the AIA with the same language. The reasons for creating the exception have also not changed.

71. The nonobviousness standard involves a qualitative judgment regarding the differences between the prior art and the claimed invention. The invention must involve a significant creative or inventive step beyond what was already known. Section 103 of the Patent Act sets forth the general nonobviousness requirement:

> A patent for a claimed invention may not be obtained, notwithstanding that the claimed invention is not identically disclosed as set forth in section 102, if the differences between the claimed invention and the prior art are such that the claimed invention as a whole would have been obvious before the effective filing date of the claimed invention to a person having ordinary skill in the art to which the claimed invention pertains. Patentability shall not be negated by the manner in which the invention was made.

The landmark case addressing nonobviousness is *Graham v. John Deere Co.*, 383 U.S. 1, 17–18 (1966). The Court set forth the following framework for assessing whether section 103 is satisfied:

> Under § 103, the scope and content of the prior art are to be determined; differences between the prior art and the claims at issue are to be ascertained; and the level of ordinary skill in the pertinent art resolved. Against this background the obviousness or nonobviousness of the subject matter is determined.

72. "Secondary considerations" are relevant to the determination of nonobviousness, a fundamental requirement for patent validity. In *Graham v. John Deere Co.*, 383 U.S. 1, 17–18 (1966), the Supreme Court set forth the standard for nonobviousness, as discussed above. The Court then stated: "Such secondary considerations as commercial success, long felt but unsolved needs, failure of others, etc., might be utilized to give light to the circumstances surrounding the origin of the subject matter sought to be patented." In other words, these considerations can help shed light on whether or not the invention satisfies the nonobviousness standard. In 2007, the Supreme Court again addressed the subject of nonobviousness in *KSR International Co. v. Teleflex Inc.*, 550 U.S. 398, 415 (2007):

> Throughout this Court's engagement with the question of obviousness, our cases have set forth an expansive and flexible approach.... To be sure, *Graham* recognized the need for 'uniformity and definiteness.' Yet the principles laid down in *Graham* reaffirmed the 'functional approach' of *Hotchkiss*. To this end, *Graham* set forth a broad inquiry and invited courts, where appropriate, to look at any secondary considerations that would prove instructive.

73. The written description requirement is one of the requirements for a patent application; if the written description requirement is not satisfied for claim in an issued patent, it may be held invalid in later litigation (other than "best mode," as noted below). *See* 35 U.S.C. §282(b)(3)(A). The written description requirement appears in Section 112 of the Patent Act, which requires a patent application to contain, in addition to the claims, a complete and enabling written description of the invention (the description must be in "full, clear, concise, and exact terms"). *See* 35 U.S.C. §112(a). The enablement requirement focuses upon the completeness and clarity of the specification from a skilled person's point of view. Because it is written for an audience composed of persons skilled in the relevant art, the "patent need not disclose what is well known in the art." *In re Wands*, 858 F.2d 731, 735 (Fed. Cir. 1988). The skilled person should merely be able to make and use the invention without "undue experimentation." In a 2010 case, the Federal Circuit also emphasized that the specification must include sufficient information to demonstrate that, as of the filing date, the inventor "had possession of the claimed subject matter" or had, in a manner of speaking, completely intellectually taken hold of it as of that date—which would show genuine conception by the filing date. According to the Federal Circuit, how much information and detail section 112 requires will vary from patent to patent, depending on the type of the invention, the scope of the claims, the existing prior art, and how complex or predictable the relevant field of technology may be.

Additional notes: Section 112 states in relevant part:

> The specification shall contain a written description of the invention, and of the manner and process of making and using it, in such full, clear, concise, and exact terms as to enable any person skilled in the art to which it pertains, or with which it is most nearly connected, to make and use the same, and shall set forth the best mode contemplated by the inventor or joint inventor of carrying out the invention.

35 U.S.C. §112(a). Although the specification is statutorily required to "set forth the best mode" known to the inventor, the patent can no longer be invalidated for failure to do so in proceedings commenced

on or after September 16, 2011 (the effective date of the America Invents Act). *See* 35 U.S.C. §282(b)(3)(A). Failure to satisfy other aspects of the written description requirement, however, including questions of breadth, depth, and clarity of the specification are grounds for invalidation.

Whether a disclosure would require undue experimentation includes:

> (1) the quantity of experimentation necessary, (2) the amount of direction or guidance presented, (3) the presence or absence of working examples, (4) the nature of the invention, (5) the state of the prior art, (6) the relative skill of those in the art, (7) the predictability or unpredictability of the art, and (8) the breadth of the claims.

In re Wands, 858 F.2d 731, 737 (Fed. Cir. 1988).

In *Ariad Pharmaceuticals, Inc. v. Eli Lilly & Co.*, 598 F.3d 1336 (Fed. Cir. 2010), the Federal Circuit emphasized that the specification must also, in addition to enabling a skilled person to make and use the invention, include sufficient information to demonstrate that, as of the filing date, the "inventor had possession of the claimed subject matter.... [T]he specification must describe an invention understandable to [a person of ordinary skill in the art] and show that the inventor actually invented the invention claimed." *Id.* at 1351.

Patent Law—Ownership & Duration

74. Section 100(f) of the Patent Act defines an *inventor* as "the individual or, if a joint invention, the individuals collectively who invented or discovered the subject matter of the invention." Section 101 clearly designates inventorship as the fundamental requirement for obtaining a valid patent: "Whoever invents or discovers [patentable subject matter] may obtain a patent therefor...." And as stated by the Federal Circuit (and other courts) many times, "conception is the touchstone of inventorship," which means that an inventor is the person or persons who conceive of the invention, not any other person or persons who might assist in reducing the invention to practice without contributing to the intellectual or mental part of invention. *See, e.g., Burroughs Wellcome Co. v. Barr Laboratories, Inc.*, 40 F.3d 1223 (Fed. Cir. 1994).

Section 115 of the Patent Act requires each patent application to include an oath or declaration from each named inventor stating that the inventor "believes himself or herself to be the original inventor or an original joint inventor of a claimed invention in the application." 35 U.S.C. § 115 (a)–(b). The pre-AIA provision's required oath included a belief that the inventor was "the original *and first* inventor" (emphasis added). Section 111 of the Patent Act provides that "[a]n application for patent shall be made, or authorized to be made, by the inventor except as otherwise provided in this title," while post-AIA section 118 states, "A person to whom the inventor has assigned or is under an obligation to assign the invention may make an application for patent." Pre-AIA section 102(f) further emphasized the inventorship requirement by making derivation part of the novelty and statutory bars to patentability: "A person shall be entitled to a patent unless ... (f) he did not himself invent the subject matter sought to be patented."

75. Answer (B) is correct. When an engineer or other researcher in a research and development (R&D) department creates an invention during the normal course of employment, the rights to the invention typically belong to the employer. There are three types of employment relationships, each with different implications for ownership of the invention. Most R&D engineers and other research employees are hired specifically to perform research functions within the scope of their duties, and it is well understood that the fruits of these efforts should inure to the benefit of the employer. Thus, the inventions developed by these R&D employees within the scope of their duties are generally assigned to their employers and are then wholly owned by the employer. At the other end of the spectrum, an employee whose duties do not involve R&D work, but who develops an invention on the employee's own time and using the employee's own materials is entitled to full ownership of any resulting inventions. The third situation is known as the "shop right." This scenario involves an employee whose duties do not involve R&D work, but who develops an invention on company time or using the employer's materials, or both. In this case, the employee retains ownership of the invention, but the employer is entitled to a non-exclusive license to use the invention for its own business operations (this right is known as a "shop right").

Answer (A) is incorrect. As noted above, an engineer or other researcher in the typical R&D employment situation would not retain ownership rights in the invention on the facts presented here.

Answer (C) is incorrect. As noted above, this case does not involve a "shop rights" fact pattern.

Answer (D) is incorrect. This is not the best answer. It is true that contracts can always govern ownership, but in many employment settings the ownership issue is not addressed by contract—and no contract is mentioned in this fact pattern. The question is seeking the result in the "typical R&D employment situation," which is one with no contract altering the default rule. The default rule is the one discussed above. (Moreover, since the employer writes the contract and has most of the bargaining power in hiring most R&D employees, even where contracts are part of the employment relationship, the typical contract will not alter the ownership outcome from the default—thus leaving ownership with the employer.)

76. In the case of inventions developed by a typical research and development employee within the scope of the employee's duties (when hired to perform research and development duties), although the patent will name as inventor(s) the individual employee(s) who invented the invention, the employer will ultimately own the rights to that patent by assignment from the employee/inventor.

A patent must name as inventor(s) the particular individual employee(s) who created ("invented") the invention. Section 101 clearly designates inventorship as the fundamental requirement for obtaining a valid patent: "Whoever invents or discovers [patentable subject matter] may obtain a patent therefor...." And as stated by the Federal Circuit (and other courts) many times, "conception is the touchstone of inventorship," which means that an inventor is the person or persons who conceive of the invention, not any other person or persons who might assist in reducing the invention to practice without contributing to the intellectual or mental part of invention. *See, e.g., Burroughs Wellcome Co. v. Barr Laboratories, Inc.*, 40 F.3d 1223 (Fed. Cir. 1994). As explained in the answer to the previous question, however, the inventions developed by typical R&D employees within the scope of their duties are generally assigned to their employers and are then wholly owned by the employer.

77. **Answer (D) is correct.** Pre-AIA United States patent law, which applies to situations like these where a patent application contains only claims effectively filed before March 16, 2013, gives priority to the "first to conceive" an invention, as long as that inventor does not suppress, conceal, or act with a lack of diligence. *See* 35 U.S.C. § 102(g). Thus, even though Inventor B was the first to develop a prototype, Inventor A conceived of the invention a year before B did so (and proceeded with reasonable diligence) and would still have priority under applicable law. Under pre-AIA law, first inventors could lose their priority if they failed to exercise reasonable diligence in reducing the invention to practice or if they abandoned, suppressed, or concealed their inventions. These facts do not raise those concerns, given the close timing of the invention's conception and its reduction to practice.

Answer (A) is incorrect. As discussed above, pre-AIA priority is generally given to the first to conceive an invention, not the first to reduce it to practice.

Answer (B) is incorrect. As discussed above, pre-AIA priority is generally given to the first to conceive an invention, not the first to file a patent application.

Answer (C) is incorrect. The delay on these facts is not sufficiently long to constitute a lack of diligence.

78. Answer (D) is correct. This printed publication appeared less than one year before the patent filing date, which does not result in a statutory bar to patenting this invention. Pre-AIA section 102(b) sets forth various statutory bars under federal patent law:

> A person shall be entitled to a patent unless ... (b) the invention was patented or described in a printed publication in this or a foreign country or in public use or on sale in this country, more than one year prior to the date of the application for patent in the United States.

These rules essentially require the inventor to proceed diligently (within a year or less) in filing a patent application after initiating any of the enumerated activities, but they do not require absolute novelty at the time of filing. The Federal Circuit in *Baxter Int'l, Inc. v. COBE Laboratories, Inc.*, 88 F.3d 1054 (Fed. Cir. 1996), identified four policies underlying the rule:

> (1) discouraging the removal, from the public domain, of inventions that the public reasonably has come to believe are freely available; (2) favoring the prompt and widespread disclosure of inventions; (3) allowing the inventor a reasonable amount of time following sales activity to determine the potential economic value of a patent; and (4) prohibiting the inventor from commercially exploiting the invention for a period greater than the statutorily prescribed time.

Id. at 1058.

Answer (A) is incorrect. By the express terms of pre-AIA section 102(b), this statutory bar can be invoked against either party. The issue under pre-AIA law is not who made a public use, obtained a patent, or caused a printed publication to issue, but whether more than a year has passed since the public disclosure.

Answer (B) is incorrect. As noted above, by the express terms of pre-AIA section 102(b), this statutory bar can be invoked against either party.

Answer (C) is incorrect. Although this printed publication disclosed the invention to the public, it occurred less than one year before the relevant filing date. See explanation of correct Answer (D).

79. Answer (B) is correct. Under current U.S. law—namely, the changes to novelty and priority instituted by the AIA—the dominant means of determining priority will be the order of the applicants' effective filing dates, *see* 35 U.S.C. § 102(a)(2), although an earlier public disclosure or patent filing by a party other than the first applicant to file could immediately destroy the novelty of the claimed invention. *See* 35 U.S.C. § 102(a)–(b) (barring a patent either (1) if a third party has earlier disclosed the claimed invention as set forth in section 102(a)(1) (or described the invention in a filing as set forth in section 102(a)(2)) or (2) if the applicant's own filing is made after the section 102(b)(1) grace period (further discussed below with respect to Answer (C)) has passed). Under these facts, which did not provide that C publicly disclosed the invention after reducing it to practice, D's application, which was filed first, will not be barred by C's activities.

Answer (A) is incorrect. Under current U.S. law—namely, the changes to novelty and priority instituted by the AIA—an inventor's date of reduction to practice (regardless of abandonment, suppression, or lack of diligence) will not be determinative of either the novelty of the invention or priority of rights as between two competing inventors (unless there is an issue of derivation by one inventor from the other, which is not present in these bare facts). See above and below for more on the determination of novelty and priority under current law.

Answer (C) is incorrect. Novelty is determined by reference to the types of disclosures or patent filings listed in section 102(a), not by reference to the passage of time after a private reduction to practice. If another inventor's reduction to practice were not maintained in confidence, it could potentially qualify as a public use or "otherwise available to the public" under section 102(a)(1)—but in that case, the claimed invention would immediately be rendered not novel for all other inventors, including the first inventor to file, as there is no longer a one-year grace period in which another inventor's application may be filed after a third-party public disclosure. Current law only gives an inventor a one-year grace period in which to file an application after the inventor's own disclosure of the invention, and that grace period protects the inventor from third-party patent filings, or third-party disclosures made during the one-year grace period, if the inventor's own disclosure is a "public disclosure" and was made before any third party disclosure (or patent filing) of the same invention. *Compare* 35 U.S.C. § 102(b)(1)(A) (eliminating from the prior art the inventor's own 102(a)(1)-type disclosures within the year before the effective filing date) *with* 102(b)(1)(B) (eliminating from the prior art a third party's section 102(a)(1)-type disclosure within the year before the effective filing date only if it was preceded by the applicant's own "public" disclosure) *and* (b)(2)(B) (eliminating from the prior art a third party's patent filing only if it was preceded by the applicant's own "public" disclosure).

Answer (D) is incorrect. Novelty is determined by reference to the types of disclosures or patent filings listed in section 102(a), and whether they occurred before the applicant's effective filing date (and whether they may be excluded from the prior art under section 102(b)), not by reference to the passage of time after another inventor's private activities, whether that is a reduction to practice or conception of the invention.

80. On the facts set forth in the previous question (Question 79), but with the additional fact that inventor C had published an article fully disclosing the invention in December 2017 in an electronically distributed scientific journal—Inventor C would have priority in the invention, even though Inventor C filed an application *after* Inventor D filed.

Section 102(b)(1)(A) eliminates from the prior art an inventor's *own* section 102(a)(1)-type disclosures that are made *within the year before* the inventor's filing date (thus preserving the invention's novelty for Inventor C as of C's June 2018 filing date despite the December 2017 journal publication). The electronically distributed journal would either be considered a "printed publication" under pre-AIA case law or would be "otherwise available to the public" under the new AIA language, *see* § 102(a)(1). Section 102(b)(2)(B) eliminates from the prior art disclosures in prior filed patent applications if they are preceded by a "public" disclosure—thus eliminating D's patent application from the prior art to Inventor C's application.

Inventor D's claimed invention, although it is claimed in the first application to be filed, would be rendered not novel by C's December 2017 journal publication. Inventor D cannot exclude that publication from the prior art under these facts, because D cannot exclude third-party disclosures from the prior art, even if made within the year before D's filing date, unless D had made a prior *public* disclosure of the invention. *See* § 102(b)(1)(A) (inventor's own disclosures) and 102(b)(1)(B) (disclosures preceded by inventor's public disclosure). Inventor D, on these facts, has made no public disclosure.

81. Answer (C) is correct. The most common method for determining priority of patent ownership worldwide is that the first inventor to file a patent application is entitled to ownership of the rights.

> **Answer (A) is incorrect.** This rule was followed in the United States until March 2013, but it is not the general rule in most foreign nations and is not the rule in the United States for new applications filed on or after the AIA's March 16, 2013 effective date.

> **Answer (B) is incorrect.** This rule is not generally followed in the United States or abroad.

> **Answer (D) is incorrect.** This rule is not generally followed in the United States or abroad. Consider the transaction costs that would arise if independent inventors were forced to share rights to an invention. Although this rule may sound evenhanded or fair in an abstract way, it would create serious problems in the managing the patent rights.

82. The *shop right* involves an employee whose duties do not involve research and development, but who develops an invention on company time or using the employer's materials, or both. In *United States v. Dubilier Condenser Corp.*, 289 U.S. 178 (1933), the Supreme Court defined the employer's shop right with regard to ideas and inventions developed by employees who are not specifically hired to perform research and development:

> Recognition of the nature of the act of invention also defines the limits of the so-called shop right, which, shortly stated, is that, where a servant, during his hours of employment, working with his master's materials and appliances, conceives and perfects an invention for which he obtains a patent, he must accord his master a nonexclusive right to practice the invention. This is an application of equitable principles. Since the servant uses his master's time, facilities, and materials to attain a concrete result, the latter is in equity entitled to use that which embodies his own property and to duplicate it as often as he may find occasion to employ similar appliances in his business. But the employer in such a case has no equity to demand a conveyance of the invention, which is the original conception of the employee alone, in which the employer had no part. This remains the property of him who conceived it, together with the right conferred by the patent, to exclude all others than the employer from the accruing benefits.

Id. at 188–189.

The shop right doctrine effectively confers upon employers a free and nonexclusive license to use the employee's innovation. As Judge Wisdom observed in *Hobbs v. United States*, 376 F.2d 488, 495 (5th Cir. 1967), "[t]he classic shop rights doctrine ordains that when an employee makes and reduces to practice an invention on his employer's time, using his employer's tools and the services of other employees, the employer is the recipient of an implied, nonexclusive, royalty-free license." The shop right doctrine rests upon several policy rationales:

> First, it seems only fair that when an employee has used his employer's time and equipment to make an invention, the employer should be able to use the device without paying a royalty. Second, under the doctrine of estoppel, if an employee encourages his employer to use an invention, and then stands by and allows him to construct and operate the new device without making any claim for compensation or royalties, it would not be equitable to allow the employee later to assert a claim for royalties or other compensation.

Id. at 495. Another justification for the shop rights doctrine is the concept of implied consent. The employee has implicitly consented to allow the employer limited use of the invention based on the employee's acceptance of assistance or resources from the employer while developing the invention. *See Solomons v. United States*, 137 U.S. 342 (1890).

83. Answer (D) is correct. Joint inventors are required to work together in some way (i.e., to be collaborative). Section 116 of the Patent Act states in relevant part:

> When an invention is made by two or more persons jointly, they shall apply for patent jointly and each make the required oath, except as otherwise provided in this title. Inventors may apply for a patent jointly even though (1) they did not physically work together or at the same time, (2) each did not make the same type or amount of contribution, or (3) each did not make a contribution to the subject matter of every claim of the patent.

The statute expressly disavows any requirement that joint inventors work in the same location, make the same amount or type of contribution to the invention, or contribute something as to every claim in the patent. This statutory language allows for a wide range of collaborative settings, as long as there is at least some degree of collaboration or connection between the inventors. *See Kimberly-Clark Corp. v. Procter & Gamble Distributing Co.*, 973 F.2d 911 (Fed. Cir. 1992).

Answer (A) is incorrect. As noted above, section 116 expressly disavows any requirement that joint inventors work in the same location.

Answer (B) is incorrect. As noted above, section 116 expressly disavows any requirement that joint inventors make the same amount or type of contribution to the invention.

Answer (C) is incorrect. As noted above, section 116 expressly disavows any requirement that joint inventors contribute something as to every claim in the patent.

84. Answer (A) is correct. Section 154(a)(2) of the Patent Act provides that the basic term of protection for a *utility patent* (or a plant patent) under present law is *20 years from the date of patent filing* (not counting any extensions of the patent term allowed by law). The statute provides:

Subject to the payment of fees under this title, such grant shall be for a term beginning on the date on which the patent issues and ending 20 years from the date on which the application for the patent was filed in the United States or, if the application contains a specific reference to an earlier filed application or applications under section 120, 121, or 365(c) of this title, from the date on which the earliest such application was filed.

The Uruguay Round Agreements Act of 1994 ("URAA") (which was the Act that Congress used to implement changes to U.S. law necessary to join the WTO, which included significant IP obligations for WTO member nations) established the present term for patents sought after June 8, 1995. Before the URAA, the standard patent term was 17 years from the date of patent issuance. Note that a patent cannot be enforced until it has been issued by the PTO. Thus, the delay that occurs after filing, while a patent application is being examined and before it issues, reduces the effective term of the patent, usually by a period of several years. Thus, the actual term of enforceable patent rights may or may not be longer now than it was under the earlier regime, depending on the extent of the delay in gaining patent issuance.

Answer (B) is incorrect. See the explanation in Answer (A) above.

Answer (C) is incorrect. See the explanation in Answer (A) above.

Answer (D) is incorrect. As discussed above, before the enactment of the URAA, the standard patent term was 17 years from the date of patent issuance. Thus, this was the governing term for utility patents that issued *before* June 8, 1995, but it is not the basic term under current law. As a transitional measure, section 154(c) also gave an option for applications pending at the time of the change: "the term of a patent that is in force on or that results from an application filed before [June 8, 1995] shall be the greater of the 20-year term as provided in subsection (a), or 17 years from grant."

85. Answer (C) is correct. The current term for newly filed design patents is 15 years from the date of issuance. Section 173 of the Patent Act states: "Patents for designs shall be granted for the term of 15 years from the date of grant." In contrast to utility and plant patents discussed above, the design patent term was not addressed by the URAA, and it continued to be governed by the prior law—which meant a term of 14 years from issuance. Then in December 2012, Congress amended section 173 to add another year to the term, but only after the United States formally acceded to an international agreement on industrial designs. ("Industrial designs" are what many countries use to protect the IP that the United States protects with design patents). The change became effective in May 2015; all design patents issued in the United States on applications filed on or after May 13, 2015 have a term of 15 years from the grant.

Answer (A) is incorrect. See the explanation in Answer (C) above.

Answer (B) is incorrect. See the explanation in Answer (C) above. This is the old term for a design patent, not the current term.

Answer (D) is incorrect. See the explanation in Answer (C) above.

86. Answer (A) is correct. If Congress attempted to grant a perpetual patent, this action would be directly contrary to the clearly expressed "limited times" language of the Intellectual Property

Clause (Art. I, sec. 8, cl. 8) of the Constitution, which states: "The Congress shall have Power … To promote the Progress of Science and useful Arts, by securing for limited Times to Authors and Inventors the exclusive Right to their respective Writings and Discoveries."

Answer (B) is incorrect. Because the Intellectual Property Clause does expressly include a "limited times" requirement, it is highly likely that Congress *could not* avoid the problem by relying upon the Commerce Clause as an end run around this express limitation on its power.

Answer (C) is incorrect. This is the second-best answer, as it *might* be argued that Congress could rely on the Commerce Clause. It is *likely*, however, that such a law would be struck down by the Supreme Court, because it contravenes a clear, express limitation of power under the Intellectual Property Clause—"limited times."

Answer (D) is incorrect. Congress has not granted perpetual patents or unlimited patent renewals in any field.

Patent Law—Infringement & Remedies

87. Answer (C) is correct. Review both section 154(a)(1) and section 271(a) for a list of the exclusive rights of the patent owner and the scope of directly infringing acts, respectively. In section 271(a), the language is "whoever without authority makes, uses, offers to sell, or sells any patented invention, within the United States or imports into the United States any patent invention during the term of the patent therefor, infringes the patent."

> **Answer (A) is incorrect.** This list does not include the act of infringing "use" of the invention, and it lists reconstruction—which means this list essentially twice says "making." If an activity is true reconstruction and is therefore infringing, the activity constitutes "making a new article"; acts of reconstruction are not conceptually separate from acts that constitute "making the invention." *See Aro Mfg Co. v. Convertible Top Replacement Co.*, 365 U.S. 336, 346 (1961). On the other hand, activities that are sometimes argued by patent owners to be reconstruction are not reconstruction at all; the acts are merely repair of a lawfully owned good and are non-infringing due to exhaustion of rights. *See id.*

> **Answer (B) is incorrect.** This list does not include the act of infringing use of the invention, and it lists exporting the invention, which is not a right of the patent owner under U.S. law.

> **Answer (D) is incorrect.** This list does not include the act of an infringing offer to sell the invention, and it lists exporting the invention, which is not a right of the patent owner under U.S. law.

88. Answer (C) is correct. This answer includes both literal infringement and infringement through the doctrine of equivalents, both of which would allow a patentee to show that an accused infringer's making and selling activities violated the patentee's rights under section 271(a). Literal infringement, as the term implies, involves a showing that the accused device (i.e., the defendant's product) reads on every element of the claimed invention—it is a duplication of the invention as it was described in the claim. While a precise definition of the doctrine of equivalents is elusive, it is clear that it must be applied individually to each element of a patent claim—not to the claim or to the invention as a whole.

> In our view, the particular linguistic framework used [seeking to assess whether an element serves the same function, in the same way, to reach the same result; versus "insubstantial differences"] is less important than whether the test is probative of the essential inquiry: Does the accused product or process contain elements identical or equivalent *to each claimed element* of the patented invention? Different linguistic frameworks may be more suitable to different cases, depending on their particular

facts. A *focus on individual elements* and a special vigilance against allowing the concept of equivalence to eliminate completely any such elements should reduce considerably the imprecision of whatever language is used. An *analysis of the role played by each element* in the context of the specific patent claim will thus inform the inquiry as to whether a substitute element matches the function, way, and result of the claimed element, or whether the substitute element plays a role substantially different from the claimed element.

Warner Jenkinson Co., Inc. v. Hilton Davis Chemical Co., 520 U.S. 17, 39–40 (1997) (emphasis added).

Answer (A) is incorrect. This response closely corresponds to the way in which the Federal Circuit has described the test for design patent infringement—not utility patent infringement. Citing *Gorham Co. v. White*, 81 U.S. 511 (1871), the court first states that the most basic test of design patent infringement is: "If, in the eye of an ordinary observer, giving such attention as a purchaser usually gives, two designs are substantially the same, if the resemblance is such as to deceive such an observer, inducing him to purchase one supposing it to be the other, the first one patented is infringed by the other"; but the Federal Circuit then supplemented that test with the influence of prior art, an influence drawn from later Supreme Court decisions, by analyzing the decisions and observing that "Subsequent cases ... interpret[ed] the ordinary observer test of *Gorham* to require that the perspective of the ordinary observer be informed by a comparison of the patented design and the accused design in light of the prior art." *Egyptian Goddess, Inc. v. Swisa, Inc.* 543 F.3d 665 (Fed. Cir. 2008) (en banc).

Answer (B) is incorrect. This is not a test for any form of patent infringement.

Answer (D) is incorrect. An essential feature of utility patent law is that each element in a claim is material to its scope. As discussed above in connection with correct Answer (C), the doctrine of equivalents cannot be applied through an assessment of "overall" equivalence; instead, the doctrine of equivalents must be applied to individual claim elements and not to the invention "as a whole."

89. Answer (D) is correct. As further explained below for each of the options, all of the options provided actually provide an example of infringement of a patent under U.S. law.

Answer (A) is incorrect. Practicing an invention for purely experimental purposes does not impinge on any of the exclusive rights of the patent holder, but it is a very narrow exception, under Federal Circuit case law. *See, e.g., Madey v. Duke University*, 307 F.3d 1351 (Fed. Cir. 2002) ("[T]he defense [i]s limited to actions performed 'for amusement, to satisfy idle curiosity, or for strictly philosophical inquiry.'... [U]se is disqualified if it has the 'slightest commercial implication.' Moreover, use in keeping with the legitimate business of the alleged infringer does not qualify for the experimental use defense." Since most universities have a "legitimate business" in doing research work to further scientific inquiry, and that research can lead to new patents, and the research is not done "for amusement, to satisfy idle curiosity," and the like, the court did not seem to think that most university research work would qualify. It also ruled against Duke University on the specific facts of the case cited.).

Answer (B) is incorrect. Selling a product manufactured using a patented process would infringe on the exclusive right provided in section 271(g). Of course, the use of the patented process to manufacture the product would also infringe under section 271(a). To understand the distinction between section 271(g) infringing sales and 271(a) infringing process use, and why both might be important rights to have, is to realize that there might be two different direct infringers by the end of this line of activities and commercial transactions. The ultimate seller of the unpatented product made by the process might not always be the same party that used the process to manufacture it and engaged in the first infringing sale. Exhaustion would not apply to make downstream sales noninfringing since the sale of the product by the infringing manufacturer would not be under the authority of the patent owner.

Answer (C) is incorrect. Importing a product covered by a patent would infringe on one of the exclusive rights provided in section 271(a).

90. Reverse engineering a patented product can potentially constitute a violation of patent law—but it depends on how far the activity is taken.

If the product being reverse engineered was purchased lawfully, then the initial act of reverse engineering, if it constitutes simple "use" and examination of the product, would not infringe the patent. This is because the right of use of that item is "exhausted" following the patentee's sale of the unit of the product. This is true even though "using" the product is one of the patentee's exclusive rights. *See* 35 U.S.C. §§ 154(a)(1) & 271(a); *Impression Prods., Inc. v. Lexmark Int'l, Inc.*, 137 S. Ct. 1523 (2017) (tracing the history and theory of exhaustion of the use and sale rights after ownership of a product passes to a lawful purchaser, and holding that it applies to both domestic and foreign sales and it is "uniform and automatic. Once a patentee decides to sell—whether on its own or through a licensee—that sale exhausts its patent rights, regardless of any post-sale restrictions the patentee purports to impose, either directly or through a license.")

But if the competitor who has lawfully engaged in such protected "use" of a lawfully owned product *thereafter* proceeds to do what most "reverse engineers" wish to do with the information learned, which is to *then proceed to make, use, sell, offer to sell, or import new copies* of the patented invention, *these actions* violate the exclusive rights of the patent owner.

91. The prosecution history estoppel (or file wrapper estoppel) doctrine places a limit on the extent to which the patentee can use the doctrine of equivalents to expand the scope of claims under the patent. It is therefore invoked by the accused infringer to restrain use of the doctrine of equivalents for any claim that was amended during prosecution. One basic explanation of the "prosecution history" or "file wrapper" appears in *Autogiro Co. of America v. United States*, 384 F.2d 391, 398–99 (Ct. Cl. 1967):

> The file wrapper contains the entire record of the proceedings in the Patent Office from the first application papers to the issued patent. Since all express representations of the patent applicant made to induce a patent grant are in the file wrapper, this material provides an accurate charting of the patent's pre-issuance history. One use of the file wrapper is file wrapper estoppel, which is the application of familiar estoppel principles to Patent Office prosecution and patent infringement litigation.

Prosecution history estoppel thus comes into play when the patent applicant has made amendments to its application to avoid prior art or to address other objections (such as obviousness) that might render the claimed subject matter unpatentable. Applying estoppel principles, the patent holder cannot then use the doctrine of equivalents to reassert during infringement litigation the scope or breadth of a claim that the patent applicant "gave up" during the patent application process. For instance, in *Keystone Driller Co. v. Northwest Engineering Corp.*, 294 U.S. 42, 48 (1935), the allegedly infringing equivalent element or feature (asserted during litigation) was part of the prior art that formed the basis for the rejection of the originally filed patent claims. The revised claims did not include the feature, and this narrowing revision had allowed the patent to issue over that prior art. The Court applied the prosecution history estoppel doctrine to prevent use of the doctrine of equivalents to encompass in later patent litigation the element or feature that had been eliminated during prosecution. In *Warner Jenkinson Co., Inc. v. Hilton Davis Chemical Co.*, 520 U.S. 17, 39–40 (1997), the Court stated:

> Prosecution history estoppel continues to be available as a defense to infringement, but if the patent holder demonstrates that an amendment required during prosecution had a purpose unrelated to patentability, a court must consider that purpose in order to decide whether an estoppel is precluded. Where the patent holder is unable to establish such a purpose, a court should presume that the purpose behind the required amendment is such that prosecution history estoppel would apply.

More recently, in *Festo Corp. v. Shoketsu Kinzoku Kogyo Kabushiki Co., Ltd.*, 535 U.S. 722 (2002), the Court held that prosecution history estoppel applies to any amendment made to satisfy the requisites of patent law, but that the amendment is not an absolute bar to a claim of infringement under the doctrine of equivalents. Instead, the patent holder has the burden of proving that the particular amendment did not surrender the equivalent material at issue.

92. Answer (C) is correct. The facts here did indicate that Seller's product was especially adapted for making lenses using this type of plastic—based on the size of the pieces of plastic—but that does not mean that Seller knows or has reason to know that there is a process patent covering a process for manufacturing a soft contact lens using this composition, or that the Manufacturers do not have a license to use the process. Although the direct infringement liability provision, section 271(a), does not include a knowledge element, the secondary or indirect infringement provisions of section 271(b)–(c) both do. *See Aro Mfg. Co. v. Convertible Top Replacement Co.*, 377 U.S. 476 (1964) (*Aro II*) ("[A] majority of the Court is of the view that §271(c) does require a showing that the alleged contributory infringer knew that the combination for which his component was especially designed was *both* patented *and* infringing.") (emphasis added); *Global-Tech Appliances, Inc. v. SEB S.A.*, 563 U.S. 754 (2011) (relying on *Aro II*'s interpretation of §271(c) and the history of the acts later separated by Congress into subsections (b) and (c) of section 271 to conclude that knowledge of the patent is also required for inducement under section 271(b)). This fact pattern best fits the section 271(c) contributory infringement pattern, but there can be overlap with section 271(b) inducement on some facts, which could, depending on circumstances, include facts like these.

Answer (A) is incorrect. This response simply points out that Seller is not a direct infringer. Not being a direct infringer is good for Seller, but it does not mean that Seller cannot be found liable for inducing infringement under section 271(b) or contributory infringement under 271(c), depending on other facts.

Answer (B) is incorrect. This would be the second-best answer, but it is still incomplete. This answer only addresses one form of indirect infringement, section 271(b) inducement. It is true that these facts do not make it clear whether there is any encouragement or inducement activity,but part of the reason inducement is not clearly present is that there is no evidence of Seller's knowledge of the patent, which is relevant for both inducement and contributory infringement—it is not relevant for inducement alone. See the explanation for correct Answer (C).

Answer (D) is incorrect. Although this answer identifies some of the elements of section 271(c) that are satisfied on these facts (the plastic being sold is useful in practicing the patented process, the pieces are especially adapted to the patented process, and seemingly material to it, etc.), this answer does not acknowledge the role of knowledge of the patent for liability under section 271(c). As explained in correct Answer (C) above, the Supreme Court has held that the alleged contributory infringer must know that the combination or process for which the material was especially designed or adapted was both patented and infringing. Direct patent infringement is "strict liability," but contributory patent infringement and infringement by inducement are not.

93. **Answer (A) is correct.** Appellate jurisdiction in patent cases is within the exclusive purview of the United States Court of Appeals for the Federal Circuit, with certiorari review (discretionary) by the Supreme Court. This unusual feature of patent law is set forth in 28 U.S.C. § 1295:

> The United States Court of Appeals for the Federal Circuit shall have exclusive jurisdiction—(1) of an appeal from a final decision of a district court of the United States, the District Court of Guam, the District Court of the Virgin Islands, or the District Court of the Northern Mariana Islands, in any civil action arising under, or in any civil action in which a party has asserted a compulsory counterclaim arising under, any Act of Congress relating to patents or plant variety protection.

Thus, appeals from any district court's patent infringement rulings must be filed in the Federal Circuit, rather than the regional court of appeals in which the parties are located or in which the case was litigated. By virtue of its exclusive appellate jurisdiction, decisions of the Federal Circuit on patent law issues are effectively controlling throughout the United States, unless they are overruled by the Supreme Court (or by the Federal Circuit itself sitting en banc). Decisions by the Court of Customs and Patent Appeals (a predecessor of the Federal Circuit) are also considered as governing precedent. Neither federal copyright nor federal trademark law vests appellate jurisdiction in this manner—appeals generally go the regional circuit, just as with any ordinary federal case. The Federal Circuit's exclusive jurisdiction serves to increase the national uniformity of patent law, although that court's patent law decisions have been overruled by the Supreme Court on a number of occasions in the last decade.

Answer (B) is incorrect. As discussed above, the Federal Circuit does have exclusive appellate jurisdiction, but the Supreme Court has the final say by virtue of its certiorari review.

Answer (C) is incorrect. As discussed above, the Federal Circuit has exclusive appellate jurisdiction over patent appeals.

Answer (D) is incorrect. As discussed above, the Federal Circuit has exclusive appellate jurisdiction over patent appeals.

94. Answer (A) is correct. In patent cases, injunctive relief is available upon a showing of a four-factor equitable test. This conclusion reflects recent Supreme Court guidance on the issue. In *eBay, Inc. v. MercExchange, L.L.C.*, 547 U.S. 388, 393–94 (2006), the Supreme Court held that a patent holder must make a four-part showing in order to receive injunctive relief:

> (1) that it has suffered an irreparable injury; (2) that remedies available at law, such as monetary damages, are inadequate to compensate for that injury; (3) that, considering the balance of hardships between the plaintiff and defendant, a remedy in equity is warranted; and (4) that the public interest would not be disserved by a permanent injunction.

The Court rejected the Federal Circuit's presumption that injunctions should be granted except in unusual cases. Injunctive relief is a very important remedy because it permits the patent holder to maintain its exclusivity in the marketplace, which is the essence of the patent reward. Section 283 of the Patent Act states: "The several courts having jurisdiction of cases under this title may grant injunctions in accordance with the principles of equity to prevent the violation of any right secured by patent, on such terms as the court deems reasonable."

Answer (B) is incorrect. As discussed above, the Supreme Court in *eBay, Inc. v. MercExchange, L.L.C.*, rejected the Federal Circuit's presumption that injunctions should be granted except in unusual cases.

Answer (C) is incorrect. There is no authority for automatic grants of injunctive relief in patent cases.

Answer (D) is incorrect. As discussed above, the Supreme Court in *eBay, Inc. v. MercExchange, L.L.C.*, required a four-part showing in order to grant injunctive relief. Although the defendant's bad faith could be a consideration, it is not required in order for equitable relief to be granted. The statutory language regarding equitable relief does not make reference to "exceptional cases."

95. Section 284 of the Patent Act sets forth the types of damages recoveries available to patent holders: "Upon finding for the claimant the court shall award the claimant damages adequate to compensate for the infringement but in no event less than a reasonable royalty for the use made of the invention by the infringer, together with interest and costs as fixed by the court." This provision expressly contemplates the use of expert testimony to determine either damages or a reasonable royalty, the minimum recovery to which patent holders are entitled: "The court may receive expert testimony as an aid to the determination of damages or of what royalty would be reasonable under the circumstances." *Id.*

In order to receive lost profits in a patent case, the plaintiff generally makes a four-part showing: (1) demand for the patented product; (2) absence of acceptable non-infringing substitutes; (3) manufacturing and marketing capability to exploit the demand; and (4) the amount of the profit it would have made. *See Panduit Corp. v. Stahlin Bros. Fibre Works, Inc.*, 575 F.2d 1152, 1156 (6th

Cir. 1978). This four-part showing establishes that the patent holder would have earned the lost profits "but for" the defendant's infringing activities. The *Panduit* test is, however, not the exclusive test. Lost profits may be awarded in any situation where the patentee establishes that the infringement *caused* economic harm. Section 284's requirement is that the damages awarded be compensating for the infringement by the infringer (including when the patent holder's damages are measured by how much profit the patent holder has lost). For example, competition from an infringer could force the patentee to lower prices or leave prices flat rather than raising them as planned. This loss of profits would still be caused by the infringement. And if a third party offers acceptable noninfringing substitutes (see the second *Panduit* factor), lost profits could potentially still be recovered if the patent holder could gather the sales data from the market as a whole to prove that the infringement caused a drop in the patentee's market share.

96. In order to receive attorney's fees and costs in a patent case, the prevailing party seeking the award—which could be either the victorious patent owner or the vindicated, previously accused infringer—must satisfy section 285 of the Patent Act, which states: "The court in exceptional cases may award reasonable attorney fees to the prevailing party." In *Octane Fitness, LLC v. Icon Health & Fitness, Inc.*, 134 S. Ct. 1749, 1756 (2014), the Supreme Court construed an "exceptional" case to mean simply one "that stands out from others with respect to the substantive strength of a party's litigating position (considering both the governing law and the facts of the case) or the unreasonable manner in which the case was litigated." In a footnote, the Court provided a bit more information about the types of evidence that could be relevant—it referred to one of its prior decisions in which it said it:

> explained that in determining whether to award fees under a similar provision in the Copyright Act, district courts could consider a "nonexclusive" list of "factors," including "frivolousness, motivation, objective unreasonableness (both in the factual and legal components of the case) and the need in particular circumstances to advance considerations of compensation and deterrence."

Id. at 1756 n.6 (citing and quoting *Fogerty v. Fantasy, Inc.*, 510 U.S. 517, 534 n.19 (1994). Note that section 285 does not mandate a fee award, and in *Octane*, the Supreme Court clearly held that the determination is for the district court to make using the totality of the circumstances on a case-by-case basis.

In *Octane*, the Supreme Court rejected the Federal Circuit's prior rigid formulation for attorney's fees awards; without rehashing the details of the overturned standard here, it suffices to say that the Federal Circuit had created categorical rules about when a case became "exceptional" as a result of willful infringement, litigation misconduct, bad faith litigation, and the like. The Supreme Court, on the other hand, held that based on the open statutory language selected by Congress, section 285 is not highly constraining of district court discretion. It construed the statute largely by reference to the "ordinary meaning" of "exceptional," which is set forth above. In a different decision handed down the same day as *Octane*, the Court determined that the same discretionary statutory language required appellate review of fee awards using an abuse-of-discretion standard. *See Highmark Inc. v. Allcare Health Mgmt. Sys., Inc.*, 134 S. Ct. 1744, 1749 (2014).

Patent Law—Defenses & Limitations

97. Answer (A) is correct. Although a patent is presumed to be valid, *see* 35 U.S.C. § 282(a), invalidity is a defense provided in section 282(b)(2)–(3) of the Patent Act.

Answer (B) is not correct. For a claim of infringement based on the defendant's making, using, or selling a patented invention, all of which are infringing under section 271(a), knowledge is irrelevant to liability (although relevant to the possible enhancement of damages under section 284). Knowledge is relevant to claims of inducement of infringement and contributory infringement under section 271(b)–(c). *See Aro Mfg. Co. v. Convertible Top Replacement Co.*, 377 U.S. 476 (1964) (contributory infringement); *Global-Tech Appliances, Inc. v. SEB S.A.*, 131 S. Ct. 2060 (2011) (inducement).

Answer (C) is not correct. The Patent Act does not contain a statute of limitations that bars the filing of claims after a certain period of time has passed. Section 286 limits monetary recovery to infringing acts committed within six years of filing of the claim of infringement. Section 286 does not prevent the owner of a valid patent from suing for infringement that began more than six years before filing the action; owners of valid patents can obtain an injunction barring future infringement (through the end of the term) and can obtain monetary recovery for infringing acts within the six-year recovery period.

Answer (D) is not correct. See above.

98. Answer (D) is correct. If a medical practitioner makes use of a patented process in order to provide medical treatment, the physician is not liable because of statutory immunity for medical providers. Section 287(c) of the Patent Act immunizes medical practitioners for liability for the unauthorized use of medical and surgical procedures:

> With respect to a medical practitioner's performance of a medical activity that constitutes an infringement under section 271(a) or (b) of this title, the provisions of sections 281, 283, 284, and 285 of this title shall not apply against the medical practitioner or against a related health care entity with respect to such medical activity.

35 U.S.C. § 287(c). The statute defines medical activity as:

> the performance of a medical or surgical procedure on a body, but shall not include (i) the use of a patented machine, manufacture, or composition of matter in violation of such patent, (ii) the practice of a patented use of a composition of matter in violation of such patent, or (iii) the practice of a process in violation of a biotechnology patent.

Under U.S. law, unlike that of some foreign nations, patents can be issued on medical procedures, such a new method for treating a physical ailment, as well as to medical devices. The statutory immunity prevents physicians from being liable for patent infringement when they provide medical treatment by using a patented treatment process. Note that the immunity applies to medical procedures, but not to the production or use of the underlying physical products that might be used in the course of medical treatment, such as a medical device or a pharmaceutical product. A medical practitioner is defined as "any natural person who is licensed by a State to provide the medical activity described in subsection (c)(1) or who is acting under the direction of such person in the performance of the medical activity." A *related health care entity* is "an entity with which a medical practitioner has a professional affiliation under which the medical practitioner performs the medical activity, including but not limited to a nursing home, hospital, university, medical school, health maintenance organization, group medical practice, or a medical clinic." The statute applies to treatment of "a human body, organ or cadaver, or a nonhuman animal used in medical research or instruction directly relating to the treatment of humans." Given this language, the law does not generally exempt veterinarians from liability. The statute is also inapplicable to patents filed prior to September 30, 1996.

Answer (A) is incorrect. As discussed above, the medical practitioner has statutory immunity.

Answer (B) is incorrect. As discussed above, the medical practitioner has statutory immunity.

Answer (C) is incorrect. As discussed above, the medical practitioner has statutory immunity.

99. Answer (D) is correct. A prior user (who is acting in good faith) of a later-patented manufacturing process is not liable—in the statutorily prescribed circumstances—because of statutory immunity for good faith prior users of certain types of inventions. Section 273(a) of the Patent Act states:

> A person shall be entitled to a defense under section 282(b) with respect to subject matter consisting of a process, or consisting of a machine, manufacture, or composition of matter used in a manufacturing or other commercial process, that would otherwise infringe a claimed invention being asserted against the person if—
>
> (1) such person, acting in good faith, commercially used the subject matter in the United States, either in connection with an internal commercial use or an actual arm's length sale or other arm's length commercial transfer of a useful end result of such commercial use; and
>
> (2) such commercial use occurred at least 1 year before the earlier of either—
>
>> (A) the effective filing date of the claimed invention; or
>>
>> (B) the date on which the claimed invention was disclosed to the public in a manner that qualified for the exception from prior art under section 102 (b).

35 U.S.C. § 273(a). Here, B began to use "subject matter consisting of a process … acting in good faith, [and] commercially used the subject matter in the United States, … in connection with an

internal commercial use … [that] occurred at least 1 year before the … effective filing date of the claimed invention." Before the AIA, or America Invents Act, section 273 provided a narrower defense for certain good faith users of business methods that were patented by another after the good faith use began.

Answer (A) is incorrect. Although using a process is among the ways in which direct infringement can occur under section 271(a), in this situation, section 273(a) provides a defense—as further explained above.

Answer (B) is incorrect. Although section 271(g) provides for an infringement action for the act of importing into the United States "a product which is made by a process patented in the United States," there is no counterpart right of exportation of a product made by a patented process after that process is used in the United States. Infringement liability arises at a moment in time before any exportation could occur (or not, on these facts, as explained above for correct Answer (D)), namely at the moment when the patented process is used within the United States. *See* § 271(a). In fact, there is no "export" right in U.S. patent law. Infringers must be caught in the patent owner's net in other ways.

Answer (C) is incorrect. There is no general defense of innocent infringement in patent cases. But as discussed above, section 273(a) generally provides a specific statutory defense in this situation.

100. Answer (D) is correct. Company A, which licensed its patent to B, should not succeed with a patent infringement suit related to the fasteners manufactured by B under the license, because the license to B (which does not, on these facts, contain any limitation on the scope of the license) exhausts A's right to control the later sale and use of B's fasteners. Even though A seeks to sue C, not B, the exhaustion doctrine still applies to the licensed goods after they are sold to another party and combined with other parts. *See, e.g., Quanta Computer, Inc. v. LG Electronics, Inc.*, 553 U.S. 617 (2008).

Answer (A) is not correct. Although selling and using are indeed both infringing activities under section 271(a), and only B has an express license under the patent, the license to B exhausts A's use and sale rights with respect to the fasteners that B manufactures and sells under that license. A's right to control the making of new fasteners by other parties is not exhausted.

Answer (B) is not correct. Active inducement is a form of infringement, actionable under section 271(b), but on these facts, C is not inducing B (although on other facts, a customer could induce a manufacturer to infringe a patent in the production of goods for that customer). Moreover, B has a license from A, so its making and selling of goods embodying the patent is noninfringing.

Answer (C) is not correct. This is the second-best answer. It is true that C is not making fasteners, and that C is not inducing B to manufacture them, but that is not the fundamental reason why A will not succeed. If C were not using B's licensed fasteners, then C's use and sale of other, unlicensed fasteners would infringe, even if C were not making them or inducing their manufacture.

101. The patent misuse doctrine is a defense to patent infringement. It can be asserted based on a showing that the plaintiff has acted in a manner that is anticompetitive or otherwise inequitable. Conduct that is related to use of the patent or patent rights allegedly infringed and that violates the antitrust laws is likely to constitute patent misuse. Courts and commentators are divided on whether any conduct that does not violate antitrust laws can nonetheless constitute patent misuse. If patent misuse can be proven, the defendant is not liable for its otherwise infringing acts, at least until the patent owner is able to "purge" the effects of the misuse from the marketplace. One unique feature of the misuse doctrine is that the defendant can assert the defense even if the defendant itself was not the target of the conduct alleged to be misuse.

Copyright Law—Subject Matter & Validity

102. Answer (C) is correct. Section 102(b) of the Copyright Act expressly precludes copyright protection for ideas, stating: "In no case does copyright protection for an original work of authorship extend to any idea, procedure, process, system, method of operation, concept, principle, or discovery, regardless of the form in which it is described, explained, illustrated, or embodied in such work." 17 U.S.C. § 102(b).

Answer (A) is incorrect. Section 102(a) of the Copyright Act provides a general statement of copyrightable subject matter and then identifies specific types of subject matter that are eligible for copyright protection, including literary works. It states:

Copyright protection subsists, in accordance with this title, in original works of authorship fixed in any tangible medium of expression, now known or later developed, from which they can be perceived, reproduced, or otherwise communicated, either directly or with the aid of a machine or device. Works of authorship include the following categories:

  (1) literary works;

  (2) musical works, including any accompanying words;

  (3) dramatic works, including any accompanying music;

  (4) pantomimes and choreographic works;

  (5) pictorial, graphic, and sculptural works;

  (6) motion pictures and other audiovisual works;

  (7) sound recordings; and

  (8) architectural works.

17 U.S.C. § 102(a).

Answer (B) is incorrect. Section 102(a) of the Copyright Act provides a general statement of copyrightable subject matter and then identifies specific types of subject matter that are eligible for copyright protection. As quoted above, musical works are included in this list.

Answer (D) is incorrect. Section 102(a) of the Copyright Act provides a general statement of copyrightable subject matter and then identifies specific types of subject matter that are eligible for copyright protection. As quoted above, architectural works are included in this list.

103. Answer (A) is correct. Section 101 of the Copyright Act states that a work is "fixed in a tangible medium of expression" for copyright law purposes when

> its embodiment in a copy or phonorecord, by or under the authority of the author, is sufficiently permanent or stable to permit it to be perceived, reproduced, or otherwise communicated for a period of more than transitory duration. A work consisting of sounds, images, or both, that are being transmitted, is "fixed" for purposes of this title if a fixation of the work is being made simultaneously with its transmission.

17 U.S.C. § 101. Materials that are handwritten on paper, recorded on film, stored on a hard drive, or even stored in a computer's random-access memory (RAM—i.e., memory that would be lost if the computer lost power) all satisfy this requirement. The first three of these examples are rather straightforward, and the last was addressed in the case of *MAI Systems Corp. v. Peak Computer, Inc.*, 991 F.2d 511, 518–19 (9th Cir. 1993) (storage in RAM sufficient for purposes of fixation requirement).

> **Answer (B) is incorrect.** This is the second-best answer, as it correctly recognizes that the first three situations would clearly satisfy the "fixation" requirement of the Copyright Act. As discussed above, however, material stored on a computer's RAM has been found to be sufficiently permanent to satisfy the statutory (fixation) and constitutional (writing) standard.

> **Answer (C) is incorrect.** A work that is merely handwritten on paper still satisfies the requirements of copyright law—indeed, many early works were handwritten, and some folks still use this form of technology even today.

> **Answer (D) is incorrect.** As discussed above, all four of these methods of recording a work in a tangible form are sufficient to satisfy the requirements of copyright law.

104. Answer (C) is correct. The Directory is not copyrightable, but the Guide is copyrightable. Applying the minimum standard of creativity for copyright protection as set forth in *Feist*, a directory listing (in alphabetical order) the names, addresses, web address, and telephone numbers of all New Orleans restaurants is not copyrightable. Such a directory is very similar to the white pages telephone directory found to be uncopyrightable in *Feist*. As the Court stated in that case:

> The selection, coordination, and arrangement of Rural's white pages do not satisfy the minimum constitutional standards for copyright protection. As mentioned at the outset, Rural's white pages are entirely typical.... In preparing its white pages, Rural simply takes the data provided by its subscribers and lists it alphabetically by surname. The end product is a garden-variety white pages directory, devoid of even the slightest trace of creativity.

Id. at 362. The Guide, however, is copyrightable under the *Feist* standard, as it satisfies the requirement of an original selection and arrangement of factual information—creative judgment is involved in selecting the best New Orleans restaurants, and no facts here indicate that GFG copied the selection or arrangement from another source. Moreover, the full explanations by GFG would very likely constitute additional copyrightable expression, even beyond the selection and judgment involved in identifying the 50 best New Orleans restaurants.

Answer (A) is incorrect. As discussed above, the Guide is copyrightable under the *Feist* standard, but the Directory is not.

Answer (B) is incorrect. As discussed above, the Guide is copyrightable under the *Feist* standard, but the Directory is not.

Answer (D) is incorrect. It is true that the Guide will be copyrightable, as discussed above, but the Directory is not copyrightable, even if it is carefully maintained and regularly updated. The Guide satisfies the *Feist* requirement of an original selection and arrangement of factual information—creative, intellectual judgment is involved in selecting the best New Orleans restaurants, and no facts here indicate that GFG copied the selection or arrangement from another source. As to the Directory, however, as set forth in *Feist* itself, no amount of effort, labor, "sweat of the brow," or other non-creative or non-intellectual output can confer the requisite minimum level of originality required for copyright protection. See the answer to Question 108 under this Topic regarding "sweat of the brow."

105. Answer (B) is correct. The law student has a valid copyright on the images and video captured by the camera, assuming they are minimally creative or involve some judgment. For example, in *Mannion v. Coors Brewing Co.*, 377 F. Supp. 2d 444 (S.D.N.Y. 2005), the court identified three aspects of creativity in photographs: rendition, composition, and timing. Rendition involves photographic skill, composition involves setting the scene, and timing involves when to press the shutter, even though that may sometimes have an element of luck as well. The photographs and videos in question involve at least some selection of scene, angle, and timing.

Answer (A) is incorrect. This answer reaches the right result but for the wrong reasons. The law student does indeed have a valid copyright, but there a minimum level of creativity required, as set forth in the discussion above. Although it is true that courts do not assess the artistic merit of works, a purely mechanical reproduction involving no creative element does not satisfy the copyright standard for originality. *See Bridgeman Art Library, Ltd. v. Corel Corp.*, 36 F. Supp. 2d 191, 197 (S.D.N.Y. 1999) (exact photographic duplication of public domain art works not copyrightable).

Answer (C) is incorrect. Section 102(a) of the Copyright Act expressly lists photographs and audiovisual works among the types of copyrightable subject matter. Although photographs and videos necessarily involve a mechanical process, as noted above, there can be creativity in terms of rendition, composition, and timing.

Answer (D) is incorrect. It is incorrect to state that only artistic and creative works of recognized stature are protected by copyright law. As Justice Holmes wrote in *Bleistein v. Donaldson Lithographing Co.*, 188 U.S. 239, 251–52 (1903), "[i]t would be a dangerous undertaking for persons trained only to the law to constitute themselves final judges of the worth of pictorial illustrations, outside of the narrowest and most obvious limits." There is consideration of the public recognition of a work only in the context of moral rights protections under the Visual

Artists Rights Act. *See* 17 U.S.C. § 106A(a)(3)(B) (providing for limited rights to prevent the destruction of a "work of visual art" when it is "of recognized stature").

106. Answer (A) is correct. This scenario presents a rare example of material that might arguably be protected under state copyright law. A famous celebrity meets a friend for a casual lunch. Unbeknownst to the celebrity, the "friend" has surreptitiously audio-taped the conversation (the celebrity did most of the talking). *See Estate of Hemingway v. Random House, Inc.*, 244 N.E.2d 250, 254 (N.Y. 1968) (state law claim involving similar facts). The key to the lack of federal protection here is understanding who the "author" is—the celebrity, for the celebrity's comments—and how that affects the definition of "fixed" and the extent of federal protection under section 102(a). "A work is 'fixed in a tangible medium of expression' when its embodiment in a copy or phonorecord, *by or under the authority of the author*, is sufficiently permanent or stable to permit it to be perceived, reproduced, or otherwise communicated for a period of more than transitory duration." 17 U.S.C. § 101 (emphasis added). Copyright preemption under section 301 of the Copyright Act does not preclude the state copyright law claim, as that claim does not involve "fixed" material:

> On and after January 1, 1978, all legal or equitable rights that are equivalent to any of the exclusive rights within the general scope of copyright as specified by section 106 in works of authorship that are *fixed in a tangible medium of expression* and come within the subject matter of copyright as specified by sections 102 and 103, whether created before or after that date and whether published or unpublished, are governed exclusively by this title. Thereafter, no person is entitled to any such right or equivalent right in any such work under the common law or statutes of any State.

17 U.S.C. § 301(a) (emphasis added). The legislative history of the 1976 Act recognizes the possibility of a state law copyright in the case of unfixed works: "section 301(b) explicitly preserves common law copyright protection for one important class of works: works that have not been 'fixed in any tangible medium of expression.'... [Unfixed works] would continue to be subject to protection under State statute or common law until fixed in tangible form." H.R. Rep. No. 94 1476, at 131 (1976), *reprinted in* 1976 U.S.C.C.A.N. 5659, 5747.

Answer (B) is incorrect. Section 101 of the Copyright Act specifically requires that a work be fixed in tangible form by authority of the author in order for federal copyright protection to attach. *See* above.

Answer (C) is incorrect. It is true that state law might offer protection. As noted above, however, section 101 of the Copyright Act specifically states that a work be fixed in tangible form by authority of the author in order for copyright protection to attach.

Answer (D) is incorrect. As discussed above, state copyright law might offer protection in this situation. Copyright preemption under section 301 of the Copyright Act does not preclude the state copyright law claim, as it does not involve copyrightable subject matter under federal law (material fixed in a tangible form of expression).

107. Answer (C) is correct. The 1790 Copyright protected only three types of works, stating: "Be it enacted ... That from and after the passing of this act, the author and authors of any map, chart, book or books ... shall have the sole right and liberty of printing, reprinting, publishing and vending such map, chart, book or books, for the term of fourteen years from the recording the title thereof in the clerk's office, as is herein after directed...." Copyright Act of 1790, Section 1, 1 Statutes at Large 124.

Answer (A) is incorrect. Books are expressly protected under the 1790 Copyright Act.

Answer (B) is incorrect. Charts are expressly protected under the 1790 Copyright Act.

Answer (D) is incorrect. Maps are expressly protected under the 1790 Copyright Act.

108. The "sweat of the brow" theory for copyright protection suggests that copyright is a reward for the hard work or industrious collection involved in compiling facts. The Supreme Court has unanimously rejected this doctrine: "'The sweat of the brow' doctrine had numerous flaws, the most glaring being that it extended copyright protection in a compilation beyond selection and arrangement—the compiler's original contributions—to the facts themselves. Under the doctrine, the only defense to infringement was independent creation. A subsequent compiler was 'not entitled to take one word of information previously published,' but rather had to 'independently wor[k] out the matter for himself, so as to arrive at the same result from the same common sources of information.' ... 'Sweat of the brow' courts thereby eschewed the most fundamental axiom of copyright law—that no one may copyright facts or ideas." *Feist Publications, Inc. v. Rural Telephone Service Co.*, 499 U.S. 340, 345 (1991).

109. **Answer (B) is correct.** The current importance of a copyright notice for a work first written and published in 1980 can best be stated as follows: copyright notices are required and works published without the copyright notice fall into the public domain unless "cured" under the Copyright Act of 1976. The Copyright Act of 1976 provisions in effect in 1980 essentially still apply to this work because it was published in that year. The 1976 Act ameliorated the harsh effect of the copyright notice requirement under the 1909 Copyright Act, under which a work published without notice fell into the public domain. The 1976 Act continued to require copyright notice, but it allowed for a cure of, or excuse for the omission of, the notice in some circumstances. The cure provision continues to be relevant even though current law no longer requires copyright notice. Section 405(a) of the Copyright Act, which would govern the work in question, states:

(a) Effect of Omission on Copyright.—With respect to copies and phonorecords publicly distributed by authority of the copyright owner before the effective date of the Berne Convention Implementation Act of 1988, the omission of the copyright notice described in sections 401 through 403 from copies or phonorecords publicly distributed by authority of the copyright owner does not invalidate the copyright in a work if—

(1) the notice has been omitted from no more than a relatively small number of copies or phonorecords distributed to the public; or

(2) registration for the work has been made before or is made within five years after the publication without notice, and a reasonable effort is made to add notice to all copies or phonorecords that are distributed to the public in the United States after the omission has been discovered; or

(3) the notice has been omitted in violation of an express requirement in writing that, as a condition of the copyright owner's authorization of the public distribution of copies or phonorecords, they bear the prescribed notice.

17 U.S.C. §405(a). *See generally Hasbro Bradley, Inc. v. Sparkle Toys, Inc.*, 780 F.2d 189 (2d Cir. 1985) (applying 1976 Act notice requirement and cure provisions).

Answer (A) is incorrect. As discussed above, a strict notice requirement applied prior to the effective date of the Copyright Act of 1976 but was modified by that statute.

Answer (C) is incorrect. This rule only applies to works published after March 1, 1989, when the Berne Convention Implementation Act of 1988 ("BCIA") took effect. If the 1980 work were *re*-published after March 1, 1989, the new copies of the work would not need copyright notices, but the copyright status of the work would still be affected by any uncured omissions in the 1980 publication.

The BCIA was enacted to bring the United States into compliance with the Berne Convention, thereby eliminating the notice requirement for works published after its effective date. Article 5(2) of the Berne Convention states:

The enjoyment and the exercise of these rights shall not be subject to any formality; such enjoyment and such exercise shall be independent of the existence of protection in the country of origin of the work. Consequently, apart from the provisions of this Convention, the extent of protection, as well as the means of redress afforded to the author to protect his rights, shall be governed exclusively by the laws of the country where protection is claimed.

Answer (D) is incorrect. As noted above, the BCIA eliminated the notice requirement for works published after March 1, 1989. The Sonny Bono Copyright Term Extension Act made a number of modifications to copyright law, but it did not address the notice requirement.

110. The copyright notice requirement was mandatory under the 1909 Copyright Act. Works published without the copyright notice fell into the public domain and thus could be freely used without permissions or payment. Later amendments have not retroactively changed this result, meaning that a work published without notice before the effective date of the 1976 Copyright Act (the effective date was January 1, 1978) is still deemed to be in the public domain.

111. The copyright notice is no longer mandatory under present law. The BCIA eliminated the mandatory notice requirement and applies to works published after March 1, 1989, the BCIA's effective date. Section 401(a) of the Copyright Act states:

Whenever a work protected under this title is published in the United States or elsewhere by authority of the copyright owner, a notice of copyright as provided by this section *may be placed* on publicly distributed copies from which the work can be visually perceived, either directly or with the aid of a machine or device.

17 U.S.C. §401(a) (emphasis added). Copyright notice still serves important informational purposes, including identification of the copyright owner and practical notice of the claim of copy-

right. Thus, although the notice is entirely optional, it is a simple way to assert ownership of a copyrighted work. It can also eliminate mitigation of damages based on a defense of innocent infringement, as provided in section 401(d):

> If a notice of copyright in the form and position specified by this section appears on the published copy or copies to which a defendant in a copyright infringement suit had access, then no weight shall be given to such a defendant's interposition of a defense based on innocent infringement in mitigation of actual or statutory damages, except as provided in the last sentence of section 504(C)(2).

17 U.S.C. § 401(d).

112. The so-called "poor man's copyright" is a layperson's term that one can hope will one day dwindle away entirely. It represents an author's practice of placing a copy of a work in a sealed envelope and then mailing it back to the author through regular postal mail. This action has no direct legal significance under the Copyright Act, but is based on the notion that the mailed, postmarked, return-addressed (and unopened) copy can serve as a record of the work's authorship or provenance. Although the mailed copy might be introduced into evidence in a dispute over authorship, the poor man's copyright has no formal recognition in copyright law. An author's postage money and time would be better applied toward a proper copyright registration with the Copyright Office (which is very low cost, and relatively simple in most instances).

113. Answer (C) is correct. The Visual Artists Rights Act of 1990 ("VARA") does not protect limited-edition or single copies of architectural plans. VARA provides protections for a "work of visual art," a term of art defined in the Copyright Act as follows:

> (1) a painting, drawing, print, or sculpture, existing in a single copy, in a limited edition of 200 copies or fewer that are signed and consecutively numbered by the author, or, in the case of a sculpture, in multiple cast, carved, or fabricated sculptures of 200 or fewer that are consecutively numbered by the author and bear the signature or other identifying mark of the author; or

> (2) a still photographic image produced for exhibition purposes only, existing in a single copy that is signed by the author, or in a limited edition of 200 copies or fewer that are signed and consecutively numbered by the author.

17 U.S.C. § 101. Thus, sculptures, prints, and photographs are eligible for protection under VARA, but architectural plans are not.

Answer (A) is incorrect. As noted above, VARA expressly protects sculptures as works of visual art as long as they are signed and numbered limited-editions or single copies.

Answer (B) is incorrect. As noted above, VARA expressly protects prints as works of visual art as long as they are signed and numbered limited-editions or single copies.

Answer (D) is incorrect. As noted above, VARA expressly protects photographs as works of visual art as long as they are signed and numbered limited-editions or single copies.

114. Answer (B) is correct. An original design for a picnic table and benches is protectable if the original, aesthetic features are either physically or conceptually separable from the utilitarian aspects of the picnic table and benches. The table and benches can be viewed as "useful articles" under the Copyright Act. *See* 17 U.S.C. § 101 ("A 'useful article' is an article having an intrinsic utilitarian function that is not merely to portray the appearance of the article or to convey information."). A useful article can gain copyright protection as a "pictorial, graphic, or sculptural work" if, "and only to the extent that, [the design of the useful article] incorporates pictorial, graphic, or sculptural features that can be identified separately from, and are capable of existing independently of, the utilitarian aspects of the article." 17 U.S.C. § 101 (definition of "pictorial, graphic, and sculptural works").

Case law has interpreted the "identified separately from" and "capable of existing independently of" requirements to mean that the original, creative aspects of the work must be either conceptually or physically separable (or both) from the underlying function of the article. As the Supreme Court recently stated:

> a feature incorporated into the design of a useful article is eligible for copyright protection only if the feature (1) can be perceived as a two- or three-dimensional work of art separate from the useful article and (2) would qualify as a protectable pictorial, graphic, or sculptural work—either on its own or fixed in some other tangible medium of expression—if it were imagined separately from the useful article into which it is incorporated.

Star Athletica, L.L.C. v. Varsity Brands, Inc., 137 S. Ct. 1002, 1007 (2017); *see also Brandir Int'l., Inc. v. Cascade Pacific Lumber Co.*, 834 F.2d 1142 (2d Cir. 1987) (affirming copyright protection via either physical or conceptual separability, and stating that: "[I]f design elements reflect a merger of aesthetic and functional considerations, the artistic aspects of a work cannot be said to be conceptually separable from the utilitarian elements. Conversely, where design elements can be identified as reflecting the designer's artistic judgment exercised independently of functional influences, conceptual separability exists."); *Kieselstein-Cord v. Accessories by Pearl, Inc.*, 632 F.2d 989, 993 (2d Cir. 1980).

Answer (A) is incorrect. It is true that the design would be protectable if the original, aesthetic features were physically separable from the utilitarian aspects of the picnic table and benches, but this is not the best answer because conceptual separability can also lead to protection, as explained above.

Answer (C) is incorrect. Although the original, aesthetic features must show a modicum of creativity in order to meet the minimum standard for copyright protection as a work of authorship, *see Feist Publications, Inc. v. Rural Telephone Service Co.*, 499 U.S. 340 (1991), the relative artistic or aesthetic merits of those features are not assessed in determining whether a work will be protected. *See Bleistein v. Donaldson Lithographing Co.*, 188 U.S. 239, 251–52 (1903).

Answer (D) is incorrect. Copyright law does not protect functional *features* of an article, *see, e.g.*, 17 U.S.C. § 102(b) (excluding ideas, procedures, processes, concepts, etc. from copyright protection of a work "regardless of the form in which" they are "embodied in such work"), but the Copyright Act does expressly provide for protection of the non-utilitarian, non-functional features of a useful article if the original pictorial, graphic, or sculptural features of that article are separable from the utilitarian or functional aspects of the article, as explained above.

115. The copyright doctrine of "scenes a faire" recognizes that certain inevitable background scenes may be necessary in order to depict the setting of a particular type of work at issue. Two movies about the Civil War, for example, might both include characters depicting Presidents Lincoln and Davis, Union and Confederate flags and regalia, Southern plantations, and generals such as Grant and Lee. These inevitable similarities would not be a basis for a claim of copyright infringement. *See Hoehling v. Universal Studios*, 618 F.2d 972 (2d Cir. 1980) (noting that movie depicting pre-World War II Germany would include beer hall scenes, Nazi uniforms and greetings, and other stock background items).

116. The idea/expression distinction as it relates to copyright law provides that ideas are not copyrightable, but the expression of those ideas is protected. In other words, an idea or concept cannot be protected under the Copyright Act, but the particular manner of expressing it can be—the word choices, phrasing, and other particular ways in which an author might express a point. The idea/expression distinction is expressly stated in the Copyright Act: "In no case does copyright protection for an original work of authorship extend to any idea, procedure, process, system, method of operation, concept, principle, or discovery, regardless of the form in which it is described, explained, illustrated, or embodied in such work." 17 U.S.C. § 102. *See generally Hoehling v. Universal Studios*, 618 F.2d 972 (2d Cir. 1980) (theory of how Hindenberg disaster occurred constitutes an uncopyrightable idea).

117. The case of a recipe book presents a good opportunity to consider the scope and limits of copyright protection. Several elements in a recipe book are clearly copyrightable, as would be the material found in any type of book. Any substantial literary expression—thoughts, comments, and observations by the chefs—would clearly be eligible for copyright protection. Any original artworks (for example, the cover design or photograph) or photographs contained in the book would also be copyrightable.

The more challenging aspect of this question involves the recipes. Although section 102(a) of the Copyright Act includes literary works (such as cookbooks) as copyrightable subject matter, Section 102(b) excludes processes, systems, and methods of operation (e.g., recipes). A compilation copyright protects the selection, order, and manner of the presentation of the compilation's elements—here, the overall selection of recipes in the cookbook—but not the individual recipes. *See Publications Intern. Ltd. v. Meredith Corp.*, 88 F. 3d 473 (7th Cir. 1996); *Lambing v. Godiva*, 142 F.3d 434 (6th Cir. 1998) (unpublished opinion). Expressive commentary related to the recipes may contain copyrightable expression, though the specific steps and ingredients involved in making a dish would clearly not be protected. *See Barbour v. Head*, 178 F. Supp. 2d 758 (S.D. Tex. 2001).

Copyright Law—Ownership & Duration

118. Answer (B) is correct. The United States government can own rights to works assigned to it by non-governmental authors. Section 105 of the Copyright Act expressly precludes copyright protection for works of United States government employees acting in the scope of their duties, but allows the government to receive copyrights from others: "Copyright protection under this title is not available for any work of the United States Government, but the United States Government is not precluded from receiving and holding copyrights transferred to it by assignment, bequest, or otherwise." 17 U.S.C. § 105. A "work of the United States Government" is defined as "a work prepared by an officer or employee of the United States Government as part of that person's official duties." 17 U.S.C. § 101.

Answer (A) is incorrect. As discussed above, these works are in the public domain.

Answer (C) is incorrect. There is no special copyright rule or carve-out from section 105 (precluding copyright protection for works of U.S. government employees acting in the scope of their duties) related to the ownership of works dealing with national secrets.

Answer (D) is incorrect. As discussed above in incorrect Answer (C), only (B) is correct.

119. Answer (C) is correct. A student is hired to do research for a professor and provides 10 pages of material, which the professor copies largely verbatim into a 30-page article. The professor is most likely the sole author of the work under the Copyright Act, given that there was no intent to form a joint work. Section 101 of the Copyright Act defines a joint work as "a work prepared by two or more authors with the intention that their contributions be merged into inseparable or interdependent parts of a unitary whole." 17 U.S.C. § 101. As discussed in *Childress v. Taylor*, 945 F.2d 500 (2d Cir. 1991), two elements must be proven to form a joint work—(1) each author must make independently copyrightable contributions to the work and (2) there must be mutual intention that the contributions be combined into a unitary whole as a joint work. Although the student assistant did contribute copyrightable material, it is unlikely that there was a mutual intention to form a joint work. *See, e.g., Thomson v. Larson*, 147 F.3d 195 (2d Cir. 1998); *Clogston v. American Academy of Orthopaedic Surgeons*, 930 F. Supp. 1156 (W.D. Tex. 1996).

Answer (A) is incorrect. As discussed above, even though the student assistant did contribute copyrightable material, it is unlikely that there was a mutual intention to form a joint work.

Answer (B) is incorrect. It is likely that the professor or institution either paid the assistant or gave academic credit for the work, and the work performed is unlikely to have been taken without express or implied authorization.

Answer (D) is incorrect. There is no specific quantitative requirement for joint authorship, as long as the requirements discussed above are met.

120. If two coauthors specifically wish to have joint authorship of the copyright in their work, courts typically require that they meet the two-part test enunciated in *Childress v. Taylor*, 945 F.2d 500 (2d Cir. 1991)—(1) each author must make independently copyrightable contributions to the work and (2) there must be mutual intention that the contributions be combined into a unitary whole as a joint work. Thus, for example, there are many famous songwriting teams—such as John Lennon/Paul McCartney, Elton John/Bernie Taupin, Mick Jagger/Keith Richards, Alan Jay Lerner/Frederick Lowe, and George and Ira Gershwin. When these songwriters create joint works, they both contribute copyrightable material (whether one writes music or song lyrics or both), and they both intend to combine their efforts into a song.

121. If (for whatever reason) one person is sole author of a work, but desires to allow a second person to have an equal ownership interest in that work, this result can be accomplished by an assignment of a one-half interest in the copyright to the second person. The assignment should be in writing and signed by the author. Like many default rules in copyright law, the initial ownership of a work by one person can be altered by contract. For purposes such as the term of copyright, however, the copyright continues to be measured by the life of the original author, regardless of whether that author has assigned or licensed all or part of the copyright to others.

122. Answer (D) is correct. A famous author writes a new novel in the year 2020. The novel is written in the author's own name (i.e., not anonymously or under a pseudonym) and is not a work made for hire. The current term of copyright protection for this work (as of the date of this study guide) is the life of the author plus 70 years. Section 302(a) of the Copyright Act states: "Copyright in a work created on or after January 1, 1978, subsists from its creation and, except as provided by the following subsections, endures for a term consisting of the life of the author and 70 years after the author's death." 17 U.S.C. §302(a).

> **Answer (A) is incorrect.** This is the term for a work made for hire or a work not in an author's actual name (such as one published anonymously or under a pseudonym).

> **Answer (B) is incorrect.** This is not a copyright term under present law.

> **Answer (C) is incorrect.** This was the original term of protection under the Copyright Act of 1976, but the Sonny Bono Copyright Term Extension Act of 1998 (CTEA) added 20 years to the term of all existing copyrights. The Supreme Court upheld the constitutionality of the CTEA's term extension in *Eldred v. Ashcroft*, 537 U.S. 186 (2003).

123. Answer (D) is correct. The current copyright duration (as of the date of this study guide) for a joint work is the life of the last surviving author plus 70 years. *See* 17 U.S.C. §302(b) ("In the case of a joint work prepared by two or more authors who did not work for hire, the copyright endures for a term consisting of the life of the last surviving author and 70 years after such last surviving author's death.").

> **Answer (A) is incorrect.** This is the term for a work made for hire or a work not in an author's actual name (such as one published anonymously or under a pseudonym).

> **Answer (B) is incorrect.** This is not a copyright term under present law.

Answer (C) is incorrect. This was the original term of protection under the Copyright Act of 1976, but the Sonny Bono Copyright Term Extension Act of 1998 added 20 years to the term of all existing copyrights.

124. Answer (C) is correct. A movie is produced in the year 2020. The movie is a "work made for hire," which is true of nearly all movies released commercially. The current term of copyright protection for this work (as of the date of this study guide) is 95 years from date of publication, or 120 years from date of creation, whichever term is shorter. *See* 17 U.S.C. § 302(c) ("In the case of an anonymous work, a pseudonymous work, or a work made for hire, the copyright endures for a term of 95 years from the year of its first publication, or a term of 120 years from the year of its creation, whichever expires first.").

Answer (A) is incorrect. This was the original term of protection under the Copyright Act of 1976, but the Sonny Bono Copyright Term Extension Act of 1988 added 20 years to the term of all existing copyrights.

Answer (B) is incorrect. This is not a copyright term under present law.

Answer (D) is incorrect. This is the current term for a work by a single identified author.

125. Answer (B) is correct. You can freely use the 1915 Latin version, as the copyright in that published version has necessarily expired and the poem is in the public domain, but the 1935 English version may still be protected by copyright.

Copyrights for works published before January 1, 1978 are governed by the Copyright Act of 1909, with extensions provided by later amendments, for a maximum of 95 years from publication (28-year initial term plus 67 years in the renewal term). Works published under the 1909 Act, which provided for renewal terms, can thus still be copyrighted as long as the copyright renewal was effectuated. (If a work was originally copyrighted between January 1, 1964, and December 31, 1977, a 1992 amendment made the renewal automatic.) Works published on or after January 1, 1978 are governed by the Copyright Act of 1976.

Copyrighted works published before 1923 have been in the public domain since January 1, 1998, as they expired at the end of 1997, before the 1998 term extension took effect and added 20 years to the duration of all unexpired copyright terms (1922 + then-current maximum term of 75 years if renewal was properly filed, see above). And then on January 1, 2019, works published in 1923 entered the public domain, since their terms expired at the end of the last day of 2018 (1923 + 95-year maximum total-term if the renewal was properly filed, *see* above.)

A work first published in 1935, then, can still be under copyright protection. Moreover, the fact that the 1935 work is a translation does not preclude protection under copyright law, as a translation can be protectable as a derivative work. *See* 17 U.S.C. § 101 (derivative work is "a work based upon one or more preexisting works, such as a translation, musical arrangement, dramatization, fictionalization, motion picture version, sound recording, art reproduction, abridgment, condensation, or any other form in which a work may be recast, transformed, or adapted. A work consisting of editorial revisions, annotations, elaborations, or other modifications which, as a whole, represent an original work of authorship, is a 'derivative work.'").

And if the Latin poem had been written in 1915 *but not published before* 1923, then the Latin poem, once later published, would still be protected by copyright today, assuming the later publication contained proper notice and a renewal was timely filed.

Section 304 of the Copyright Act sets forth the rather complex and specific rules governing copyrighted works that were already published when the 1976 Act took effect on January 1, 1978. *See* 17 U.S.C. § 304.

Answer (A) is incorrect. As noted above, the copyright in the published 1915 Latin version has necessarily expired and the poem is in the public domain, but the 1935 English version may still be protected by copyright.

Answer (C) is incorrect. As noted above, the copyright in the published 1915 Latin version has necessarily expired and the poem is in the public domain, but the 1935 English version may still be protected by copyright.

Answer (D) is incorrect. Using the work in its entirety is unlikely to satisfy the fair use defense, absent additional facts and circumstances not described here. Thus, this blanket statement is incorrect. Certainly, the expiration of the copyright is a much stronger defense than the fact-specific fair use defense.

126. A "work made for hire" under copyright law is defined as follows:

(1) a work prepared by an employee within the scope of his or her employment; or

(2) a work specially ordered or commissioned for use as a contribution to a collective work, as a part of a motion picture or other audiovisual work, as a translation, as a supplementary work, as a compilation, as an instructional text, as a test, as answer material for a test, or as an atlas, if the parties expressly agree in a written instrument signed by them that the work shall be considered a work made for hire. For the purpose of the foregoing sentence, a "supplementary work" is a work prepared for publication as a secondary adjunct to a work by another author for the purpose of introducing, concluding, illustrating, explaining, revising, commenting upon, or assisting in the use of the other work, such as forewords, afterwords, pictorial illustrations, maps, charts, tables, editorial notes, musical arrangements, answer material for tests, bibliographies, appendixes, and indexes, and an "instructional text" is a literary, pictorial, or graphic work prepared for publication and with the purpose of use in systematic instructional activities.

17 U.S.C. § 101. Works made for hire come in two categories under the statutory definition—(1) works by employees and (2) works by independent contractors—with works in the second category being required to meet a range of other requirements, such as being specially ordered or commissioned, being subject to a written agreement, and falling within one of nine statutory types of uses. When a work is a "work made for hire," the hiring party is considered the author of the work under U.S. law. *See* 17 U.S.C. § 201(b). Work-for-hire status affects not only initial ownership, *see* § 201(b), but also the term of the copyright, *see* § 302(c), and termination of transfers, *see* § 203 (transfers and licenses of works made for hire are not subject to termination).

127. Answer (C) is correct. The Supreme Court has adopted the common law agency test for defining a "work made for hire" by an employee under copyright law. *See Community for Creative Non-Violence v. Reid*, 490 U.S. 730 (1989). The case involved a homeless advocacy group, which hired a well-known sculptor to create a work depicting the homeless. The Court ultimately held that the sculptor owned the copyright to the work, even though the advocacy group owned the physical sculpture itself. To determine whether a work is created by an independent contractor or whether it is a work made for hire (in which case the hiring party would own the copyright), the Court considered all four of the tests listed in this question, but adopted the common law agency standard. This test involves analysis of the following factors:

> In determining whether a hired party is an employee under the general common law of agency, we consider the hiring party's right to control the manner and means by which the product is accomplished. Among the other factors relevant to this inquiry are the skill required; the source of the instrumentalities and tools; the location of the work; the duration of the relationship between the parties; whether the hiring party has the right to assign additional projects to the hired party; the extent of the hired party's discretion over when and how long to work; the method of payment; the hired party's role in hiring and paying assistants; whether the work is part of the regular business of the hiring party; whether the hiring party is in business; the provision of employee benefits; and the tax treatment of the hired party.

Id.

> **Answer (A) is incorrect.** As discussed above, the Court in *Community for Creative Non-Violence v. Reid*, 490 U.S. 730 (1989), considered all four of the tests listed in this question, but adopted the common law agency standard.

> **Answer (B) is incorrect.** As discussed above, the Court in *Community for Creative Non-Violence v. Reid*, 490 U.S. 730 (1989), considered all four of the tests listed in this question, but adopted the common law agency standard.

> **Answer (D) is incorrect.** As discussed above, the Court in *Community for Creative Non-Violence v. Reid*, 490 U.S. 730 (1989), considered all four of the tests listed in this question, but adopted the common law agency standard.

128. Answer (D) is correct. Both an assignment and an exclusive license are required to be in writing under the Copyright Act. Section 204 states:

> (a) A transfer of copyright ownership, other than by operation of law, is not valid unless an instrument of conveyance, or a note or memorandum of the transfer, is in writing and signed by the owner of the rights conveyed or such owner's duly authorized agent.

> (b) A certificate of acknowledgment is not required for the validity of a transfer, but is prima facie evidence of the execution of the transfer if—

>> (1) in the case of a transfer executed in the United States, the certificate is issued by a person authorized to administer oaths within the United States; or

(2) in the case of a transfer executed in a foreign country, the certificate is issued by a diplomatic or consular officer of the United States, or by a person authorized to administer oaths whose authority is proved by a certificate of such an officer.

17 U.S.C. § 204. For purposes of section 204, an exclusive license is deemed a transfer, but a nonexclusive license is not (and thus need not be meet the writing requirement). *See* 17 U.S.C. § 101 (defining a transfer of copyright ownership as "an assignment, mortgage, exclusive license, or any other conveyance, alienation, or hypothecation of a copyright or of any of the exclusive rights comprised in a copyright, whether or not it is limited in time or place of effect, but not including a nonexclusive license").

> **Answer (A) is incorrect.** As discussed above, both an assignment and an exclusive license are required to be in writing under the Copyright Act.

> **Answer (B) is incorrect.** As discussed above, a non-exclusive license is not required to be in writing under the Copyright Act.

> **Answer (C) is incorrect.** As discussed above, both an assignment and an exclusive license are required to be in writing under the Copyright Act.

129. The termination of transfers provision of the Copyright Act allows the author of a work who has assigned or licensed it to others essentially to cancel that transfer during a five-year time frame from 35 to 40 years after the transfer. This provision gives an author (or the author's heirs) a non-waivable "second chance" to negotiate a better deal. Section 203(a) sets forth the conditions in which terminations can occur:

> Conditions for Termination.—In the case of any work other than a work made for hire, the exclusive or nonexclusive grant of a transfer or license of copyright or of any right under a copyright, executed by the author on or after January 1, 1978, otherwise than by will, is subject to termination under the following conditions:

> > (1) In the case of a grant executed by one author, termination of the grant may be effected by that author or, if the author is dead, by the person or persons who, under clause (2) of this subsection, own and are entitled to exercise a total of more than one half of that author's termination interest. In the case of a grant executed by two or more authors of a joint work, termination of the grant may be effected by a majority of the authors who executed it; if any of such authors is dead, the termination interest of any such author may be exercised as a unit by the person or persons who, under clause (2) of this subsection, own and are entitled to exercise a total of more than one half of that author's interest.

> > (2) [Setting forth procedure when the author is deceased] ...

> > (3) Termination of the grant may be effected at any time during a period of five years beginning at the end of thirty five years from the date of execution of the grant; or, if the grant covers the right of publication of the work, the period begins at the end of thirty five years from the date of publication of the work under the

grant or at the end of forty years from the date of execution of the grant, whichever term ends earlier.

(4) [Setting forth notice requirements.] …

(5) Termination of the grant may be effected notwithstanding any agreement to the contrary, including an agreement to make a will or to make any future grant.

17 U.S.C. § 203(a). The termination provision serves a similar to the renewal term under copyright law prior to the enactment of the 1976 Copyright Act.

130. Answer (B) is correct. This is a straightforward application of the rule, stated in the prior question, that

[t]ermination of the grant may be effected at any time during a period of five years beginning at the end of thirty five years from the date of execution of the grant; or, if the grant covers the right of publication of the work, the period begins at the end of thirty five years from the date of publication of the work under the grant or at the end of forty years from the date of execution of the grant, whichever term ends earlier.

17 U.S.C. § 203(a). Here, the work was created, published, and transferred by license in the year 2000, and therefore the termination window consists of the years 2035 to 2040.

Answer (B) is incorrect. As noted above, the termination window consists of the years 2035 to 2040.

Answer (C) is incorrect. As noted above, the termination window consists of the years 2035 to 2040.

Answer (D) is incorrect. As noted above, the termination window consists of the years 2035 to 2040. There are no "renewal" terms for works created in the year 2000.

131. Answer (A) is correct. The duration for rights under VARA for post-VARA works is the life of the author. *See* 17 U.S.C. § 106A(d)(1) ("With respect to works of visual art created on or after the effective date set forth in section 610(a) of the Visual Artists Rights Act of 1990, the rights conferred by subsection (a) shall endure for a term consisting of the life of the author."). Thus, the VARA moral rights of post-VARA authors are not given the same term as the economic rights under section 106—life plus 70 years. Interestingly, and likely unintentionally, the VARA moral rights for a pre-VARA work sold by an author after June 1, 1991 extend for the entire copyright term of the work.

Answer (B) is incorrect. As noted above, the duration for rights under VARA is the life of the author.

Answer (C) is incorrect. As noted above, the duration for rights under VARA is the life of the author.

Answer (D) is incorrect. As noted above, the duration for rights under VARA is the life of the author.

Copyright Law—Infringement & Remedies

132. Answer (B) is correct. Your client wishes to record and sell 1000 copies of a cover version of a copyrighted song (like the Blackberry Smoke and Amanda Shires version of Tom Petty's song, "You Got Lucky"). The easiest way to do this is to obtain a mechanical (reproduction) license from the Harry Fox Agency. Section 115 of the Copyright Act provides for compulsory mechanical licenses both to make and distribute new sound recordings based on musical works that have been previously recorded and released (i.e., cover versions of songs). *See* 17 U.S.C. § 115(a). The cover version cannot "change the basic melody or fundamental character of the work." § 115(a)(2). The Harry Fox Agency is the easiest way to obtain and pay the statutory royalty for such a license. *See* http://www.harryfox.com. This type of license to reproduce musical works is not available for other types of copyrightable works. There are very important limits on the scope of what can be done with a mechanical license; if the makers of a cover song wish to have additional rights, they will need to negotiate directly with the owners of the rights to the song.

> **Answer (A) is incorrect.** Public performance rights from BMI, ASCAP, or SESAC do not include the right to make new CDs or digital downloads.

> **Answer (C) is incorrect.** The client is seeking to make the reproductions of the composition, not just distribute them. The mechanical license discussed above includes a right to distribute the resulting sound recordings.

> **Answer (D) is incorrect.** The public display right is not relevant to this fact pattern.

133. Answer (D) is correct. Sally's Hair Salon wants to hook up a CD player to its telephone system so that people placed on hold can hear music being played on the CD player in the store. The most accurate conclusion is that Sally has violated the Copyright Act by publicly performing copyrighted works. The section 106 public performance right is implicated when a work is (1) performed in some way and (2) that performance is deemed to be public. Each of these two terms is defined in the Copyright Act. To perform a work, as defined in section 101, "means to recite, render, play, dance, or act it, either directly or by means of any device or process or, in the case of a motion picture or other audiovisual work, to show its images in any sequence or to make the sounds accompanying it audible." Playing songs on a CD player and telephone line would clearly perform the musical works in question. The second prong is more complicated:

> To perform or display a work "publicly" means—

> > (1) to perform or display it at a place open to the public or at any place where a substantial number of persons outside of a normal circle of a family and its social acquaintances is gathered; or

(2) to transmit or otherwise communicate a performance or display of the work to a place specified by clause (1) or to the public, by means of any device or process, whether the members of the public capable of receiving the performance or display receive it in the same place or in separate places and at the same time or at different times.

17 U.S.C. § 101. Thus, a work can be publicly performed if any one of the following three events has taken place: (1) the work is performed in a public place ("a place open to the public"); (2) the work is performed in a semipublic place ("any place where a substantial number of persons outside of a normal circle of a family and its social acquaintances is gathered"); or (3) the work is transmitted or otherwise communicated to the public or to a public place, which includes radio and television broadcasts, as well as cable and satellite transmissions. On the present facts, the songs on the CD are essentially being "transmitted" to the public via the telephone line. This constitutes a public performance of the work.

Answer (A) is incorrect. There is a "safe harbor" provision for small businesses, but it does not apply to further transmissions of the work or to the playing of a CD, both of which are taking place in this fact scenario. *See* 17 U.S.C. § 110(5).

Answer (B) is incorrect. The "first sale" defense does not apply to violations of the public performance right. *See* 17 U.S.C. § 109.

Answer (C) is incorrect. As discussed above, playing a CD over a telephone line in the manner described here is a public performance.

134. Answer (D) is correct. If Bob were to turn a published and copyrighted novel into a movie without authorization and then sell DVDs of the movie, he would likely violate three rights of the author of the novel—derivative works, reproduction, and distribution. The movie version would be a derivative work based on the novel. *See* 17 U.S.C. § 101 (derivative work is "a work based upon one or more preexisting works, such as a translation, musical arrangement, dramatization, fictionalization, motion picture version, sound recording, art reproduction, abridgment, condensation, or any other form in which a work may be recast, transformed, or adapted"). It would also very likely reproduce significant amounts of copyrightable expression from the novel (such as scenes, dialogue, detailed plot development, and characters). Finally, the sale of the DVD copies would constitute distribution of the copied portions of the work.

Answer (A) is incorrect. As discussed above, all three rights are violated.

Answer (B) is incorrect. As discussed above, all three rights are violated.

Answer (C) is incorrect. As discussed above, all three rights are violated.

135. Answer (C) is correct. If Sally sells or rents a bootleg DVD (which Sally purchased from an anonymous seller who had the bootleg DVDs in the back of his van) she likely violates the distribution right of the copyright owner of the movie/DVD. Section 106 grants to copyright owners the right "to distribute copies or phonorecords of the copyrighted work to the public by sale or other transfer of ownership, or by rental, lease, or lending." This provision would be violated on the facts above.

Answer (A) is incorrect. No derivative work has been created on these facts.

Answer (B) is incorrect. The sale or rental of the bootleg DVD violates the distribution right, but the act of copying or reproducing the DVD was committed by someone else.

Answer (D) is incorrect. As noted above, only an unauthorized distribution has taken place on these facts.

136. **Answer (D) is correct.** A public performance takes place when a copyrighted work is performed by any of the following: (a) being played on CD in a semipublic place, (b) being played live in a place open to the public, or (c) being transmitted beyond the place it is located by electronic means. As discussed earlier, a work can be publicly performed if any one of the following three events has taken place: (1) the work is performed in a public place ("a place open to the public")—here, the live performance; (2) the work is performed in a semipublic place ("any place where a substantial number of persons outside of a normal circle of a family and its social acquaintances is gathered")—here, the playing of the CD; or (3) the work is transmitted or otherwise communicated to the public or to a public place, which includes radio and television broadcasts, as well as cable and satellite transmissions—here, the transmission by electronic means.

Answer (A) is incorrect. As noted above, all three actions are public performances.

Answer (B) is incorrect. As noted above, all three actions are public performances.

Answer (C) is incorrect. As noted above, all three actions are public performances.

137. **Answer (C) is correct.** A typical download or stream of a song file embodies two different copyrighted works: a musical composition and a sound recording. The musical composition involves the words and music, created by songwriters. Swift co-wrote the song with its producers, Max Martin and Karl Johan Schuster (known professionally as Shellback). Swift then created the sound recording, the version of the song that fans would be familiar with. Thus, most downloaded or streamed song files embody two different copyrighted works.

Answer (A) is incorrect. As explained above, a typical song file embodies both a musical composition and a sound recording.

Answer (B) is incorrect. As explained above, a typical song file embodies both a musical composition and a sound recording.

Answer (D) is incorrect. As explained above, a typical song file embodies both a musical composition and a sound recording.

Neither of these works is necessarily a work made for hire (a work created in the scope of an employment relationship; check section 101 for the list of uses for which a "work made for hire" can be specially ordered or commissioned from an independent contractor to see why that pathway to creating a work made for hire would not apply here).

138. Answer (B) is correct. Under present law, the owner of a copyright in a sound recording possesses the following rights—reproduction, distribution, and public performance by digital transmission, but not general public performance or public display. It is important to recognize that there are two copyrights on any song that has been recorded—the copyright in the musical work and the copyright in the sound recording. Authors of sound recordings do not have the full range of rights, whereas songwriters receive the full bundle of sticks. Section 106 grants the following rights:

> (1) to reproduce the copyrighted work in copies or phonorecords; (2) to prepare derivative works based upon the copyrighted work; (3) to distribute copies or phonorecords of the copyrighted work to the public by sale or other transfer of ownership, or by rental, lease, or lending; (4) in the case of literary, *musical*, dramatic, and choreographic works, pantomimes, and motion pictures and other audiovisual works, to perform the copyrighted work publicly; (5) in the case of literary, musical, dramatic, and choreographic works, pantomimes, and pictorial, graphic, or sculptural works, including the individual images of a motion picture or other audiovisual work, to display the copyrighted work publicly; and (6) *in the case of sound recordings,* to perform the copyrighted work publicly by means of a digital audio transmission.

17 U.S.C. § 106 (emphasis added). As a careful review of the language indicates, sound recordings do not have general public performance rights under section 106(4) or public display rights under section 106(5), but there are limited public performance rights for digital audio transmissions—such as satellite or internet music—under section 106(6). Musical works, in contrast, have full rights under sections 106(4) and 106(5). There have been bills put forward to provide broader public performance rights in sound recordings, but none has been enacted thus far. *See generally* Gary Myers & George Howard, *The Future of Music: Reconfiguring Public Performance Rights*, 17 J. INTELL. PROP. L. 207 (2010).

> **Answer (A) is incorrect.** As discussed above, there are limited public performance rights for digital audio transmissions—such as satellite or internet music—under section 106(6).

> **Answer (C) is incorrect.** As discussed above, there are no full public performance rights under section 106(4).

> **Answer (D) is incorrect.** As discussed above, there are no full public performance or display rights under section 106(4)–(5).

139. Answer (B) is correct. The Music Modernization Act ("MMA") streamlines the music licensing process to make it easier for rights holders to get paid when their music is streamed online and provides federal copyright protection for sound recordings made before 1972. Included in the MMA is the Compensating Legacy Artists for their Songs, Service, and Important Contributions to Society (CLASSICS) Act. This provision addressed the problem that sound recordings made prior to February 15, 1972 were not covered under federal copyright law, leaving it to the individual states to pass laws for recording protection. The CLASSICS Act established that pre-1972 sound recordings are covered by federal copyright law.

Answer (A) is incorrect. Some, but not all, elements of the "Fair Play Fair Pay Act," H.R. 1836 (2017), introduced by Rep. Jerrold Nadler, were included in the MMA. The Fair Play Fair Pay Act had been designed to harmonize the royalty obligations of terrestrial radio broadcasters and Internet streaming services. The Fair Play Fair Pay Act included language that would allow recording artists to receive full performance royalties (i.e., royalties for radio air play). These provisions of the Fair Play Fair Pay Act were not, however, included in the MMA as adopted by Congress and signed by the President.

Answer (C) is incorrect. The MMA did not create a "small claims court" for any alleged copyright violation involving small amounts of money. Representatives Hakeem Jeffries (D-NY) and Doug Collins (R-GA) have introduced H.R. 2426, the Copyright Alternative in Small-Claims Enforcement (CASE) Act, but the CASE Act has not been enacted as this book goes to press. The Senate version of the bill has also been introduced by a bipartisan group of sponsors. The bill seeks to establish an alternative forum for resolving disputes involving small claims of copyright infringement.

Answer (D) is incorrect. As noted above, Answer (A) is incorrect, and thus this is an incorrect answer.

140. Answer (D) is correct. Two types of moral rights are protected under the Visual Artists Rights Act of 1990 ("VARA")—attribution and integrity. Section 106A(a) states as follows:

Rights of attribution and integrity.

Subject to section 107 and independent of the exclusive rights provided in section 106, the author of a work of visual art—

(1) shall have the right—

(A) to claim authorship of that work, and

(B) to prevent the use of his or her name as the author of any work of visual art which he or she did not create;

(2) shall have the right to prevent the use of his or her name as the author of the work of visual art in the event of a distortion, mutilation, or other modification of the work which would be prejudicial to his or her honor or reputation; and

(3) subject to the limitations set forth in section 113(d), shall have the right—

(A) to prevent any intentional distortion, mutilation, or other modification of that work which would be prejudicial to his or her honor or reputation, and any intentional distortion, mutilation, or modification of that work is a violation of that right, and

(B) to prevent any destruction of a work of recognized stature, and any intentional or grossly negligent destruction of that work is a violation of that right.

17 U.S.C. § 106A(a). Attribution is protected under subsections 106A(a)(1) and (a)(2) and integrity is protection under subsection 106A(a)(3).

Answer (A) is incorrect. As noted above, both attribution and integrity are protected moral rights under VARA.

Answer (B) is incorrect. As noted above, both attribution and integrity are protected moral rights under VARA.

Answer (C) is incorrect. VARA does not provide a right as to divulgation or disclosure of the work. The much broader conception of moral rights in France includes this right. *See* Gary Myers, Principles of Intellectual Property Law 138 (3d ed. 2017) ("France recognizes four type[s] of moral rights: (1) droit de divulgation, or the right of disclosure; (2) droit de repentir ou de retrait, or the right to withdraw or correct works previously disclosed to the public; (3) droit de paternite, or the right of attribution, which includes rights to publish anonymously or pseudonymously; and (4) droit au respect de l'oeuvre, the right of integrity ('the right to respect of the work')").

141. Answer (D) is correct. The Digital Millennium Copyright Act (DMCA) provides copyright owners with rights regarding both anticircumvention and anti-trafficking. First, under its anticircumvention provision, the DMCA prohibits a person from circumventing a technological measure that effectively controls access to a copyrighted work. This provision states: "No person shall circumvent a technological measure that effectively controls access to a work protected under this title." 17 U.S.C. § 1201(a)(1)(A). To circumvent a technological measure means: "to descramble a scrambled work, to decrypt an encrypted work, or otherwise to avoid, bypass, remove, deactivate, or impair a technological measure, without the authority of the copyright owner." 17 U.S.C. § 1201(a)(3)(A). A technological measure "effectively controls access to a work" when the measure "in the ordinary course of its operation, requires the application of information, or a process or a treatment, with the authority of the copyright owner, to gain access to the work." 17 U.S.C. § 1201(a)(3)(B). Second, the DMCA also prohibits trafficking in anticircumvention devices. *See* 17 U.S.C. § 1201(a)(2) ("No person shall manufacture, import, offer to the public, provide, or otherwise traffic in any technology, product, service, device, component, or part thereof, that—(A) is primarily designed or produced for the purpose of circumventing a technological measure that effectively controls access to a work protected under this title; (B) has only limited commercially significant purpose or use other than to circumvent a technological measure that effectively controls access to a work protected under this title; or (C) is marketed by that person or another acting in concert with that person with that person's knowledge for use in circumventing a technological measure that effectively controls access to a work protected under this title."); *Universal City Studios, Inc. v. Reimerdes*, 111 F. Supp. 2d 294 (S.D.N.Y. 2000), *aff'd sub nom., Universal City Studios, Inc. v. Corley*, 273 F.3d 429 (2d Cir. 2001).

Answer (A) is incorrect. As discussed above, the DMCA provides copyright owners with rights regarding both anticircumvention and anti-trafficking.

Answer (B) is incorrect. As discussed above, the DMCA provides copyright owners with rights regarding both anticircumvention and anti-trafficking.

Answer (C) is incorrect. The DMCA does not address moral rights.

142. Answer (C) is correct. Copyright registration for U.S. authors is required as a condition precedent to filing suit. Section 411 of the Copyright Act states:

> Except for an action brought for a violation of the rights of the author under section 106A(a), and subject to the provisions of subsection (b), no action for infringement of the copyright in any United States work shall be instituted until preregistration or registration of the copyright claim has been made in accordance with this title. In any case, however, where the deposit, application, and fee required for registration have been delivered to the Copyright Office in proper form and registration has been refused, the applicant is entitled to institute an action for infringement if notice thereof, with a copy of the complaint, is served on the Register of Copyrights. The Register may, at his or her option, become a party to the action with respect to the issue of registrability of the copyright claim by entering an appearance within sixty days after such service, but the Register's failure to become a party shall not deprive the court of jurisdiction to determine that issue.

17 U.S.C. §411(a). It should be noted that registration is a condition precedent only for a "United States work"—i.e., by its express terms, the requirement does not apply to foreign works. In *Fourth Estate Public Benefit Corp. v. Wall-Street.com, LLC*, 139 S. Ct. 881 (2019), the Supreme Court held that the mere filing of a copyright application is not sufficient to allow a copyright owner to file suit—actual approval (or at least a decision) of the copyright application by the United States Copyright Office is required before suit can be filed.

Copyright protection attaches to a work when it is fixed in a tangible medium of expression, and a copyright owner can recover compensatory and injunctive relief for infringements occurring at any time thereafter. However, a copyright plaintiff cannot recover statutory damages and attorney's fees when the infringement precedes copyright registration (except when infringement and registration take place within three months after publication). *See* 17 U.S.C. §412.

Answer (A) is incorrect. Registration is not required in order to recover compensatory damages for copyright infringement. Compensatory damages for infringement are recoverable whether they occur before or after registration. The availability of statutory damages can be affected by the timing of registration, as noted above.

Answer (B) is incorrect. Registration is not required in order to obtain injunctive relief, even if the infringement began before registration.

Answer (D) is incorrect. As noted above, copyright registration for U.S. authors is required as a condition precedent to filing suit. Moreover, registration can have an impact on the ability to recover attorney's fees and statutory damages for all works, whether domestic or foreign.

143. Answer (D) is correct. The Copyright Act preempts state law when all three of the following are shown regarding a state law—the state law (1) is equivalent to rights under copyright law, (2) is within the general scope of copyrightable subject matter, and (3) involves works of authorship fixed in a tangible medium of expression. Section 301 of the Copyright Act states:

> On and after January 1, 1978, all legal or equitable rights that are *equivalent to any of the exclusive rights* within the general scope of copyright as specified by section 106 in works of authorship that are *fixed in a tangible medium* of expression and

come *within the subject matter of copyright* as specified by sections 102 and 103, whether created before or after that date and whether published or unpublished, are governed exclusively by this title. Thereafter, no person is entitled to any such right or equivalent right in any such work under the common law or statutes of any State.

17 U.S.C. § 301(a) (emphasis added).

Answer (A) is incorrect. As discussed above, all three points must be proven to establish pre-emption of state law under section 301.

Answer (B) is incorrect. As discussed above, all three points must be proven to establish pre-emption of state law under section 301.

Answer (C) is incorrect. As discussed above, all three points must be proven to establish pre-emption of state law under section 301.

144. Answer (D) is correct. The following statement most accurately describes the approach taken by federal copyright law to questions of remedies—injunctive relief is frequently granted, and actual monetary damages and profit are available upon a showing of bad faith or actual harm. Section 502(a) of the Copyright Act authorizes courts to provide injunctive relief, albeit not presumptively: "Any court having jurisdiction of a civil action arising under this title may, subject to the provisions of section 1498 of title 28, grant temporary and final injunctions on such terms as it may deem reasonable to prevent or restrain infringement of a copyright." Section 504 of the Copyright Act permits the award of either compensatory or statutory damages, at the election of the plaintiff. Compensatory damages are provided as follows:

The copyright owner is entitled to recover the actual damages suffered by him or her as a result of the infringement, and any profits of the infringer that are attributable to the infringement and are not taken into account in computing the actual damages. In establishing the infringer's profits, the copyright owner is required to present proof only of the infringer's gross revenue, and the infringer is required to prove his or her deductible expenses and the elements of profit attributable to factors other than the copyrighted work.

17 U.S.C. § 504(b). The alternative monetary remedy of statutory damages is discussed more fully below and may be recovered regardless of proof of bad faith or actual harm.

Answer (A) is incorrect. As discussed above, both injunctions and actual monetary damages and profits can be obtained on proper proof.

Answer (B) is incorrect. As discussed above, both injunctions and actual monetary damages and profits can be obtained on proper proof. There are no presumptions for or against a remedy, as implied in this statement.

Answer (C) is incorrect. As discussed above, both injunctions and actual monetary damages and profits can be obtained on proper proof.

145. Answer (C) is correct. Section 504(a) of the Copyright Act states: "Except as otherwise provided by this title, an infringer of copyright is liable for *either*—(1) the copyright owner's actual damages and any additional profits of the infringer, as provided by subsection (b); *or* (2) statutory damages, as provided by subsection (c)." (Emphasis added.) In other words, a copyright plaintiff can elect to receive either statutory or actual damages, but not both.

> **Answer (A) is incorrect.** As noted above, a copyright plaintiff can elect to receive either statutory or actual damages.

> **Answer (B) is incorrect.** As noted above, a copyright plaintiff can elect to receive either statutory or actual damages.

> **Answer (D) is incorrect.** As noted above, a copyright plaintiff can elect to receive either statutory or actual damages, but not both.

146. Answer (A) is correct. Statutory damages can be increased or decreased based on the bad faith or good faith of the defendant. In cases of bad faith, the award can be increased to as much as $150,000; in cases of good faith, it can be reduced to as little as $200.

> In a case where the copyright owner sustains the burden of proving, and the court finds, that infringement was committed willfully, the court in its discretion may increase the award of statutory damages to a sum of not more than $150,000. In a case where the infringer sustains the burden of proving, and the court finds, that such infringer was not aware and had no reason to believe that his or her acts constituted an infringement of copyright, the court in its discretion may reduce the award of statutory damages to a sum of not less than $200.

17 U.S.C. 504(c)(2). Proper notice will eliminate mitigation for an innocent infringement defense, as noted in the answer to Question 111 in Topic 11.

> **Answer (B) is incorrect.** As discussed above, the award can either be increased or decreased based on the defendant's conduct and state of mind.

> **Answer (C) is incorrect.** As discussed above, the award can either be increased or decreased based on the defendant's conduct and state of mind.

> **Answer (D) is incorrect.** As discussed above, the award can either be increased or decreased based on the defendant's conduct and state of mind.

147. Answer (C) is correct. Section 505 of the Copyright Act provides that "the court may also award a reasonable attorney's fee to the prevailing party." 17 U.S.C. § 505. In *Fogerty v. Fantasy, Inc.*, 510 U.S. 517 (1994), the Supreme Court addressed the standards governing awards of attorney's fees in copyright cases. The Court held that fee awards are discretionary, and that the same standards should be applied in the case of a prevailing plaintiff and a prevailing defendant. In other words, the Court adopted the "even handed" approach, as opposed to giving prevailing copyright plaintiffs a greater chance of obtaining a fee award. The Supreme Court elaborated on the fee award question in *Kirtsaeng v. John Wiley & Sons, Inc.*, 136 S. Ct. 1979 (2016), holding that the district court should exercise its discretion, giving "substantial weight" to the objective reasonableness of the losing party's position, while also taking into account other relevant circumstances. These factors include the losing party's "litigation misconduct," and whether a fee award would deter repeated instances of copyright infringement or overaggressive assertions of copyright claims.

Answer (A) is incorrect. As discussed above, the Supreme Court has held that the same discretionary standard should be applied in the case of a prevailing plaintiff and a prevailing defendant (the "even handed" approach).

Answer (B) is incorrect. As discussed above, the Supreme Court has held that the same discretionary standard should be applied in the case of a prevailing plaintiff and a prevailing defendant (the "even handed" approach).

Answer (D) is incorrect. As discussed above, the Court has not applied an automatic or presumptive standard for the award of fees.

148. Answer (D) is correct. Unauthorized music file-sharing can be a violation of copyright protections against reproduction or distribution. 17 U.S.C. § 106. At first blush, it would appear that music file-sharing is primarily a problem of reproduction—making unauthorized copies of musical works. In fact, however, some courts have ruled that the uploading of a song constitutes a distribution of that song (by the person having a lawful or unauthorized copy of it) if another person ultimately downloads that file; the unauthorized downloading of the song by the recipient is a reproduction of that work. *See, e.g., Atlantic Recording Corp. v. Howell*, 554 F. Supp. 2d 976, 981–985, (D Ariz. 2008); *Capitol Records, Inc. v. Thomas*, 579 F. Supp. 2d 1210, 1214–25 (D. Minn. 2008). Thus, both rights can be implicated by unauthorized music file-sharing.

Answer (A) is incorrect. Public performance rights are not implicated by the mere act of file-sharing of music because the music is not being "performed." Under 17 U.S.C. § 101, performing a work "means to recite, render, play, dance, or act it, either directly or by means of any device or process or, in the case of a motion picture or other audiovisual work, to show its images in any sequence or to make the sounds accompanying it audible."

Answer (B) is incorrect. As discussed above, both reproduction and distribution rights can be violated by music file-sharing.

Answer (C) is incorrect. As discussed above, both reproduction and distribution rights can be violated by music file-sharing.

Copyright Law—Defenses & Limitations

149. Answer (C) is correct. Innocent copying is not a defense to a copyright infringement action. Independent creation is a crucial defense because copyright only prevents the copying from the plaintiff's work, not independent creation of a similar work. As expressed by Judge Hand: "Borrowed the work must indeed not be, for a plagiarist is not himself pro tanto an 'author'; but if by some magic a man who had never known it were to compose anew Keats's Ode on a Grecian Urn, he would be an 'author,' and, if he copyrighted it, others might not copy that poem, though they might of course copy Keats's." *Sheldon v. Metro-Goldwyn Pictures Corp.*, 81 F.2d 49, 54 (2d Cir. 1936). Common source is a second important defense, involving a showing that two works are similar because they are based on a common source—either a public domain work or a work by a third party. For example, two adaptations of a Shakespeare play are likely to have similarities resulting from their common source in the work of the Bard. Finally, consent or license involves conduct or an agreement, express or implied, by the copyright owner that would reasonably provide that the use of the copyrighted work was authorized.

> **Answer (A) is incorrect.** As discussed above, independent creation is a defense.

> **Answer (B) is incorrect.** As discussed above, common source is a defense.

> **Answer (D) is incorrect.** As discussed above, consent or license is a defense.

150. Answer (A) is correct. Public performances of an audiovisual work in a classroom are permitted so long as the copy of the work being performed is lawfully made. *See* 17 U.S.C. § 110(1) (exempting "performance or display of a work by instructors or pupils in the course of face-to-face teaching activities of a nonprofit educational institution, in a classroom or similar place devoted to instruction, unless, in the case of a motion picture or other audiovisual work, the performance, or the display of individual images, is given by means of a copy that was not lawfully made under this title, and that the person responsible for the performance knew or had reason to believe was not lawfully made").

> **Answer (B) is incorrect.** Section 110(1) does not require notice to the copyright owner.

> **Answer (C) is incorrect.** Section 110(1) does not require that the educational institution register with the copyright office.

> **Answer (D) is incorrect.** As noted above, section 110(1) does not require notice to the copyright owner.

151. Answer (D) is correct. This question is loosely based on *Horizon Comics Prods. Inc. v. Marvel Entm't, LLC,* No. 16-CV-2499 (S.D.N.Y. July 15, 2019). In that case, which involved the movie

"Iron Man 3," Marvel released a poster of actor Robert Downey Jr. kneeling and crouching in his suit of armor. Twelve years prior, comic book artists Ben and Ray Lai created a character for their comic book series called Radix, and created a picture depicting him in a "mechanized suit of armor in a kneeling pose." They alleged that Marvel infringed the copyright in the drawing, but the court granted Marvel's motion for summary judgment because the plaintiffs could not prove that the makers of the poster had access to their drawing. Thus, a lack of access is a defense to a copyright infringement claim because the work would then be independently developed. Similarly, a lack of substantial similarity would be a valid defense. Finally, the idea of a kneeling superhero in a suit of armor is an uncopyrightable idea, and any similarity in the basic images could be barred by the merger doctrine. Thus, all of the options in this question involve possible defenses that the movie production company might assert.

> **Answer (A) is incorrect.** As noted above, all of the options in this question involve possible defenses that the movie production company might assert.

> **Answer (B) is incorrect.** As noted above, all of the options in this question involve possible defenses that the movie production company might assert.

> **Answer (C) is incorrect.** As noted above, all of the options in this question involve possible defenses that the movie production company might assert.

152. **Answer (D) is correct.** The traditional "homestyle" exemption for public performances requires: (1) receipt of a radio or television broadcast (or the equivalent cable/satellite); (2) compliance with requirements regarding the number and type of receiving apparatus; and (3) no direct charge for admission. *See* 17 U.S.C. § 110(5)(a) (exempting "communication of a transmission embodying a performance or display of a work by the public reception of the transmission on a single receiving apparatus of a kind commonly used in private homes, unless—(i) a direct charge is made to see or hear the transmission; or (ii) the transmission thus received is further transmitted to the public"). The Fairness in Music Licensing Act of 1988 expanded the scope of this exemption, particularly as to the size of exempt venues (particularly bars and restaurants up to specified square footage) and the number and types of receiving apparatus that would qualify, and the basic elements of the exemption continue to remain in effect. *See* 17 U.S.C. § 110(5)(b) (exempting some larger venues with somewhat more complex sound systems).

> **Answer (A) is incorrect.** As discussed above, all three requirements must be met.

> **Answer (B) is incorrect.** As discussed above, all three requirements must be met.

> **Answer (C) is incorrect.** As discussed above, all three requirements must be met.

153. **Answer (D) is correct.** Internet service providers ("ISPs") are immune from copyright liability for user-generated material they store for their customers unless they either (1) have actual knowledge of the infringement, (2) fail to take down infringing material after sufficient notice and opportunity, or (3) have control of and receive substantial financial benefit from the infringement. In other words, failure to satisfy any of these three elements extinguishes the immunity. *See* 17 U.S.C. § 512(c). Several prior cases had addressed ISP liability, applying common law rules focusing on whether the ISP was a mere conduit for infringing material or whether it was liable be-

cause it had knowledge or control over the information. In the Digital Millennium Copyright Act, codified at 17 U.S.C. §512, Congress established various detailed safe harbors for ISPs, including the one in §512(c) related to material stored by the ISP at the direction of a user.

Answer (A) is incorrect. As discussed above, all three requirements must be met to establish immunity.

Answer (B) is incorrect. As discussed above, all three requirements must be met to establish immunity.

Answer (C) is incorrect. As discussed above, all three requirements must be met to establish immunity.

154. Answer (D) is correct. An undergraduate student buys one copy of a commercial outline, marks in it as noted in the facts, resells it to a second student, who again marks in it, and resells it a second time. The second student has not violated any copyright, because the "first sale" doctrine makes the subsequent resales of the copy non-infringing. This scenario provides the classic illustration of the first sale defense, which limits the copyright owner's right of distribution in cases involving lawful copies of the work. 17 U.S.C. §109(a) ("Notwithstanding the provisions of section 106(3), the owner of a particular copy or phonorecord lawfully made under this title, or any person authorized by such owner, is entitled, without the authority of the copyright owner, to sell or otherwise dispose of the possession of that copy or phonorecord.").

Answer (A) is incorrect. On this set of facts, the work was not reproduced.

Answer (B) is incorrect. On this set of facts, no derivative work was created. Simple markings in an outline would not constitute a derivative work, as they would not "transform" the original expression or recast or edit that expression. *See* 17 U.S.C. §101 (derivative work is "a work based upon one or more preexisting works, such as a translation, musical arrangement, dramatization, fictionalization, motion picture version, sound recording, art reproduction, abridgment, condensation, or any other form in which a work may be recast, transformed, or adapted. A work consisting of editorial revisions, annotations, elaborations, or other modifications which, as a whole, represent an original work of authorship, is a 'derivative work.' ").

Answer (C) is incorrect. As discussed above, the first sale defense limits the copyright owner's right of distribution in cases involving lawful copies of the work; the defense continues to apply to all resales downstream of the "first sale." It does not merely apply to the first resale.

155. Answer (B) is correct. In *Kirtsaeng v. John Wiley & Sons, Inc.*, 568 U.S. 519, 525 (2013), the Supreme Court held that the "first sale" doctrine applies in full force to copies of a copyrighted work lawfully made abroad and imported into the United States. Thus, the importation into the United States is lawful, and the DVD can be sold or otherwise transferred in the United States, because this action protected by the first sale doctrine.

Answer (A) is incorrect. As noted above, the importation into the United States is lawful, and the DVD can be then sold or otherwise transferred in the United States, because this action is protected by the first sale doctrine.

Answer (C) is incorrect. Based on the facts as written, there is no violation of the copyright owner's anticircumvention rights under the Digital Millennium Copyright Act (DMCA). Many copyright owners place such measures on DVDs, but the facts involve importation and sale, not any action prohibited by the DMCA.

Answer (D) is incorrect. As noted above, the importation into the United States is lawful, and the DVD can be sold or otherwise transferred in the United States, because this action is protected by the first sale doctrine.

156. Answer (A) is correct. A professor at a state college copies an entire textbook and distributes the copies to the professor's class of 30 students. The professor charges the students only for the actual cost of making the copies. The college's best defense in a suit brought by the publisher of the textbook is the argument that sovereign immunity under the Eleventh Amendment bars suits against the state college. Although this area of the law is somewhat unsettled, there is a strong argument that the Eleventh Amendment generally bars various types of claims against state institutions in federal court, including claims under intellectual property law, unless the state has waived its sovereign immunity for the relevant type of claim. *See Chavez v. Arte Publico Press*, 204 F.3d 601 (5th Cir. 2000) (dismissing copyright and Lanham Act suit against state university on grounds of Eleventh Amendment immunity). *See generally College Savings Bank v. Florida Prepaid Postsecondary Educ. Expense Bd.*, 527 U.S. 666 (1999) (Lanham Act); *Florida Prepaid Postsecondary Educ. Expense Bd. v. College Savings Bank*, 527 U.S. 627 (1999) (Patent Act). No other defense would be particularly strong on this set of facts, given the circumstances, number of copies, and blatant copying involved. As this book goes to press, the Supreme Court has on its docket *Allen v. Cooper*, to address whether the Copyright Remedy Clarification Act of 1990 ("CRCA") validly and unambiguously abrogated sovereign immunity for copyright infringement. The Fourth Circuit decision below held that Congress lacked authority to abrogate Eleventh Amendment immunity for copyright infringement by state actors. *Allen v. Cooper*, 895 F.3d 337 (4th Cir. 2018), *cert. granted*, 139 S. Ct. 2664 (2019). Oral arguments took place in November 2019, and an opinion is expected in spring 2020.

Answer (B) is incorrect. Secondary liability can be imposed in copyright cases.

Answer (C) is incorrect. Applying the various factors in the fair use analysis, it is unlikely that fair use would be found in this case, given the wholesale copying of the book, which would displace sales that would normally be made by the copyright owner. Limited copying of excerpts might result in a different outcome.

Answer (D) is incorrect. Contrary to popular belief, a copyright violation can occur even if no profit was obtained. The professor in this case reproduced entire copies of works, displacing sales that the copyright owner was likely to make.

157. Answer (A) is correct. The following statement most accurately describes the fair use defense under federal copyright law—the scope of fair use is broader for factual works (i.e., fair use is more likely to be found when the taking is from a fact work), and the commercial purpose of the defendant's taking is but one factor in the analysis. This is the first in a series of questions addressing the fair use defense. Section 107 of the Copyright Act sets forth a series of factors to be balanced in analyzing every fair use case:

Notwithstanding the provisions of sections 106 and 106A, the fair use of a copyrighted work, including such use by reproduction in copies or phonorecords or by any other means specified by that section, for purposes such as criticism, comment, news reporting, teaching (including multiple copies for classroom use), scholarship, or research, is not an infringement of copyright. In determining whether the use made of a work in any particular case is a fair use the factors to be considered shall include —

(1) the purpose and character of the use, including whether such use is of a commercial nature or is for nonprofit educational purposes;

(2) the nature of the copyrighted work;

(3) the amount and substantiality of the portion used in relation to the copyrighted work as a whole; and

(4) the effect of the use upon the potential market for or value of the copyrighted work.

The fact that a work is unpublished shall not itself bar a finding of fair use if such finding is made upon consideration of all the above factors.

17 U.S.C. § 107. Whether a work is factual or fictional is relevant to the second prong of the fair use analysis, "the nature of the copyrighted work." Because facts are not copyrightable, the scope of fair use is broader as to factual works than as to works of fiction. *See generally Feist Publications, Inc. v. Rural Telephone Service Co.*, 499 U.S. 340 (1991) (facts alone are not copyrightable). In *Campbell v. Acuff-Rose Music Inc.*, 510 U.S. 569 (1994), the Supreme Court held that a commercial purpose (such as selling CDs for profit) did not give rise to a presumption against fair use and was only one factor in the overall balancing test, which must be done on a case-by-case basis.

Answer (B) is incorrect. As noted above, the Supreme Court has rejected the presumption against commercial uses for purposes of fair use.

Answer (C) is incorrect. As noted above, the scope of fair use is broader in the case of factual works, not fictional works.

Answer (D) is incorrect. As noted above, the scope of fair use is broader in the case of factual works, not fictional works, and the Supreme Court has rejected the presumption against commercial uses for purposes of fair use.

158. Answer (A) is correct. The following statement most accurately describes the fair use defense under federal copyright law — the qualitative and quantitative amount taken in relation to the plaintiff's copyrighted work is relevant, and good faith (or bad faith) is taken into account. The third prong of the fair use analysis specifically focuses on the quantitative and qualitative amount of the taking: "the amount and substantiality of the portion used in relation to the copyrighted work as a whole." In *Harper & Row v. Nation Enterprises*, 471 U.S. 539 (1985), the well-known fair use case involving President Gerald Ford's memoir, "A Time to Heal," the Supreme Court found that excerpts quoted by the Nation magazine did not involve a large number of words quantitatively (three to four hundred words were taken from the lengthy Ford memoir). The Court nonetheless held that the quoted excerpts were the *heart of the work*, the most important and significant aspects of the copyrighted book in a qualitative sense:

> In absolute terms, the words actually quoted were an insubstantial portion of "A Time to Heal." The District Court, however, found that "[T]he Nation took what was essentially the heart of the book." We believe the Court of Appeals erred in overruling the District Judge's evaluation of the qualitative nature of the taking. A Time editor described the chapters on the pardon as "the most interesting and moving parts of the entire manuscript." The portions actually quoted were selected by Mr. Navasky as among the most powerful passages in those chapters.

Id. at 565 (citing *Roy Export Co. Establishment v. Columbia Broadcasting System, Inc.*, 503 F. Supp. 1137, 1145 (S.D.N.Y. 1980) (taking of 55 seconds out of 1.5-hour film deemed qualitatively substantial). The first prong of the fair use analysis takes into consideration the good faith or bad faith of the defendant: "the purpose and character of the use." Once again, the Court's analysis in *Harper & Row v. Nation Enterprises*, is relevant — the Court took into account the defendant's bad faith in having made use of a stolen manuscript in order to write its story. The Court's overall conclusion was that the Nation failed to prove the fair use defense despite its news reporting purpose and factual and historical nature of the Ford memoir.

Answer (B) is incorrect. The third prong of the fair use test focuses on the amount in relation to the copyrighted work, not as to the defendant's alleged infringing work.

Answer (C) is incorrect. As discussed above, good faith or bad faith is relevant to the first prong of the fair use test (the character of the use).

Answer (D) is incorrect. As discussed above, the third prong of the fair use test focuses on the amount in relation to the copyrighted work, not as to the defendant's alleged infringing work. Moreover, good faith or bad faith is relevant to the first prong of the fair use test (the character of the use).

159. Answer (C) is correct. The following statement most accurately describes the fair use defense under federal copyright law — a legitimate parody is taken into account in analyzing the fair use factors on a case-by-case basis. In *Campbell v. Acuff-Rose Music Inc.*, 510 U.S. 569 (1994), which involved a Two Live Crew rap parody version of the copyrighted song "Oh Pretty Woman," the Court specifically addressed parodies. Analyzing whether the parody was a fair use under the Copyright Act, the Court emphasized the need to analyze each fair use situation on a case-by-case, fact-specific basis. The Court viewed the parody as a favored purpose in fair use analysis, to be weighed in the overall balancing:

> The fact that *parody can claim legitimacy for some appropriation* does not, of course, tell either parodist or judge much about where to draw the line. Like a book review quoting the copyrighted material criticized, parody may or may not be fair use, and petitioners' suggestion that any parodic use is presumptively fair has no more justification in law or fact than the equally hopeful claim that any use for news reporting

should be presumed fair, see *Harper & Row*. The Act has no hint of an evidentiary preference for parodists over their victims, and no workable presumption for parody could take account of the fact that parody often shades into satire when society is lampooned through its creative artifacts, or that a work may contain both parodic and nonparodic elements. Accordingly, parody, like any other use, has to work its way through the relevant factors, and be *judged case by case, in light of the ends of the copyright law.*

Id. at 581 (emphasis added).

Answer (A) is incorrect. As discussed above, the Court rejected any assertion that parody is automatically fair use.

Answer (B) is incorrect. As discussed above, the Court rejected the presumption that parody is fair use.

Answer (D) is incorrect. As discussed above, the Court weighed parody as a favorable factor in the fair use analysis.

160. Answer (C) is correct. The following statement most accurately describes the fair use defense under federal copyright law—whether a work is published or unpublished is a factor in a fair use analysis, and fair use is more likely to be found if a work is published rather than unpublished. Whether a work is published is relevant to the second prong of the fair use analysis—the nature of the copyrighted work. In *Harper & Row v. Nation Enterprises*, 471 U.S. 539 (1985), the Court weighed the fact that the Ford memoir had not yet been published as a factor against finding fair use. The Court found that the Nation magazine had usurped book publisher Harper & Row's right of first publication. In other words, the defendant interfered with the copyright owner's right to decide when and how the book is first published. After this ruling, some lower courts interpreted the *Harper & Row v. Nation Enterprises* decision as imposing a presumption against finding fair use when the copyrighted work was unpublished. In response, Congress added the last sentence to the section 107 standard: "The fact that a work is unpublished shall not itself bar a finding of fair use if such finding is made upon consideration of all the above factors." 17 U.S.C. §107.

Answer (A) is incorrect. The Copyright Act protects works as soon as they are fixed in a tangible medium of expression. Thus, unpublished works are protected under federal copyright law.

Answer (B) is incorrect. As discussed above, whether a work is published or unpublished is a factor in a fair use analysis, although it is not determinative by itself.

Answer (D) is incorrect. As discussed above, fair use is more likely to be found if a work is published, not unpublished.

161. Answer (D) is correct. The following copyrighted works are not eligible for commercial rental under the first sale doctrine—both computer programs and sound recordings of musical works. Although the first sale doctrine under section 109 of the Copyright Act generally permits the rental or other disposition of lawful copies of works, there is a specific exception in section 109(b) for the commercial rental of computer software and sound recordings in any form:

Notwithstanding the provisions of subsection (a), unless authorized by the owners of copyright in the sound recording or the owner of copyright in a computer program (including any tape, disk, or other medium embodying such program), and in the case of a sound recording in the musical works embodied therein, neither the owner of a particular phonorecord nor any person in possession of a particular copy of a computer program (including any tape, disk, or other medium embodying such program), may, for the purposes of direct or indirect commercial advantage, dispose of, or authorize the disposal of, the possession of that phonorecord or computer program (including any tape, disk, or other medium embodying such program) by rental, lease, or lending, or by any other act or practice in the nature of rental, lease, or lending. Nothing in the preceding sentence shall apply to the rental, lease, or lending of a phonorecord for nonprofit purposes by a nonprofit library or nonprofit educational institution. The transfer of possession of a lawfully made copy of a computer program by a nonprofit educational institution to another nonprofit educational institution or to faculty, staff, and students does not constitute rental, lease, or lending for direct or indirect commercial purposes under this subsection.

17 U.S.C. § 109(b).

Answer (A) is incorrect. A DVD can be rented commercially under the general provisions of the first sale doctrine.

Answer (B) is incorrect. As discussed above, both computer software and music CDs cannot be offered for commercial rental under the first sale provision.

Answer (C) is incorrect. As discussed above, both computer software and music CDs cannot be offered for commercial rental under the first sale provision.

Answers

Practice Final Examination

Exam Answer 1. The "first to file" method for determining ownership of patents is effectively the law in the United States, with an important exception for inventions whose applications were effectively filed on or after March 16, 2013. *See* U.S.C. § 102(a)(2). Introducing a modified "first to file" system was the major feature of the America Invents Act, or AIA, which was enacted in September 2011. Inventions within applications containing only claims with effective filing dates before March 16, 2013 will continue to be evaluated for novelty, nonobviousness, and priority under prior law, which awarded priority to the first to conceive the invention, absent abandonment or suppression or lack of diligence.

The above-mentioned "important exception" in the AIA's modified "first to file" system is that priority will be awarded to an inventor who filed second, compared to a competing inventor of the same invention, if the second-filing inventor publicly disclosed the invention *before* the first-to-file inventor filed an application (or publicly disclosed the invention). *See* 35 U.S.C. § 102(b)(2)(B). The application must still, like all applications, be filed within a year of the inventor's disclosure, or it will be barred under section 102(a). *See* 35 U.S.C. § 102(a) and 102(b)(1).

Exam Answer 2. Answer (A) is correct. A fundamental rule in trade secret law is that reverse engineering is a lawful means of competition. Thus, a competitor is free to purchase a sample of a product and attempt to determine its composition, structure, and chemical makeup. Similarly, independent development is a lawful method of competition. In either case, the owner of the original trade secret has no cognizable claim under trade secret law. In contrast, patent law does not include exceptions for reverse engineering or independent development.

> **Answer (B) is incorrect.** This answer could be second best, because many recipes for food items are in fact too well known to be protected as trade secrets. There are, however, many exceptions to this rule. The formula for Coca-Cola (arguably a food item) is a long-time trade secret; so too is the recipe for Kentucky Fried Chicken, although persons have suggested that they have uncovered that formula or recipe by reverse engineering.

> **Answer (C) is incorrect.** As discussed above, reverse engineering is a lawful means of competition and does not constitute improper means.

> **Answer (D) is incorrect.** A defendant's knowledge that information was a trade secret and intended to be held in confidence is only relevant if knowledge of the information (the secret) was obtained by accident or mistake. Reverse engineering is lawful and not within "accident" or "mistake."

Exam Answer 3. Answer (C) is correct. A lawfully purchased music CD can be distributed to the public by a nonprofit public library through lending based on the copyright law doctrine of first sale. The copyright owner's otherwise exclusive right of distribution is limited by the "first sale" doctrine enunciated in section 109 of the Copyright Act: "Notwithstanding the provisions of section 106(3), *the owner of a particular* copy or *phonorecord* lawfully made under this title, or any person authorized by such owner, is entitled, without the authority of the copyright owner, to sell *or otherwise dispose of the possession of that copy or phonorecord.*" Although *commercial* rental of music CDs would be prohibited under § 109(b), that provision does not restrain nonprofit lending libraries from loaning music CDs:

> Notwithstanding the provisions of subsection (a), unless authorized by the owners of copyright *in the sound recording* or the owner of copyright in a computer program (including any tape, disk, or other medium embodying such program), *and in the case of a sound recording in the musical works embodied therein,* neither the owner of a particular phonorecord nor any person in possession of a particular copy of a computer program (including any tape, disk, or other medium embodying such program), may, for the purposes of direct or indirect commercial advantage, dispose of, or authorize the disposal of, the possession of that phonorecord or computer program (including any tape, disk, or other medium embodying such program) by rental, lease, or lending, or by any other act or practice in the nature of rental, lease, or lending. *Nothing in the preceding sentence shall apply to the rental, lease, or lending of a phonorecord for nonprofit purposes by a nonprofit library or nonprofit educational institution.*

17 U.S.C. § 109(b)(1)(A).

Answer (A) is incorrect. De minimis use is inapplicable here; the directly relevant defense relates to the fact that the library lawfully purchased and now owns the copy that it is loaning. See the explanation for Answer (C) above.

Answer (B) is incorrect. Fair use is not the most directly relevant defense to this set of facts, given the clear defense provided by the first sale doctrine. Moreover, the third and fourth factor outcomes might not be favorable in light of modern fair use case law.

Answer (D) is incorrect. "Noncommercial use" is not itself a recognized defense. Whether a use is noncommercial can affect a defense of fair use, under the first and fourth factors, but it is not alone a defense.

Exam Answer 4. Answer (A) is correct. An accounting system is not protected by copyright law. *See, e.g., Baker v. Selden,* 101 U.S. 99 (1879).

Answer (B) is incorrect. Architectural works are expressly identified as a category of copyrightable subject matter. *See* 17 U.S.C. § 102(a)(8).

Answer (C) is incorrect. Sound recordings are expressly identified as a category of copyrightable subject matter. 17 U.S.C. § 102(a)(7). The "depth" of the protection in such a recording would be thin, meaning others could still make their own sound recording of insect sounds, even though those new recordings would inevitably sound quite similar. *See* 17 U.S.C. § 114.

Answer (D) is incorrect. Computer code is protectable under copyright law. Although code often has "useful" functions, those functional elements will not be what copyright protects. Copyright will only protect the expression used, not that underlying functionality. Interestingly, the code is treated as a literary work. This may seem odd at first, but a software designer could express a work, a computer program, in a variety of different ways, and any given computer program expresses the work (or the visual elements and other goals of the programmer) in a particular coding language. (A literary work is also expressed in a particular language, and it might be expressing functional matter as well.) A computer program can be expressed and protected in its source code form, but it is protected as a literary work even when the computer "language" in question is the 1s and 0s of object code. User interfaces or visual elements generated by computer code are also protected. *See generally Justmed, Inc. v. Byce*, 600 F. 3d 1118 (9th Cir. 2010).

Exam Answer 5. The minimum standard of originality for copyright protection, as announced in the Supreme Court's decision in *Feist Publications, Inc. v. Rural Telephone Service Co.*, 499 U.S. 340, 345 (1991), can be explained as follows:

> The *sine qua non* of copyright is originality. To qualify for copyright protection, a work must be original to the author. Original, as the term is used in copyright, means only that the work was independently created by the author (as opposed to copied from other works), and that it possesses at least some minimal degree of creativity.

The Court announced this rule in the context of a case involving a factual compilation—a "white pages" telephone directory. As the Court noted,

> (1) facts are not copyrightable; and (2) compilations of facts generally are copyrightable. Each of these propositions possesses an impeccable pedigree. That there can be no valid copyright in facts is universally understood. The most fundamental axiom of copyright law is that "[n]o author may copyright his ideas or the facts he narrates."

Id. at 344–45. Most creative works, particularly non-factual works, easily satisfy this minimum standard for originality.

Exam Answer 6. Answer (B) is correct. The Visual Artists Rights Act of 1990 ("VARA") does not protect limited-edition or single copies of films. VARA, at 17 U.S.C. § 106A, provides protections for a "work of visual art," a term of art defined in the Copyright Act as follows:

> (1) a painting, drawing, print, or sculpture, existing in a single copy, in a limited edition of 200 copies or fewer that are signed and consecutively numbered by the author, or, in the case of a sculpture, in multiple cast, carved, or fabricated sculptures of 200 or fewer that are consecutively numbered by the author and bear the signature or other identifying mark of the author; or

> (2) a still photographic image produced for exhibition purposes only, existing in a single copy that is signed by the author, or in a limited edition of 200 copies or fewer that are signed and consecutively numbered by the author.

17 U.S.C. § 101. Thus, painting, prints, and drawings are eligible for protection under VARA, but films are not. Moral rights laws in some foreign nations, such as France, do offer protection for films.

> **Answer (A) is incorrect.** As noted above, drawings, paintings, and photographs are eligible for protection under VARA.

> **Answer (C) is incorrect.** As noted above, drawings, paintings, and photographs are eligible for protection under VARA.

> **Answer (D) is incorrect.** As noted above, drawings, paintings, and photographs are eligible for protection under VARA.

Exam Answer 7. The Lanham Act defines a certification mark as a mark "used upon or in connection with the products or services of one or more persons other than the owner of the mark to certify regional or other origin, material, mode of manufacture, quality, accuracy or other characteristics of such goods or services." 15 U.S.C. § 1127.

Examples of certification marks are the "UL Listed" and "UL Certified" marks (where the letters U and L appear in a circle, with the U just slightly higher than the L). These UL marks indicate that products sold by third parties meet certain safety standards set by a company called UL LLC, a subsidiary of Underwriters Laboratories, Inc., which has existed for more than 100 years (and which certified its first vacuum cleaner in 1909, according to the company's website).

Exam Answer 8. Answer (B) is correct. A new mathematical algorithm cannot be protected with a utility patent under the Patent Act, even if it can be put to a useful end. The Patent Act offers protection for the practical applications of ideas or concepts, i.e., it might offer protection to a specific structure or method when the algorithm has been worked into a specific built system or a specific process having certain other components or routines, but it will not protect the abstract idea or concept itself. *See Diamond v. Diehr*, 450 U.S. 175 (1981) (finding patentable a specific manufacturing method that relied upon a mathematical algorithm); *see also Alice Corp. v. CLS Bank Int'l*, 573 U.S. 208 (2014) (holding unpatentable, as abstract ideas, a patentee's claims to a financial settlement method and to a computer system implementing that method. The Court did not find in the claims "an element or combination of elements that [was] 'sufficient to ensure that the patent in practice amounts to significantly more than a patent upon the [ineligible concept] itself.'").

> **Answer (A) is incorrect.** A new genetically modified animal—one not naturally occurring—such as a faster growing strain of Angus beef cattle would be patentable subject matter. *See generally Diamond v. Chakrabarty*, 447 U.S. 303 (1980).

> **Answer (C) is incorrect.** A new process for producing a motor oil, even a known composition, would be patentable subject matter as a "process." *See* 35 U.S.C. § 101.

> **Answer (D) is incorrect.** A new type of paperclip would be patentable subject matter, *see* 35 U.S.C. § 101, although of course a *minor* improvement to or variation on the paperclip might not meet the section 103 requirement of nonobviousness.

Exam Answer 9. Answer (C) is correct. Reselling a product covered by a patent is not an example of an infringement of a patent. Patent infringement does occur when a party makes, uses, sells, offers to sell, or imports the product into the United States. This is the "bundle of sticks" or collection of rights provided for in the Patent Act. The resale of a product still under patent, however, would not violate this patent based on the exhaustion doctrine. *See Impression Prods., Inc. v. Lexmark Int'l, Inc.*, 137 S. Ct. 1523 (2017). The principle involved is that the patent owner has already had the opportunity to reap a legally protected reward from the patent at the time of the original sale of the product, and the owner of the physical item or good (in common law property terms, the chattel) has the right of a property owner to resell that physical item or good to another person free of restraint.

Answer (A) is incorrect. Importing a product covered by a patent would violate section 271(a), which clearly lists a right of import: "Except as otherwise provided in this title, whoever without authority makes, uses, offers to sell, or sells any patented invention, within the United States, *or imports into the United States* any patented invention during the term of the patent therefor, infringes the patent." 35 U.S.C. § 271(a) (emphasis added).

Answer (B) is incorrect. Offering to make and sell a product covered by a patent during the term of a patent would violate section 271(a), as set forth above in the explanation to Answer (A), even if the product was not actually produced or sold by the defendant.

Answer (D) is incorrect. Selling a product manufactured using a patented process would violate section 271(g), which provides in relevant part:

> Whoever without authority imports into the United States or offers to sell, sells, or uses within the United States a product which is made by a process patented in the United States shall be liable as an infringer, if the importation, offer to sell, sale, or use of the product occurs during the term of such process patent.

35 U.S.C. § 271(g).

Exam Answer 10. Answer (D) is correct. An injunction in most trade secrets cases should last as long as it would take to reverse engineer the subject matter of the trade secret. A prevailing trade secret plaintiff is only entitled to an injunction lasting as long as the "head start" that the defendant received by usurping the trade secret via unlawful behavior. Thus, the injunction should remain in place for the time period that would have been needed to reverse engineer the product, which might be a short period or might be indefinite, depending on the facts. *See Lamb-Weston, Inc. v. McCain Foods, Ltd.*, 941 F.2d 970 (9th Cir. 1991). (It could be indefinite only if there were no evidence of a capacity for the trade secret to be reverse engineered.)

Answer (A) is incorrect. Allowing an injunction in most cases to continue indefinitely, as long as the requisite reasonable efforts to maintain secrecy and a competitive advantage exist, would require that the court engage in continuing supervision of the status of most trade secrets, since most trade secret claimants will proffer their efforts at secrecy and argue for the advantage the secret provides. Courts are unlikely to grant this open-ended term for injunctive relief unless the defendant has offered no evidence that reverse engineering is within reach. If they did grant such relief when reverse engineering was likely, this could put one competitor at a permanent disadvantage (through the injunction) based on one moment of bad behavior (the misappropriation), leaving other competitors not part of the litigation to reverse engineer the information and hold the information in "secret."

Answer (B) is incorrect. Although sanctioning unlawful behavior and deterring future bad behavior are both objectives of the law, a perpetual injunction would far exceed the likely time period in which most information could be maintained as trade secrets.

Answer (C) is incorrect. There is no set term in trade secret law. It is true that patent protection lasts for 20 years from the date of filing; an injunction in a patent case would have a relationship to the time remaining on that term.

Exam Answer 11. The level of secrecy required in order for information to be protected as a trade secret is that it must be sufficiently secret for its owner to derive an advantage, actual or potential, from the fact that the information is not generally known to others who might use it. Whether information qualifies as proprietary thus depends on the extent of secrecy of the information in the industry. If the information can readily be duplicated by those with general skills and knowledge in the field, it is not a protectable trade secret. *See Kewanee Oil Co. v. Bicron Corp.*, 416 U.S. 470 (1974). In comparison, the patent law standard of novelty is both more demanding and arguably less so — the invention must be something new to the public and the marketplace, but the invention might have been held in secret by another and yet be novel. Section 102(a) of the Patent Act states: "A person shall be entitled to a patent unless — (i) the claimed invention was patented, described in a printed publication or in public use, on sale, or otherwise available to the public before the effective filing date of the claimed invention." It also bars a patent if the claimed invention was described in a prior-filed patent application, even if the information was not public. *See* 35 U.S.C. § 102(a)(2). Thus, while trade secret law requires that the information *not be generally known*, patent law requires that the invention *not be known to the public*.

Exam Answer 12. Answer (A) is correct. The best way to protect an idea for a new video game is through contract law, which would also include confidentiality agreements. An idea can be conveyed confidentially to third parties who expressly agree to be bound; they may also agree to provide compensation for the conveyance of the idea. The enforceability of this type of agreement will depend on state law, which can vary by jurisdiction. *See, e.g., Desny v. Wilder*, 299 P.2d 257 (Cal. 1956); *Wrench LLC v. Taco Bell Corp.*, 256 F.3d 446 (6th Cir. 2001) (Michigan law); *Nadel v. Play-by-Play Toys & Novelties, Inc.*, 208 F.3d 368 (2d Cir. 2000) (New York law); *see also Lapine v. Seinfeld*, 918 N.Y.S. 2d 313 (N.Y. Sup. Ct. 2011) (disagreeing with *Nadel*).

Answer (B) is incorrect. Copyright law cannot be used to protect an idea for a new video game — only the expression used to convey that idea. As § 102(b) of the Copyright Act states: "In no case does copyright protection for an original work of authorship extend to any idea, procedure, process, system, method of operation, concept, principle, or discovery, regardless of the form in which it is described, explained, illustrated, or embodied in such work." 17 U.S.C. § 102(b).

Answer (C) is incorrect. Trademark law cannot be used to protect an idea for a new video game — trademark law requires use in commerce of a source-identifying word or other device.

Answer (D) is incorrect. As noted above, contracts and confidentiality agreements can be used to protect an idea for a new video game.

Exam Answer 13. Answer (A) is correct. Trade secret misappropriation can occur by either breach of confidence or soliciting that breach of confidence.

Answer (B) is incorrect. When sales employees are discussing a company's strategies in the boarding area of the airport in voices loud enough to be overheard by others, then simply sitting and listening in a public place would *not* appear to be improper means (and neither would the information appear to be held as a trade secret, since reasonable efforts to maintain secrecy are not being observed). This is not misappropriation. For a useful comparison, where the defendant's otherwise lawful flight activity was nevertheless held to constitute improper means, see *E.I. DuPont DeNemours & Co. v. Christopher*, 431 F.2d 1012 (5th Cir. 1970) (stating. "To obtain knowledge of a process without spending the time and money to discover it independently is improper unless the holder voluntarily discloses it or fails to take reasonable precautions to ensure its secrecy," and, "We ... need not proclaim a catalogue of commercial improprieties. Clearly, however, one of its commandments does say 'thou shall not appropriate a trade secret through deviousness under circumstances in which countervailing defenses are not reasonably available.'").

Answer (C) is incorrect. Taking apart and examining a publicly available product is classic reverse engineering, which is a permissible and proper means of discovering a trade secret.

Answer (D) is incorrect. See explanation above for why Answers (B) and (C) are not good choices.

Exam Answer 14. Answer (C) is correct. The overall appearance, presentation, and sales techniques of a retail store can be protected as trade dress, as long as this collection of features is either inherently distinctive or has acquired distinctiveness (also called secondary meaning). This was the holding of the Supreme Court's decision in *Two Pesos, Inc. v. Taco Cabana, Inc.*, 505 U.S. 763 (1992); the Court did not back away from that holding in *Wal-Mart Stores v. Samara Bros.*, 529 U.S. 205 (2000). It must also be nonfunctional.

Answer (A) is incorrect. The overall appearance, presentation, and sales techniques of a retail store would not quality as a collective mark. A "collective mark" does not refer to a collection of features used as a mark. Instead, it:

> means a trademark or service mark—(1) used by the members of a cooperative, an association, or other collective group or organization, or (2) which such cooperative, association, or other collective group or organization has a bona fide intention to use in commerce and applies to register on the principal register established by this Act, and includes marks indicating membership in a union, an association, or other organization.

15 U.S.C. § 1127 (definition of "collective mark"). For a bit more information, see Question 5 and its associated answer in Topic 1.

Answer (B) is incorrect. The retail store's overall appearance, presentation, and sales techniques, even if primarily ornamental, would not be the "ornamental design for an *article of manufacture*" as required for design patent subject matter. 35 U.S.C. § 171 (emphasis added).

Answer (D) is incorrect. By virtue of being part of what consumers directly encounter at the store—especially the appearance and presentation aspects here, which consumers will certainly see—this overall subject matter could not qualify as a trade secret.

Exam Answer 15. The merger doctrine in copyright law provides that "when there is essentially only one way to express an idea, the idea and its expression are inseparable, and copyright is no bar to copying that expression." *ATC Distribution Group, Inc. v. Whatever It Takes Transmissions & Parts, Inc.*, 402 F.3d 700 (6th Cir. 2005). Thus, the copyright owner cannot obtain exclusive rights to an idea when that idea cannot be expressed in sufficient alternative ways. For example, in *Herbert Rosenthal Jewelry Corp. v. Kalpakian*, 446 F.2d 738 (9th Cir. 1971), the court applied the merger doctrine in a case involving a jewel pin in the shape of a bee, where the idea of a jeweled bee pin can only be expressed in a very limited number of ways.

Exam Answer 16. Answer (A) is correct. A business method that is useful for accountants because it quickly and repeatedly applies a mathematical algorithm would not be patentable subject matter under the most recent Supreme Court case law. In *Alice Corp. v. CLS Bank Int'l*, 134 S. Ct. 2347 (2014), the Court applied its decision in *Mayo Collaborative Services v. Prometheus Labs. Inc.*, 566 U.S. 66 (2012), to determine that claims to both a method and a system were not patentable subject matter under the exclusion for abstract ideas. Although it is a controversial decision in some corners, it remains the law. The framework used in *Alice* first asks whether "the claims at issue are directed to one of those patent-ineligible concepts [namely, laws of nature, natural phenomena, and abstract ideas]. If so, we then ask '[w]hat else is there in the claims before us?'.... We have described step two of this analysis as a search for an 'inventive concept'—i.e., an element or combination of elements that is 'sufficient to ensure that the patent in practice amounts to significantly more than a patent upon the [ineligible concept] itself.'" In *Alice Corp.*, the patentee's claims were to a method for intermediated settlement, where a third party's participation in the transaction settlement mitigated risk, and for a computer system configured to perform that method. The court found intermediated settlement to be an "abstract idea," and it did not find that the "generic computer implementation" of the settlement concept was enough to ensure that the claimed process or system would avoid monopolizing the abstract idea itself. It therefore rejected the claims as unpatentable subject matter. The same would happen to the business method described above, which is simply a repeated application of an unpatentable algorithm. *See also Bilski v. Kappos*, 130 S. Ct. 3218 (2010) (rejecting an exclusion of "business methods" from patentable subject matter but nevertheless holding that the particular claims in question (which involved a method for hedging against risk) were directed to abstract ideas and were ineligible for patent protection).

Answer (B) is incorrect. A newly created complementary DNA sequence useful in testing for certain forms of lung cancer is patentable subject matter under the reasoning of *Association for Molecular Pathology v. Myriad Genetics, Inc.*, 133 S. Ct. 2107 (2013), although the newly discovered human gene sequences from which the cDNA was synthesized would not be. The sequences discovered from analyzing human DNA are not patentable subject matter because they would not have been created or modified by the discoverer; the Court differentiated the cDNA by reasoning that "the lab technician unquestionably creates something new when cDNA is made. cDNA retains the naturally occurring exons of DNA, but it is distinct from the DNA from which it was derived. As a result, cDNA is not a 'product of nature' and is patent eligible under § 101." (In a footnote, the court did note that it "express[ed] no opinion whether cDNA satisfies the other statutory requirements of patentability," which it noted would include sections 102 and 103.)

Answer (C) is incorrect. A distinct, even if not useful, plant created by hybridization would be patentable subject matter under the plant patent provisions. *See* 35 U.S.C. § 161 ("Whoever invents or discovers and asexually reproduces any distinct and new variety of plant, including cultivated sports, mutants, hybrids, and newly found seedlings, other than a tuber propagated plant or a plant found in an uncultivated state, may obtain a patent therefor, subject to the conditions and requirements of this title." Asexual reproduction methods include rooting of cuttings, layering, and grafting methods.

Answer (D) is incorrect. An ornamental design for an automobile battery would be protectable by a design patent, which does not require that the underlying article of manufacture to which the design is applied be new, or that the design be visible during all phases of the product's life. *See* 35 U.S.C. § 171.

Exam Answer 17. Answer (C) is correct. The following statement most accurately describes the approach taken by federal patent law to questions of remedies: injunctive relief is frequently granted, and money damages are generally available.

As to injunctive relief, section 283 of the Patent Act states: "The several courts having jurisdiction of cases under this title may grant injunctions in accordance with the principles of equity to prevent the violation of any right secured by patent, on such terms as the court deems reasonable." Thus, injunctive relief is available based upon a four-factor equitable test. As noted in *eBay, Inc. v. MercExchange, L.L.C.*, 547 U.S. 388, 393–94 (2006), the patent holder must show:

> (1) that it has suffered an irreparable injury; (2) that remedies available at law, such as monetary damages, are inadequate to compensate for that injury; (3) that, considering the balance of hardships between the plaintiff and defendant, a remedy in equity is warranted; and (4) that the public interest would not be disserved by a permanent injunction.

The Court rejected the Federal Circuit's presumption that injunctions should be granted except in unusual cases. Injunctive relief is a very important remedy because it permits the patent holder to maintain its exclusivity in the marketplace, which is the essence of the patent reward.

Section 284 of the Patent Act identifies the monetary damages available to patent holders: "Upon finding for the claimant the court shall award the claimant damages adequate to compensate for the infringement but in no event less than a reasonable royalty for the use made of the invention by the infringer, together with interest and costs as fixed by the court." 35 U.S.C. § 284. Note the mandatory wording but note also that the patentee would still need to prove causation and the connection to compensation; nevertheless, a floor of a "reasonable royalty" is provided. In cases that the district court finds to be out of the ordinary in some way, whether for the blatant nature of the infringement, bad faith, or bad litigation behavior, section 285 of the Patent Act allows for the recovery of reasonable attorney's fees: "The court in exceptional cases may award reasonable attorney fees to the prevailing party." (Do note that this fee-shifting possibility runs both ways and might favor a prevailing defendant.) Enhanced damages are also available in cases of willful infringement.

Answer (A) is incorrect. As discussed above with respect to Answer (C), injunctive relief is not presumed in patent cases, and monetary damages are generally awarded to compensate the patent owner.

Answer (B) is incorrect. As discussed above with respect to Answer (C), damages are not "presumed" in patent cases, even though the statute sets a floor of a reasonable royalty (the amount of which a patentee must still prove), and injunctions are frequently issued to vindicate the patent owner's exclusive rights.

Answer (D) is incorrect. As discussed above with respect to Answer (C), damages are generally awarded to compensate the patent owner, even in the absence of bad faith or actual loss of profits — section 284 makes a "reasonable royalty for the use made of the invention by the infringer" the minimum monetary award.

Exam Answer 18. Answer (D) is correct. If Congress wished to grant a perpetual copyright, the Intellectual Property Clause (Art. I, sec. 8, cl. 8) would expressly preclude such a law, and Congress could not avoid the problem by relying on the Commerce Clause to circumvent the express limits of the Intellectual Property Clause. In *Eldred v. Ashcroft*, 537 U.S. 186 (2003), the Supreme Court held that Congress did not exceed its constitutional authority when it added 20 years to all existing and future copyrights. Justice Ginsburg found that "[t]ext, history, and precedent, confirm that the Copyright Clause empowers Congress to prescribe 'limited Times' for copyright protection and to secure the same level and duration of protection for all copyright holders, present and future." This holding, however, does not mean that Congress could enact a *perpetual* copyright statute, or allow *unlimited* renewals, as that would be beyond its power under the Intellectual Property Clause, which gives Congress the power "[t]o promote the Progress of Science and useful Arts, by securing for *limited Times* to Authors and Inventors the exclusive Right to their respective Writings and Discoveries." U.S. Const. art. I, sec. 8, cl. 8. It seems unlikely that Congress could evade this express limit on its power by invoking the Commerce Clause (or any other clause) to enact unlimited terms within its copyright legislation.

Answer (A) is incorrect. By its clear terms, the Intellectual Property Clause does not itself permit such a law.

Answer (B) is incorrect. Congress has not enacted any perpetual or unlimited-term copyright legislation, including for works of foreign authors. It restored foreign authors' copyrights to the remainder of what would have otherwise been the statutory term for those works in certain instances, *see* 17 U.S.C. § 104A, but the *restoration of the remaining period* of protection that was lost is not the same as a *perpetual* or *unlimited* term. *See Golan v. Holder*, 132 S. Ct. 873 (2012).

Answer (C) is incorrect. As discussed above in connection with Answer (D), it is highly unlikely that Congress could avoid the problem by relying upon the Commerce Clause.

Exam Answer 19. Answer (D) is correct. Assume that someone writes a new novel under a pseudonym in the year 2010. The current term of copyright protection for this work not published in the author's own name is 95 years from the date of publication or 120 years from the date of creation, whichever comes first. 17 U.S.C. § 302(c) ("In the case of an anonymous work, a pseudonymous work, or a work made for hire, the copyright endures for a term of 95 years from the year of its first publication, or a term of 120 years from the year of its creation, whichever expires first.").

Answer (A) is incorrect. Life plus 50 years was the term of copyright given in the 1976 Act to works published in the author's own name, but only before the 1998 copyright term extension added 20 years to those terms (as well as all other extant terms). The life-based term for works published in the author's own name is now life plus 70 years.

Answer (B) is incorrect. Life plus 70 years is the term of copyright for works published in the author's own name. 17 U.S.C. § 302(c) ("Copyright in a work created on or after January 1, 1978, subsists from its creation and, except as provided by the following subsections, endures for a term consisting of the life of the author and 70 years after the author's death.") If the identity of the initially pseudonymous work is revealed in the registration records for the work during the term of copyright, then the term will change to "life plus seventy." *See* 17 U.S.C. § 302(c).

Answer (C) is incorrect. As discussed above, the copyright term is 95 years from the date of publication or 120 years from the date of creation, whichever comes first. Between January 1, 1978 and 1998, before the 1998 Copyright Term Extension Act added 20 years to all copyright terms, this would have been correct, but it has not been correct for over 20 years now.

Exam Answer 20. Answer (D) is correct. Your client wishes to use a copyrighted song and sound recording in a movie. This would require synchronization and master use licenses from the copyright owners. A synchronization (or "synch") license from the music publisher allows the moviemaker to place the musical work (the lyrics and melody) alongside the visual aspects of the movie. Assuming the moviemaker wishes to use a particular sound recording that has already been made by a performer, a master use license from the record company is needed to make use of this work. Two licenses are needed because there are two copyrights embodied in the recorded version of a song—the musical work copyright and the copyright in the sound recording.

Answer (A) is incorrect. The right of distribution, standing alone, would not allow the use of the song on the film. The right to distribute the movie containing the musical work and sound recording is included in the synch license and master use license.

Answer (B) is incorrect. A mechanical license allows a performer to record and sell "cover" versions (new sound recording) of a previously recorded musical work. It would not permit placing the song on a film or other audiovisual work without a synch license.

Answer (C) is incorrect. Public performance rights from BMI, ASCAP, or SESAC do not cover synchronization of musical works. *See, e.g., Frank Music Corp. v. Metro-Goldwyn-Mayer, Inc.,* 772 F.2d 505 (9th Cir. 1985) (casino with a musical revue featuring copyrighted songs had ASCAP public performance license, which did not cover rights needed to set music to the theatrical production on stage).

Exam Answer 21. Answer (C) is correct. Under these facts, where the president of the corporation distributes five copies of an article within days of initial publication, with the copies to be used by fellow senior executives to prepare for a meeting taking place the same week, the action should not violate copyright law, in light of the fair use defense. This appears to be a classic case of fair use under section 107, involving a single journal article reproduced for immediate, one-time use in limited quantity, and not distributed to the public. Although not specified in the facts, one difficulty for the corporation could be that it may be a for-profit corporation rather than a not-for-profit corporation, and its uses would then likely have elements that are "commercial" under the first § 107 factor, even if that commerciality is attenuated. Nevertheless, commerciality of a use does not doom a fair use defense to failure, as explained in *Campbell v. Acuff-Rose Music, Inc.*, 510 U.S. 569 (1994). Another difficulty may be that some copyright owners of publications make photocopying and other licenses available through collective endeavors like the Copyright Clearance Center, a fact that at least one court used in connection with the fourth factor (effect on the market) en route to finding the copying of journal articles not to be fair use. *See American Geophysical Union v. Texaco, Inc.*, 60 F.3d 913 (2d Cir. 1994). The facts of that case were markedly different, however, as the copying of the articles was for long-term storage in researcher files, seemingly as a substitute for multiple subscriptions. *See id.* (contrasting "spontaneous" copying with "archival" copying). At the same time, the court in that case took pains in refusing to call the defendant's use of the articles solely "commercial use" while simultaneously not ignoring the for-profit nature of defendant Texaco.

Answer (A) is incorrect. While it is true that the act is a reproduction of the work in copies, and the corporation is responsible for the infringing acts of the president, fair use should eliminate liability in these circumstances as explained above in connection with Answer (C).

Answer (B) is incorrect. There can be secondary or indirect infringement liability under various theories under the Copyright Act, *see Metro-Goldwyn-Mayer Studios v. Grokster, Ltd.*, 545 U.S. 913 (2005). In addition, no copyright violation occurred on these facts (as explained above in connection with Answer (C)).

Answer (D) is incorrect. The absence of profit being made by the corporation on these specific copies does not make the use noncommercial and is not dispositive of whether the act is infringing, although it is a factor in the fair use analysis. Noncommercial and nonprofit activities that exceed the scope of fair use based on a balancing of all relevant factors can violate the Copyright Act.

Exam Answer 22. Answer (A) is correct. A company hires a freelance professional website designer to create and design its website. The website designer most likely owns the copyright to the work, absent an agreement to the contrary. An independent contractor who creates a copyrighted work for a client ordinarily owns the copyright to the work, even though the client pays for copies of the work and provides some input into its creation. A complete analysis of this question requires application of the common law agency standard set forth in the Supreme Court's decision in *Community for Creative Non-Violence v. Reid*, 490 U.S. 730 (1989). The case involved a homeless advocacy group, which hired a well-known sculptor to create a work depicting the homeless. The Court ultimately held that the sculptor owned the copyright to the work, even though the advocacy group owned the physical sculpture itself. To determine whether a work is created by an independent contractor or whether it is a "work made for hire" by an employee (in which case the hiring party would own the copyright), the Court adopted the common law agency standard. This test involves analysis of the following factors:

> In determining whether a hired party is an employee under the general common law of agency, we consider the hiring party's right to control the manner and means by which the product is accomplished. Among the other factors relevant to this inquiry are the skill required; the source of the instrumentalities and tools; the location of the work; the duration of the relationship between the parties; whether the hiring party has the right to assign additional projects to the hired party; the extent of the hired party's discretion over when and how long to work; the method of payment; the hired party's role in hiring and paying assistants; whether the work is part of the regular business of the hiring party; whether the hiring party is in business; the provision of employee benefits; and the tax treatment of the hired party.

Id. Applying this test on the present limited set of facts, it appears the web designer would be deemed an independent contractor and would be entitled to copyright ownership. The "specially ordered or commissioned" branch of the definition of a "work made for hire" will not apply here because a website, without more facts to alter the common understanding of that term, is not a work that will be used "as a contribution to a collective work, as a part of a motion picture or other audiovisual work, as a translation, as a supplementary work, as a compilation, as an instructional text, as a test, as answer material for a test, or as an atlas." 17 U.S.C. § 101 (definition of a "work made for hire"). Moreover, even commissioned works that are made for the uses listed above, are only works made for hire authored and owned by the hiring party if the parties agree in writing to such treatment. This conclusion would have serious implications for the company, particularly as to future modifications or use of the website. This result is, however, simply the default rule in copyright law and can be modified by agreement of the parties.

Answer (B) is incorrect. As discussed above, the web designer would be deemed an independent contractor and would be entitled to copyright ownership of a website.

Answer (C) is incorrect. Without additional facts, it is highly unlikely that the company's contributions to the work were independently copyrightable or that the web designer ever intended a joint authorship arrangement. Section 101 of the Copyright Act defines a joint work as "a work prepared by two or more authors with the intention that their contributions be merged into inseparable or interdependent parts of a unitary whole." 17 U.S.C. § 101. As discussed in *Childress v. Taylor*, 945 F.2d 500 (2d Cir. 1991), two elements must be proven to form a joint work—(1) each author must make independently copyrightable contributions to the work, and (2) there must be mutual intention that the contributions be combined into a unitary whole as a joint work. Thus, it is highly unlikely that the website was a joint work.

Answer (D) is incorrect. Copyright law provides default rules in this situation, as discussed above. The outcome under the default rule can of course be modified by express agreement.

Exam Answer 23. Answer (C) is correct. The general term of protection for a plant patent under the Plant Patent Act is 20 years from the date of patent filing. *See* 35 U.S.C. §§ 154 (a)(2) and 161.

This is the same term as provided for utility patents. These patent terms were established in the Uruguay Round Agreements Act of 1994 ("URAA"), which established the term for patents sought after June 8, 1995.

Answer (A) is incorrect. This does not correctly state the patent term, as noted above.

Answer (B) is incorrect. This was the term for plant and utility patents under prior law, but the patent term was amended by the URAA, as noted above.

Answer (D) is incorrect. This does not correctly state the patent term, as noted above.

Exam Answer 24. Answer (D) is correct. The significance of a copyright notice under current law for a work first written and published in 2020 is that copyright notice is no longer required, but the notice provides some amount of potential remedial benefit. The Berne Convention Implementation Act of 1988 ("BCIA") eliminated the requirement. Section 401(a) of the Copyright Act currently states:

> Whenever a work protected under this title is published in the United States or elsewhere by authority of the copyright owner, a notice of copyright as provided by this section *may* be placed on publicly distributed copies from which the work can be visually perceived, either directly or with the aid of a machine or device.

17 U.S.C. §401(a) (emphasis added). A similar provision applies to phonorecords. *See* 17 U.S.C. §402 (a). A remedial benefit is possible, although it is somewhat remote in most typical circumstances, in that notice can eliminate a claim of innocence for those defendants who might have been able to demonstrate their lack of knowledge of the protected status of the work and then use it to mitigate statutory damages or avoid paying the owner's attorney's fees. For example, the provision governing statutory damages specifically notes that the statutory damages may be reduced to a fairly nominal sum where the infringer can prove that the "infringer was not aware and had no reason to believe that his or her acts constituted an infringement of copyright." *See* 17 U.S.C. §§401(d), 402(d), and 504(c) (particularly §504(c)(2)).

The elimination of a mandatory notice requirement applies to works published after March 1, 1989, when the BCIA took effect. *See* 17 U.S.C. §405. The BCIA brought the United States into compliance with article 5(2) of the Berne Convention by eliminating the notice requirement for works published after its effective date. Article 5(2) of the Berne Convention states: "The enjoyment and the exercise of these rights shall not be subject to any formality." Mandatory copyright notice would be a prohibited "formality."

Answer (A) is incorrect. As discussed above, works published under current law are not subject to a mandatory notice requirement.

Answer (B) is incorrect. As discussed above, works published under current law are not subject to a mandatory notice requirement.

Answer (C) is incorrect. As noted above, there is a potential remedial benefit to the use of the notice.

Exam Answer 25. Answer (A) is correct. A law student prepares a written outline of a course based on the casebook readings and classroom discussion. The law student has a valid copyright on the outline because it is minimally creative and involves some judgment. The originality standard of *Feist Publications, Inc. v. Rural Telephone Service Co.*, 499 U.S. 340, 345 (1991), provides as follows:

> The *sine qua non* of copyright is originality. To qualify for copyright protection, a work must be original to the author. Original, as the term is used in copyright, means only that the work was independently created by the author (as opposed to copied from other works), and that it possesses at least some minimal degree of creativity.

The outline is independently created and has a minimal degree of creativity, based on the selection and arrangement of the material in the outline. Even though much of the content of the outline might be derived from the class lecture and casebook, the law student has an implied right to prepare notes from the class and from the readings, and fair use would be implicated as well. Of course, a verbatim reproduction of the class lecture or casebook that is used beyond the scope of section 107 fair use would raise copyright issues, but most student outlines do not fall into this category.

Answer (B) is incorrect. As noted above, there is an originality requirement, but the outline is very likely to satisfy the threshold for creativity.

Answer (C) is incorrect. This is the second-best answer. As noted above, although much of the content of the outline might be derived from the class lecture and casebook, the law student has an implied right to prepare notes from the class and from the readings. Of course, a verbatim reproduction (or nearly so) of the class lecture or casebook that is used beyond the scope of section 107 fair use would raise copyright issues, but most student outlines do not fall into this category.

Answer (D) is incorrect. As the Court made clear in *Feist*, factual works that meet the originality standard are copyrightable.

Exam Answer 26. Answer (C) is correct. An original and ornamental feature of a useful device is eligible for protection under either copyright or design patent law. Section 171 of the Patent Act states: "Whoever invents any new, original, and ornamental design for an article of manufacture may obtain a patent therefor, subject to the conditions and requirements of this title." And as long as the original and ornamental feature is either physically or conceptually separable from the utilitarian aspects of the device, it will also be eligible for copyright protection, as further explained in the answer to Question 114 in Topic 11.

Answer (A) is incorrect. Both forms of protection are available. The creator of such an original and ornamental design or feature is not required to elect one form of protection over the other. *See, e.g., Application of Richard Q. Yardley*, 493 F.2d 1389 (C.C.P.A. 1974) (noting that there is an area of overlap between copyright and design patent subject matter, and rejecting the argument that an author-inventor must elect between the two available forms of protection).

Answer (B) is incorrect. As noted above, both forms of protection are available.

Answer (D) is incorrect. As noted above, both forms of protection are available.

Exam Answer 27. Answer (B) is correct. The best description of the role of evidence as to the "sophistication of consumers" in trademark infringement cases is that a low level of consumer sophistication weighs in favor of the trademark owner's claim of infringement. A less "sophisticated" consumer is presumed to take less time or care with the purchasing decision, and is therefore presumed to be more likely to be confused by similar marks on similar goods or services, while a more sophisticated purchaser, such as a specialized or professional buyer or a procurement expert, is deemed less likely to suffer consumer confusion than would an ordinary consumer. Thus, if the relevant universe of purchasers is more sophisticated than an average consumer, then consumer confusion is less likely to take place. *See, e.g., In re N.A.D.*, 754 F.2d 996 (Fed. Cir. 1985) (taking into account purchaser sophistication in reversing refusal to register NARKOMED for anesthesia machines because of purported confusion with NARKO medical supply mark).

> **Answer (A) is incorrect.** Consumer sophistication, or a factor related thereto, is only one factor in the likelihood of confusion analysis; no one factor is a "must have" in the analysis of trademark infringement. *See, e.g., Polaroid Corp. v. Polarad Electronics Corp.*, 287 F.2d 492, 495 (2d Cir. 1961).

> **Answer (C) is incorrect.** As discussed above, a high level of consumer sophistication weighs against, not in favor of, a finding of likelihood of confusion and therefore it does not favor the owner's claim of infringement.

> **Answer (D) is incorrect.** A high level of consumer sophistication is merely one factor in the likelihood of confusion analysis; given that it weighs against the trademark owner (see above), it is certainly not required in order for the trademark owner to succeed.

Exam Answer 28. Answer (C) is correct. If a term is proven to be generic, whereby its primary significance to consumers is to identify the product itself, then competitors can use the term freely. *See King-Seeley Thermos Co. v. Aladdin Industries, Inc.*, 321 F.2d 577 (2d Cir. 1963). Genericism is set aside as grounds to contest an otherwise "incontestable" mark within the statutes providing for incontestability and for the defenses that survive incontestability, as well as the statute governing cancellation proceedings. *See* 15 U.S.C. §§ 1064(3) (cancellation), 1065(4) (incontestability), and 1115(b)(2) (defenses to incontestability, referring to marks that have been "abandoned," the definition of which in 15 U.S.C. § 1127 includes situations where "the mark [has] become the generic name for the goods"). The fact that Prince Software has identified options it could use other than "PowerPoint" would not detract from the generic status of the term if it could otherwise prove generic status. The test for whether a mark has become generic focuses on the primary significance to consumers, not on whether there are alternative words that can be used to identify the product. (Note: The authors of this study guide are not claiming that "PowerPoint" has, in fact, become a generic term in the marketplace.)

> **Answer (A) is incorrect.** To prove a trademark descriptive fair use defense, a competitor must show (1) use of the term other than as a mark, (2) in good faith, and (3) use of the term descriptively. *See* 15 U.S.C. § 1115(b)(4). Here the term "PowerPoint" is being used too prominently to be "other than as a mark."

Answer (B) is incorrect. "Nominative fair use" is, in a broad sense, an argument by a defendant that the defendant's use of another owner's mark was intended to refer to—or in other words to denominate or "nominate"—the other trademark owner in the mind of the consumer, rather than to create a likelihood of consumer confusion. To prove nominative fair use, in those jurisdictions that recognize that argument or that type of use of a mark as a separate concept (as opposed to taking it into account within the likelihood of confusion analysis), a competitor would prove some variation on the following test: (1) the product or service was not "readily identifiable" without use of the other trademark owner's mark; (2) the defendant did not use more of the mark than necessary; and (3) the defendant did not falsely suggest sponsorship or endorsement by the trademark owner. *See, e.g., Toyota Motor Sales v. Tabari*, 610 F.3d 1171 (9th Cir. 2010). Given that here, Prince PowerPoint would be the name of Prince Software's own product, and Prince would not simply be using "PowerPoint" to compare, for example, its software product's features to those of the Microsoft product or to explain compatibility with Microsoft PowerPoint, it would be quite difficult to convince a court that this use is "nominative," or actually intended to refer customers to the Microsoft product. *Cf. Toyota v. Tabari* (noting that the Tabaris were actually referring to Lexus products and the Tabaris' service of buying Lexus products for customers as automobile brokers when they used the URLs buy-a-lexus.com and buyorleaselexus.com).

Answer (D) is incorrect. A mark can be challenged if it has become generic, even if the mark has attained incontestable status. The statutes providing for incontestability and for the defenses that survive incontestability, as well as the statute governing cancellation proceedings, all set aside genericism as grounds to contest an otherwise "incontestable" mark. *See* 15 U.S.C. §§ 1064(3) (cancellation), 1065(4) (incontestability), and 1115(b)(2) (defenses to incontestability, referring to marks that have been "abandoned," the definition of which in 15 U.S.C. § 1127 includes situations where "the mark [has] become the generic name for the goods"). The Lanham Act specifically states that "no incontestable right shall be acquired in a mark which is the generic name for the goods or services or a portion thereof, for which it is registered." 15 U.S.C. § 1065.

Exam Answer 29. Answer (C) is correct. The trademark term "Sun" for a bank is arbitrary; there is no connection at all between the sun and banking services.

Answer (A) is incorrect. The term "Sun" does not describe characteristics of the bank.

Answer (B) is incorrect. The term "Sun" does not indirectly suggest something about the bank.

Answer (D) is incorrect. The term "Sun" was not coined to serve as a trademark.

Exam Answer 30. Answer (B) is correct. The trademark term "Good Housekeeping Seal of Approval" is a certification mark. The mark is used to certify the goods or services of others (third parties other than Good Housekeeping itself).

Answer (A) is incorrect. There is no evidence that the trademark term "Good Housekeeping Seal of Approval" is used misleadingly or deceives consumers.

Answer (C) is incorrect. The trademark term "Good Housekeeping Seal of Approval" does not signify membership in an association or cooperative organization.

Answer (D) is incorrect. Good Housekeeping does not market services under the "Good Housekeeping Seal of Approval" mark.

Exam Answer 31. Answer (B) is correct. The trademark term "Roquefort" for cheese originating in Roquefort, France—and meeting the production standard for that community's cured sheep's milk cheeses—is best characterized as a certification mark under these facts. The term signifies that this cured sheep's milk cheese meets the standards established for this variety of cheese, including having its origin in Roquefort, France. *See* 15 U.S.C. § 1127 (definition of "certification mark"). *See also Community of Roquefort v. William Faehndrich, Inc.*, 303 F.2d 494 (2d Cir. 1962).

> **Answer (A) is incorrect.** This is a second-best answer. Consumers can accurately connect "Roquefort" to Roquefort, France, as the geographic origin of the goods, but because of the additional facts regarding the community's standards, the best answer is (B).

> **Answer (C) is incorrect.** The term "Roquefort" does not signify membership in an association or cooperative organization.

> **Answer (D) is incorrect.** The term "Roquefort" is not used to market services.

Exam Answer 32. Answer (B) is correct. The term "Dallas Steak Company" for a steak restaurant in Dallas, Texas, is descriptive. It accurately identifies the geographic location of the restaurant and may be able to attain trademark status upon a showing of secondary meaning or consumer recognition.

> **Answer (A) is incorrect.** Although many may think of Texas as a place synonymous with steak, "Dallas" does not identify a particular type of steak, so the term is not generic.

> **Answer (C) is incorrect.** The term is not suggestive, as it does not have an indirect connection to the services (i.e., one that requires imagination to recognize).

> **Answer (D) is incorrect.** There is no evidence that the term is used by persons other than the owner to signify the origin of goods or services. Instead, this mark, on these facts, is used to indicate a single source of goods or services—although the facts do not indicate that the mark has acquired the distinctiveness required for registration.

Exam Answer 33. Answer (D) is correct. A candy maker produces a new product which is made with synthetic chocolate flavoring and which it would like to call "Chocolaty Chompers." This mark is likely to be found deceptive if there is no real chocolate ingredient in it. Courts apply a three-part test to assess whether a mark is deceptive under the Lanham Act: "(1) Is the term misdescriptive of the character, quality, function, composition or use of the goods? (2) If so, are prospective purchasers likely to believe that the misdescription actually describes the goods? (3) If so, is the misdescription likely to affect the decision to purchase?" *In re Budge Manufacturing Co.*, 857 F.2d 773, 775 (Fed. Cir. 1988). Applying this test, the term falsely implies that chocolate is an ingredient, purchasers are likely to believe this statement, and it is likely to affect the purchasing decision. Deceptive marks are barred from registration. *See* 15 U.S.C. § 1052 ("No trademark by which the goods of the applicant may be distinguished from the goods of others shall be refused registration on the principal register on account of its nature *unless it* (a) *consists of* or comprises immoral, *deceptive*, or scandalous *matter*; or matter which may disparage or falsely suggest a connection with persons, living or dead, institutions, beliefs, or national symbols, or bring them into contempt, or disrepute….") (emphasis added).

Answer (A) is incorrect. The term in question does not identify a category of candy.

Answer (B) is incorrect. The term in question does appear to describe a feature of the candy. Thus, if the statement were true, this term probably would be descriptive. Given its falsity in this case, however, it would be deceptive and thus barred from registration under the Lanham Act.

Answer (C) is incorrect. The term in question is not suggestive. Instead, it falsely describes the goods and is likely to be found deceptive.

Exam Answer 34. Answer (C) is correct. An automobile parts manufacturer develops a revolutionary new engine. The process of manufacturing the engine and the engine itself both involve significant improvements over existing automobile technology. The best legal advice in this situation is that the manufacturer should seek only patent protection for the engine itself and weigh its options on whether trade secret or patent law offers the best form of protection for its new manufacturing process. The engine is patentable subject matter, and it likely meets the novelty and nonobviousness standards on these bare facts. It would be susceptible to reverse engineering once on the market, however, which would render trade secret protection undesirable. The manufacturing process, on the other hand, could either be maintained as a trade secret or could be the basis for a process patent. The alternatives in this instance should be carefully weighed, taking into account the duration of its likely commercial value, whether the process is thought to be ascertainable by competitors or otherwise reasonably maintainable in secrecy, and the like.

Answer (A) is incorrect. This is incorrect in how it looks at the process. The manufacturer can maintain the manufacturing process as a trade secret even after it obtains patent protection for the engine. As long as it fully discloses the claimed features of the product, a firm can still maintain the production process for that product as a trade secret.

Answer (B) is incorrect. As discussed above in the explanation to correct Answer (C), the engine appears to be potentially patentable and would be susceptible to reverse engineering once on the market, which would render trade secret protection undesirable for the engine. There are also considerations to be balanced for how best to protect the process.

Answer (D) is incorrect. This statement incorrectly assumes that the engine itself could be maintained as a trade secret and that the best way to protect the process is through disclosure and patenting. The best advice is the direct opposite of this statement, as discussed above for correct Answer (C).

Exam Answer 35. A transformative use is an important consideration in analysis of copyright infringement cases, particularly in the determination of fair use. Transformative use was given particular emphasis in the Supreme Court's decision in *Campbell v. Acuff-Rose Music Inc.*, 510 U.S. 569 (1994). That case involved a Two Live Crew rap parody version of the copyrighted song "Oh Pretty Woman." Analyzing whether the parody was a fair use under the Copyright Act, the Court emphasized the need to analyze each fair use situation on a case-by-case, fact-specific basis. In addressing the first factor, the character of the use, the Court found that Two Live Crew's use of the copyrighted song was transformative in nature, which mitigated the effect of the commerciality of the use. More specifically, the Court noted that Two Live Crew substantially altered the original Roy Orbison song. In particular, the lyrics of the Two Live Crew song are substantially different from the original and convey a very different message. The transformative nature of the use weighs in favor of fair use.

As this book goes to press, the Supreme Court has granted certiorari in *Oracle Am., Inc. v. Google LLC*, 886 F.3d 1179 (Fed. Cir. 2018), cert. granted, 2019 WL 6042317 (U.S. Nov. 15, 2019)(No. 18-956). One of the issues on which the Court granted certiorari involves the scope and application of the fair use defense; when the Court analyzes this issue, it is likely to address once again the role of transformative use in the fair use analysis.

Exam Answer 36. Answer (A) is correct. The best form of intellectual property protection for a certain clothing design feature or fabric design is likely to be a copyright. *See Wal-Mart Stores, Inc. v. Samara Bros., Inc.*, 529 U.S. 205 (2000) (rejecting trademark claim for clothing design because of lack of secondary meaning, but not addressing the plaintiff's successful copyright claim, which it brought based on graphical features appliqued onto the articles of clothing). As commentators have noted, clothing designs have often failed to attain *any* form of protection. *See* Kal Raustiala & Christopher Sprigman, *The Piracy Paradox: Innovation and Intellectual Property in Fashion Design*, 92 Va. L. Rev. 1687 (2006); Julie P. Tsai, *Fashioning Protection: A Note on the Protection of Fashion Designs in the United States*, 9 Lewis & Clark L. Rev. 447, 447 (2005). Nonetheless, there have been instances in which some features of clothing design (particularly graphic design features or fabric patterns, but not the shape or overall "look" of the garment) have been found to be copyrightable.

In order to be eligible for copyright protection, the original, creative aspects of the clothing/fabric must be either conceptually or physically separable (or both) from the underlying function of the article. As the Supreme Court recently stated, "a feature incorporated into the design of a useful article is eligible for copyright protection only if the feature (1) can be perceived as a two- or three-dimensional work of art separate from the useful article and (2) would qualify as a protectable pictorial, graphic, or sculptural work—either on its own or fixed in some other tangible medium of expression—if it were imagined separately from the useful article into which it is incorporated." *Star Athletica, L.L.C. v. Varsity Brands, Inc.*, 137 S. Ct. 1002, 1007 (2017). Thus, for example, a shower curtain with a unique floral pattern or image of a sunset is separable from the functional features of the shower curtain; this design would be eligible for copyright protection.

There have been proposals to offer copyright-like protection for clothing designs as such, including the Design Piracy Prohibition Act, H.R. 5055, 109th Congress, 2d Session. To date, however, no fashion design bill has been enacted in the U.S.

Answer (B) is incorrect. Design patent law is ill-suited to protecting fashion designs, particularly given the high threshold for patentability (i.e., novelty and nonobviousness). While a design patent is available for an ornamental design applied to an article of manufacture, such as the design applied to the exterior of a mattress, which could be a design implemented through a patterned fabric, the claim is still limited to the design for that article of manufacture. The cost and time involved in obtaining patent protection are also unfavorable, and the duration of protection is shorter as well (just 15 years from issuance).

Answer (C) is incorrect. As discussed above, a copyright claim is likely to be more successful than a trademark claim as to certain clothing design features and fabric patterns. *See, e.g., Wal-Mart Stores, Inc. v. Samara Bros., Inc.*, 529 U.S. 205 (2000) (rejecting trademark or product-design trade dress claim for clothing design because of lack of secondary meaning but not addressing the plaintiff's successful copyright claim, which it brought based on graphical features appliqued onto the articles of clothing).

Answer (D) is incorrect. This answer is tempting, as there is an argument that no current form of intellectual property protection adequately protects clothing designs. As noted above, however, designers have had success in using copyright law to protect patterns that are then printed on fabric. Particular nonfunctional handbag designs have also occasionally gained trade dress protection.

Exam Answer 37. Answer (B) is correct. The trademark term "Lyft" is best characterized as suggestive for the service of providing temporary use of online, non-downloadable software for providing transportation services, bookings for transportation services, and dispatching motorized vehicles to customers. Although it is a misspelling of "Lift," and the word "Lyft" with that spelling did not previously exist, that does not make it a "fanciful" mark.

The overarching question in characterizing a mark for distinctiveness purposes is how—in the context of the goods and services in connection with which the mark is used—consumers will perceive the mark. As a result, the initial question when a word is a misspelling or phonetic equivalent of another word is whether—in the context of the relevant goods and services—consumers will perceive the different spelling as the equivalent of the other word or term. *See, e.g., In re State Chem. Mfg. Co.*, 225 U.S.P.Q. 687 (T.T.A.B. 1985) (holding "FOM" to be merely descriptive of foam rug shampoo because it was and would be understood to be the phonetic spelling of "foam"). Here, in the context of providing use of software that connects customers to motor vehicles, a reasonable customer would perceive "lyft" just as they would the word "lift," its phonetic equivalent. A "lift," in this context, would be thought of as a ride given to a person in a motor vehicle (usually for free, and by a friend or acquaintance).

The next question is how close the relationship is between the "car ride" meaning of "lyft/lift" and the services of the would-be trademark owner, in the mind of the reasonable consumer. Suggestive marks have some association with the relevant goods or services, but some "imagination" or "perception" (or maybe an "aha, I get it!" moment) is required to see the connection or association between the mark and the goods or services. There is a relationship between the "free car ride with a friend" meaning of "lyft/lift" and the service of use of software to find a driver who can be paid to drive a customer, but it is a somewhat indirect relationship. Because the service here is use of software to match providers and customers of motor vehicle transportation, rather than the actual provision of transportation services by motor vehicle (although the line is thin), the best categorization of this mark is suggestive. (This is true at least when the services are described as they are in the question above; it would no longer be true if the service connected to the "Lyft/Lift" mark were described as the direct provision of transportation by motor vehicle by the mark owner.)

Answer (A) is incorrect. This is the second-best answer. As explained above, this is a close call and may depend on exactly what the services are, or the way in which the services are described. A mark is merely descriptive if it describes an ingredient, quality, characteristic, function, feature, purpose, or use of an applicant's services. As explained above in connection with correct Answer (B), "lyft" is the phonetic misspelling of "lift," which is a ride given to a person in a motor vehicle, and the common understanding is that a "lift"-type of car ride is for free and from a friend, family member, or acquaintance. Although the two are fairly closely related, and the line is a fine one, the services in question in the facts are use of online software to obtain transportation, rather than transportation services themselves; also, the software-enabled connection or networking service provided under the mark ultimately connects a customer to transportation from a stranger working for hire rather than to transportation from someone driving for free (and not a friend or family member).

Answer (C) is incorrect. The trademark term "Lyft" is not arbitrary as applied to services that relate to a customer's ability to obtain a ride in a motor vehicle.

Answer (D) is incorrect. The trademark term "Lyft" is not fanciful. As noted above, a simple and easily understood misspelling will not create a fanciful mark when the mark has a relationship to the mark owner's goods or services.

Exam Answer 38. Answer (C) is correct. Injunctive relief is usually granted to successful utility patent owner plaintiffs, and actual damages can be recovered as well—and the language of the Act sets out a floor to measure those actual damages. Section 284 of the Patent Act sets forth the types of damage recoveries available to patent holders: "Upon finding for the claimant the court shall award the claimant damages adequate to compensate for the infringement *but in no event less than a reasonable royalty for the use made of the invention by the infringer,* together with interest and costs as fixed by the court." (Emphasis added).

Answer (A) is incorrect. As noted above, the measure of minimum recovery under section 284 for infringement of a utility patent is a "reasonable royalty," not the infringer's profits. Section 284, which addresses damages for utility patent infringement, does not provide for recovery of the infringer's profits as such. The Patent Act does provide an additional remedy for *design patent infringement* that looks to the infringer's profits. That provision directs the award of the infringer's "total profit" earned through the manufacture or sale of articles of manufacture to which the patented design has been applied, but not less than $250. *See* 35 U.S.C. § 289; *Samsung Electronics Co. v. Apple, Inc.*, 137 S. Ct. 429 (2016)

Answer (B) is incorrect. The patent owner's lost profits are recoverable under section 284 as part of the "damages adequate to compensate for the infringement," but the floor or *minimum* recovery in the statute is a "reasonable royalty." If the patentee's lost profits exceed a reasonable royalty, on the other hand, the patent owner can recover the higher amount.

Answer (D) is incorrect. Statutory damages are not available in the Patent Act.

Exam Answer 39. Answer (C) is correct. Nonobviousness can be best described as a showing that the invention involves an inventive step past the prior art in the view of a skilled person, not just any distinction compared to the prior art. In other words, nonobviousness of an invention requires a departure from the prior art that would not have been apparent to a person having ordinary skill in the art (PHOSITA). Section 103 of the Patent Act states: "A patent may not be obtained notwithstanding that the claimed invention is not identically disclosed as set forth in section 102, if the differences between the claimed invention and the prior art are such that the claimed invention as a whole would have been obvious before the effective filing date of the claimed invention to a person having ordinary skill in the art to which the claimed invention pertains. Patentability shall not be negated by the manner in which the invention was made." *See Graham v. John Deere Co.*, 383 U.S. 1, 17–18 (1966) ("Under § 103, the scope and content of the prior art are to be determined; differences between the prior art and the claims at issue are to be ascertained; and the level of ordinary skill in the pertinent art resolved. Against this background the obviousness or nonobviousness of the subject matter is determined.").

Answer (A) is incorrect. This statement is not relevant to either novelty or nonobviousness under the current Patent Act. Under pre-AIA patent law, there was some obviousness relevance to prior knowledge by others before the date of invention, but current law does not utilize the date of invention.

Answer (B) is incorrect. This statement is a portion of the novelty inquiry under the Patent Act. *See* 35 U.S.C. § 102(a). Moreover, nonobviousness requires a conceptual inventive step beyond novelty. See the explanation to correct Answer (C).

Answer (D) is incorrect. This standard focuses on the applicant-inventor's perspective rather than section 103's person having ordinary skill in the art.

Exam Answer 40. Answer (A) is correct. The changes to sections 102 and 103 of the Patent Act enacted as part of the America Invents Act (AIA) took effect on March 16, 2013, and they affect the validity of all patents containing claims with an effective filing date on or after March 16, 2013. The novelty and nonobviousness of inventions within applications containing only claims with effective filing dates before March 16, 2013 will continue to be judged under the pre-AIA sections 102 and 103.

Answer (B) is incorrect. As stated above, the standards of novelty and nonobviousness of patents existing on March 16, 2013, or of inventions within applications containing only claims with effective filing dates before that date, will continue to be judged under the pre-AIA sections 102 and 103 — regardless of the context in which their validity is examined, including reexamination.

Answer (C) is incorrect. As stated above, the standards of novelty and nonobviousness of patents existing on March 16, 2013, or of inventions within applications containing only claims with effective filing dates before that date, will continue to be judged under the pre-AIA sections 102 and 103 — regardless of the context in which their validity is examined, including later invalidity challenges during infringement litigation.

Answer (D) is incorrect. Answer (A) is the only correct answer.

Exam Answer 41. Answer (A) is correct. A work was published without proper copyright notice in 1970. Under present law, this work is likely in the public domain. Copyright notices were required under the 1909 Act and works published without the copyright notice fell into the public domain. Later amendments did not change this result, unless this was a foreign work whose copyright was restored under 17 U.S.C. § 104A. These facts do not allude to foreign authorship or first publication in a foreign country.

Answer (B) is incorrect. The "cure" provisions are not relevant to works that were published before the effective date of the 1976 Copyright Act, which was January 1, 1978. Instead, the "cure" provisions potentially affect works published between Jan. 1, 1978 and March 1, 1989. Thus, the work in question is still governed by the strict rule of the 1909 Act, unless restored under section 104A.

Answer (C) is incorrect. This statement as to likely protection would only apply to works that were not published before the effective date of the Berne Convention Implementation Act, which is March 1, 1989. The work in question is still governed by the strict rule of the 1909 Act.

Answer (D) is incorrect. The Sonny Bono Copyright Term Extension Act had no effect on the copyright notice issue.

Exam Answer 42. Answer (D) is correct. In most states, misappropriation of a trade secret is governed by the Uniform Trade Secrets Act (UTSA). As of 2019, 48 states and the District of Columbia, as well as the Virgin Islands, had adopted the UTSA either in whole or with only moderate changes. Under the federal civil action, often called the DTSA (for the Defend Trade Secrets Act of 2016), as well as under the UTSA, "misappropriation" includes all of the acts of obtaining, using, and disclosing the trade secret without consent. In fuller terms, the DTSA and UTSA encompass within misappropriation: obtaining another's trade secret, when the acquirer knows or has reason to know that the information was acquired by improper means; and either disclosing or using another's trade secret without the other's consent, when the discloser or user either used improper means to obtain the information or knows or has reason to know that the information had been either obtained by improper means or had been obtained as a result of a breach of confidence or outside the scope of permitted use.

Answer (A) is incorrect. Obtaining a trade secret, when the acquirer knows or has reason to know that the information was acquired by improper means, does constitute misappropriation, but using and disclosing the trade secret are also potential acts of misappropriation.

Answer (B) is incorrect. Using a trade secret of another without the other's express consent does constitute misappropriation when the user either used improper means to obtain the information or knows or has reason to know that the information had been either obtained by improper means or had been obtained as a result of a breach of confidence or outside the scope of permitted use. Both obtaining the secret and disclosing the secret are, however, also potential acts of misappropriation.

Answer (C) is incorrect. Disclosing a trade secret of another without the other's express consent does constitute misappropriation when the discloser either used improper means to obtain the information or knows or has reason to know that the information had been either obtained by improper means or had been obtained as a result of a breach of confidence or outside the scope of permitted use. Both obtaining the secret and using the secret are, however, also potential acts of misappropriation.

Exam Answer 43. Answer (C) is correct. An ordinary citizen (who is not a famous celebrity) has her name and image used on a billboard advertisement for a restaurant without her consent. Her best claim is a violation of the right of publicity or privacy under applicable state law. Note that the answer option is "right of publicity or privacy," acknowledging the shared history and basis of those actions. It is a common misconception that *only* celebrities or famous persons have a right of publicity action, as their endorsements tend to have far greater commercial value. While some states that recognize publicity rights may limit the "publicity" strand of the law to celebrities whose identities have had prior commercial value, many or most do not, and even those that do will provide a somewhat similar privacy action (even if under the common law) for an ordinary citizen. In any event, as long as the elements of a right of publicity claim are met, the claim is worth pursuing. *See, e.g.,* Restatement (Third) of Unfair Competition § 46 ("One who appropriates the commercial value of a person's identity by using without consent the person's name, likeness, or other indicia of identity for purposes of trade is subject to liability for the relief appropriate under the rules stated in §§ 48 and 49."). Those elements appear to be met on these facts.

> **Answer (A) is incorrect.** The ordinary citizen in this scenario would not have a federal copyright claim related to the photograph because she was not the author of that work—the photographer who took the image would ordinarily be the author and owner of the copyright (unless the photograph was a "work made for hire"). If the photo was taken without the subject's knowledge or consent, copyright law does not provide the subject of the photo with a remedy for the activity described.

> **Answer (B) is incorrect.** The use of an ordinary citizen's image would not lead a reasonable consumer to believe that the citizen depicted was endorsing the product or service. The ordinary citizen would not have any reasonable chance of success with a claim of false endorsement under the Lanham Act, because those claims require the plaintiff to prove a likelihood of consumer confusion, mistake, or deception as to the endorsement, sponsorship, or affiliation between the plaintiff and the defendant. *See, e.g., Albert v. Apex Fitness, Inc.,* 1997 U.S. Dist. LEXIS 8535 (S.D.N.Y. June 12, 1997). When consumers have no idea who the person on the billboard is, consumers fail to make an endorsement-type link between the person pictured and the advertiser, which means there will be no viable false endorsement claim.

> **Answer (D) is incorrect.** As discussed above, ordinary citizens can have a cause of action for violation of their right of publicity or privacy under (applicable) state law, as explained above for correct Answer (C).

Exam Answer 44. Answer (D) is correct. Section 504 of the Copyright Act sets forth the measures or types of damage recoveries available from a copyright infringer, but it does not provide a floor for the award of damages in all successful infringement cases, as does the Patent Act. (*See* Practice Exam Answer 38 above.) With respect to actual damages and profits, the Copyright Act requires proof that the owner's damages were the "result of the infringement" before they may be recovered, and it allows recovery of the infringer's profits, but only to the extent that they were "attributable to the infringement." 17 U.S.C. §504(b). Statutory damages do exist; they are addressed below in connection with incorrect Answer (C).

Answer (A) is incorrect. The Copyright Act does not provide for damages for harm to the reputation of the copyright owner of a literary work. *Cf.* 17 U.S.C. § 106A (protecting additional, non-economic interests of the author of a work of visual art).

Answer (B) is incorrect. The owner's lost profits are recoverable to the extent that they were the "result of the infringement," but that proof can be difficult, *see, e.g., Frank Music Corp. v. Metro-Goldwyn-Mayer, Inc.*, 772 F.2d 505 (9th Cir. 1985), and a court may decline to award any amount if the court believes the evidence offered is too speculative.

Answer (C) is incorrect. Although statutory damages are available in the Copyright Act, this is not the best answer because those statutory damages do not serve as a minimum recovery for all copyright owners in all successful infringement actions. For most copyright owners (with some provisions for pre-registration aside, which do not apply to most copyright owners), statutory damages are only available if the work either (1) was registered before the infringement commenced or (2) was registered within three months of first publication of the work and the infringement commenced during that short window between publication and registration. *See* 17 U.S.C. §412.

Exam Answer 45. Answer (C) is correct. Section 284 of the Patent Act provides that: "Upon finding for the claimant, the court shall award the claimant damages adequate to compensate for the infringement, but in no event less than a reasonable royalty for the use made of the invention by the infringer." The minimum award is thus a reasonable royalty, but if the plaintiff patent owner can prove lost profits on its own competitive product that were caused by the infringement, those would be recoverable as reasonably foreseeable damages. *See, e.g., Rite-Hite Corp. v. Kelley Co., Inc.*, 56 F.3d 1538 (Fed. Cir. 1995).

Answer (A) is incorrect. Section 284 does not provide for recovery of the defendant infringer's own profits. The minimum damage award of a reasonable royalty could take into account, in assessing what royalty is reasonable, the amount of profit earned by the defendant as a result of the infringement. The only portion of the Patent Act providing for the infringer's profits as such is section 289, which is only applicable to design patent infringement. *See* 35 U.S.C. § 289; *cf.* 15 U.S.C. § 1117(b) (providing, among other measures of monetary recovery under the Lanham Act, that "plaintiff shall be entitled, subject to the provisions of sections 1111 and 1114 of this title, and subject to the principles of equity, to recover (1) defendant's profits").

Answer (B) is incorrect. Under section 285, an award of attorney's fees is permitted only in "exceptional cases." 35 U.S.C. §285. While fees may be awarded in cases where infringement was not willful, the defendant would generally need to have engaged in some sort of misconduct, such as frivolous filings or vexatious litigation conduct, taking the case outside the typical case of unintentional infringement. *See Octane Fitness, LLC v. Icon Health & Fitness, Inc.*, 134 S. Ct. 1749, 1756 (2014) (holding that an "exceptional" case for an award of attorney's fees under section 285 is one "that stands out from others with respect to the substantive strength of a party's litigating position (considering both the governing law and the facts of the case) or the unreasonable manner in which the case was litigated," and that [d]istrict courts may determine whether a case is 'exceptional' in the case-by-case exercise of their discretion, considering the totality of the circumstances.").

Answer (D) is not correct. See the explanations above.

Exam Answer 46. Answer (C) is correct. If your client owns a trademark that has been used from 2010 to the present in Pennsylvania and New Jersey but never registered anywhere, you can advise the client that it may have a civil action against an infringer under both the state common law of unfair competition and under section 43(a) of the Lanham Act, which does not require federal registration by a trademark plaintiff, as long as the requisite nexus with "commerce" (defined in the Act as coextensive with Congress's commerce power) is present. *See* 15 U.S.C. § 1125(a)(1)(A). Although the facts specify that there is no federal diversity jurisdiction between the client and the infringer, you could file the claims in either federal or state court. Federal district courts have original, but not exclusive, jurisdiction over Lanham Act claims. *See* 28 U.S.C. § 1338(a). And under 28 U.S.C. § 1338(b), federal district courts have original jurisdiction over civil claims of unfair competition "when joined with a substantial and related claim under the … trademark laws." Most trademark owners prefer to bring trademark claims in federal court, because of those courts' greater familiarity with trademark law.

> **Answer (A) is incorrect.** Although your client would indeed be able to bring its claims in state court — even its Lanham Act claims — it can also bring them all in federal court, as explained above.

> **Answer (B) is incorrect.** Although your client would indeed be able to bring its claims in federal court — even its state unfair competition claims, if joined with its Lanham Act claim — it can also bring them all in state court, as explained above.

> **Answer (D) is incorrect.** Your client can bring claims in either state or federal court.

Exam Answer 47. Answer (C) is correct. If your client owns a trademark that has been used from 2010 up to the present in Pennsylvania and New Jersey and was registered in 2019 with the U.S. Patent & Trademark Office, you can advise the client that it may have a civil action against an infringer under both the state common law of unfair competition and under section 32 of the Lanham Act. Section 32, unlike section 43(a), requires federal registration of the mark being asserted. Your client could also, for good measure, assert a claim under section 43(a), particularly if its use-based rights in the mark might arguably be broader than the rights reflected in the registration. *See* 15 U.S.C. §§ 1114(1) & 1125(a)(1)(A). Although the facts specify that there is no federal diversity jurisdiction between the client and the infringer, you could file the claims in either federal or state court. Federal district courts have original, but not exclusive, jurisdiction over Lanham Act claims. *See* 28 U.S.C. § 1338(a). And under 28 U.S.C. § 1338(b), federal district courts have original jurisdiction over civil claims of unfair competition "when joined with a substantial and related claim under the … trademark laws."

Answer (A) is incorrect. Although your client would indeed be able to bring its claims in state court—even its Lanham Act claim or claims—it can also bring them all in federal court, as explained above.

Answer (B) is incorrect. Although your client would indeed be able to bring its claims in federal court—even its state unfair competition claims, if joined with its Lanham Act claim or claims—it can also bring them all in state court, as explained above.

Answer (D) is incorrect. Your client can bring claims in either state or federal court.

Exam Answer 48. Answer (C) is correct. Inventor B is likely to receive the patent rights. Inventor A conceived of an invention and reduced it to practice in the year 2001, but A did not proceed to seek patent protection. Inventor B independently conceived of the same invention in December 2009. B reduced it to practice in March 2010. Learning of B's efforts, A applied for a patent in May 2010. B applied for a patent in June 2010. Although pre-AIA U.S. patent law ordinarily gives priority to the "first to conceive" an invention, this rule does not apply if that inventor suppresses the invention, conceals it, or acts with a lack of diligence. Pre-AIA section 102(g) of the Patent Act states:

> A person shall be entitled to a patent unless— ... (1) during the course of an interference conducted under section 135 or section 291, another inventor involved therein establishes, to the extent permitted in section 104, that before such person's invention thereof the invention was made by such other inventor and not abandoned, suppressed, or concealed, or (2) before such person's invention thereof, the invention was made in this country by another inventor who had not abandoned, suppressed, or concealed it. In determining priority of invention under this subsection, there shall be considered not only the respective dates of conception and reduction to practice of the invention, but also the reasonable diligence of one who was first to conceive and last to reduce to practice, from a time prior to conception by the other.

Thus, the first inventor could lose priority if that inventor failed to exercise reasonable diligence in reducing the invention to practice or if the first inventor abandoned, suppressed, or concealed the invention. As noted in *Paulik v. Rizkalla*, 760 F.2d 1270, 1275 (Fed. Cir. 1985):

> The decisions applying section 102(g) balanced the law and policy favoring the first person to make an invention, against equitable considerations when more than one person had made the same invention: in each case where the court deprived the de facto first inventor of the right to the patent, the second inventor had entered the field during a period of either inactivity or deliberate concealment by the first inventor. Often the first inventor had been spurred to file a patent application by news of the second inventor's activities. Although "spurring" is not necessary to a finding of suppression or concealment, the courts' frequent references to spurring indicate their concern with this equitable factor.

Here, Inventor A appears to have failed to act diligently and was "spurred" into seeking patent protection by learning of the inventive efforts made by Inventor B.

Answer (A) is incorrect. As discussed above, the first to conceive of the invention received the patent rights under pre-AIA patent law, but not if there was a failure to act diligently, which can be shown in this case.

Answer (B) is incorrect. Inventor A does not appear to have acted diligently in seeking patent protection, as discussed above.

Answer (D) is incorrect. Joint inventors are required to work together in at least some way—there is no collaboration on these facts.

Exam Answer 49. Answer (A) is correct. The primary source of Congress's authority to protect semiconductors (computer chips or mask works) in the Semiconductor Chip Protection Act is the Commerce Clause. Congress sought to avoid any issue as to whether the mask works constituted a "writing" under the Intellectual Property Clause by invoking the Commerce Clause power. *See* Edward C. Walterscheid, The Nature of the Intellectual Property Clause: A Study in Historical Perspective, 463 & n.132 (2002).

Answer (B) is incorrect. As discussed above, Congress sought to avoid any issue as to whether the mask works constituted a "writing" under the Intellectual Property Clause by invoking the Commerce Clause power.

Answer (C) is incorrect. The Necessary and Proper Clause does not independently support Congress's authority to enact statutory protection for mask works.

Answer (D) is incorrect. The First Amendment is a limit on congressional power, not a general source of law-making authority.

Exam Answer 50. Answer (C) is correct. A consumer buys a copyrighted print and scans it onto a digital file and then posts a full-size image of the print on the Internet. The consumer has violated both the right of reproduction and the right of public display. By scanning the photo to create the digital file, the consumer has reproduced the work in a copy in violation of section 106(1). There is no "exception" for a private copy (and these bare facts alone do not support fair use). The consumer has also publicly displayed the work. To display a work "publicly" includes, under section 101, transmitting a display to members of the public. *See* 17 U.S.C. § 101 (definition of "publicly"). Section 101 of the Copyright Act also provides that to "display" a work "means to show a copy of it, either directly or by means of a film, slide, television image, or any other device or process or, in the case of a motion picture or other audiovisual work, to show individual images nonsequentially." Posting a work on the Internet is considered a public display. *See, e.g., Kelly v. Arriba Soft Corp.*, 280 F.3d 934 (9th Cir. 2002). The first-sale protection for public displays only applies when the display is to viewers present at the place where the lawful copy is located, not to transmissions of displays. *See* 17 U.S.C. § 109(c). Thus, both rights are likely to be violated on these facts.

Answer (A) is incorrect. As discussed above, both the right of reproduction and the right of public display are violated on these facts.

Answer (B) is incorrect. As discussed above, both the right of reproduction and the right of public display are violated on these facts.

Answer (D) is incorrect. The first sale doctrine does not apply since the consumer has not transferred or displayed the original, lawful copy of the work and has instead violated other rights of the copyright owner.

Exam Answer 51. Answer (D) is correct. A teenage computer hacker develops software code to enable anyone receiving streaming video, such as a movie watched via the Internet from Netflix, to be able to download a permanent copy onto a computer. The hacker posts the code onto the Internet, with the announcement—"I am king of the world. Anyone can download movies for free now. Have at it, people!" The hacker most likely has violated rights under the Digital Millennium Copyright Act ("DMCA") and committed secondary copyright infringement by contributory infringement or inducement. The DMCA prohibits trafficking in anti-circumvention devices. *See* 17 U.S.C. 1201(a)(2) ("No person shall manufacture, import, offer to the public, provide, or otherwise traffic in any technology, product, service, device, component, or part thereof, that—(A) is primarily designed or produced for the purpose of circumventing a technological measure that effectively controls access to a work protected under this title; (B) has only limited commercially significant purpose or use other than to circumvent a technological measure that effectively controls access to a work protected under this title; or (C) is marketed by that person or another acting in concert with that person with that person's knowledge for use in circumventing a technological measure that effectively controls access to a work protected under this title."); *Universal City Studios, Inc. v. Reimerdes*, 111 F. Supp. 2d 294 (S.D.N.Y. 2000), *aff'd sub nom., Universal City Studios, Inc. v. Corley*, 273 F.3d 429 (2d Cir. 2001). As for secondary liability, it is likely that the hacker can be found to have intentionally encouraged others to violate copyright law and to have provided the tools by which to do so (inducement). *See MGM Studios, Inc. v. Grokster, Ltd.*, 545 U.S. 913 (2005).

Answer (A) is incorrect. The facts show no direct violation of these rights.

Answer (B) is incorrect. As discussed above, the hacker has most likely committed secondary copyright infringement and violated the DMCA.

Answer (C) is incorrect. As discussed above, the hacker has most likely committed secondary copyright infringement and violated the DMCA.

Exam Answer 52. "Employee" status for one of the two forms of "work made for hire" under copyright law (i.e., a work "prepared by an employee within the scope of … employment") is to be analyzed using factors derived from the common law agency standard, as explained and set forth in *Community for Creative Non-Violence v. Reid*, 490 U.S. 730 (1989). When faced with how to define "employee," the Court's first step was to look at the two forms of "work made for hire," after which it concluded that: "The structure of § 101 indicates that a work for hire can arise through one of two mutually exclusive means, one for employees and one for independent contractors, and ordinary canons of statutory interpretation indicate that the classification of a particular hired party should be made with reference to agency law." In a later portion of the opinion the Court provided a range of considerations derived from agency law:

> In determining whether a hired party is an employee under the general common law
> of agency, we consider the hiring party's right to control the manner and means by

which the product is accomplished. Among the other factors relevant to this inquiry are the skill required; the source of the instrumentalities and tools; the location of the work; the duration of the relationship between the parties; whether the hiring party has the right to assign additional projects to the hired party; the extent of the hired party's discretion over when and how long to work; the method of payment; the hired party's role in hiring and paying assistants; whether the work is part of the regular business of the hiring party; whether the hiring party is in business; the provision of employee benefits; and the tax treatment of the hired party.

If a hired party is deemed an employee under this agency standard, then authorship vests in the employer. On the other hand, if the hired party is found to be an independent contractor, then that individual has authorship rights.

Exam Answer 53. Answer (A) is correct. Record Co. sells its copyrighted songs worldwide. It licenses a British company to make and sell CDs in the United Kingdom but not to import them into the United States. The British company makes CDs in a factory in England. One of its wholesale distributors sells them to a U.S. distributor, which sells them to buyers in the United States, resulting in a copyright suit by Record Co. against the U.S. distributor. Record Co. will likely lose because of the first sale defense. *See* 17 U.S.C. § 109(a) ("Notwithstanding the provisions of section 106(3) [the right of distribution], the owner of a particular copy or phonorecord lawfully made under this title, or any person authorized by such owner, is entitled, without the authority of the copyright owner, to sell or otherwise dispose of the possession of that copy or phonorecord."). In *Kirtsaeng v. John Wiley & Sons, Inc.*, 133 S. Ct. 1351 (2013), the Supreme Court ruled that a copy or phonorecord owned by a distributor or reseller could be "lawfully made under this title" and subject to section 109(a), even if made abroad, as long as it was made under the authority of the copyright owner and would therefore be a lawful copy of phonorecord if U.S. law had governed its making.

> **Answer (B) is incorrect.** The first sale defense applies to lawful copies of works, including musical works.

> **Answer (C) is incorrect.** As discussed above, the Supreme Court has rejected this argument.

> **Answer (D) is incorrect.** The fair use defense is not the best defense on these facts, as shown above.

Exam Answer 54. Answer (A) is correct. The type of patentable subject matter having the shortest term is the design patent. The current term for newly filed design patents is 15 years from the date of issuance. Section 173 of the Patent Act states: "Patents for designs shall be granted for the term of 15 years from the date of grant." Until relatively recently, the design patent term was 14 years from issuance, but all design patents issued in the United States on applications filed on or after May 13, 2015 now have a term of 15 years from the grant. For a bit more detail, see Question 85 and its Answer in Topic 8.

> **Answer (B) is incorrect.** Plant patents have a term of 20 years from the filing of the patent application.

Answer (C) is incorrect. Utility patents have a term of 20 years from the filing of the patent application.

Answer (D) is incorrect. See the explanations above.

Exam Answer 55. Answer (B) is correct. The following statement most accurately describes the current importance of a copyright notice for a work first published in 1982 — copyright notices are required and works published without the copyright notice fall into the public domain unless "cured" under the Copyright Act of 1976. The Copyright Act of 1976 provisions in effect in 1982 essentially still apply to this work because it was first published in that year. The 1976 Act ameliorated the harsh effect of the copyright notice requirement under the 1909 Copyright Act, under which a work published without notice fell into the public domain. The 1976 Act continued to require copyright notice, but it allowed for a cure of, or excuse for, the omission of the notice in some circumstances. The cure provision continues to be relevant if copyright protection might have been lost between 1978–1989 due to the omitted notice, even though current law no longer requires copyright notice for new copies of a work published after March 1, 1989. Section 405(a) of the Copyright Act, which would govern the work in question, states:

> (a) Effect of Omission on Copyright. — With respect to copies and phonorecords publicly distributed by authority of the copyright owner before the effective date of the Berne Convention Implementation Act of 1988, the omission of the copyright notice described in sections 401 through 403 from copies or phonorecords publicly distributed by authority of the copyright owner does not invalidate the copyright in a work if —
>
> > (1) the notice has been omitted from no more than a relatively small number of copies or phonorecords distributed to the public; or
> >
> > (2) registration for the work has been made before or is made within five years after the publication without notice, and a reasonable effort is made to add notice to all copies or phonorecords that are distributed to the public in the United States after the omission has been discovered; or
> >
> > (3) the notice has been omitted in violation of an express requirement in writing that, as a condition of the copyright owner's authorization of the public distribution of copies or phonorecords, they bear the prescribed notice.

17 U.S.C. § 405(a). *See generally Hasbro Bradley, Inc. v. Sparkle Toys, Inc.*, 780 F.2d 189 (2d Cir. 1985) (applying 1976 Act notice requirement and cure provisions).

Answer (A) is incorrect. As discussed above, a strict notice requirement applied prior to the effective date of the Copyright Act of 1976. The requirement was modified by that statute for works first published on or after that date — January 1, 1978.

Answer (C) is incorrect. This rule — the lack of a notice requirement whatsoever — only applies to works first published after March 1, 1989, when the Berne Convention Implementation Act of 1988 took effect.

Answer (D) is incorrect. As noted above, the BCIA eliminated the notice requirement for copies of works published after March 1, 1989. The Sonny Bono Copyright Term Extension Act made a number of modifications to copyright law, but it did not address the notice requirement.

Exam Answer 56. Answer (C) is correct. Protection of intellectual property rights can be described as solving a public goods problem. The standard public goods problem involves a product or service that has a number of basic characteristics. In a state of nature (i.e., without legal protections), a public good created by one person can easily be appropriated by another, which can lead to "free rider" problems. In other words, people can make use of the efforts of others without compensating them. Because of this problem, there is underinvestment in public goods absent property rights or another mechanism to reward innovation. Ironically, another feature of a public good such as intellectual property is that it is not exhaustible. The use of the good (or service) by some does not diminish the ability of others to enjoy the substance of the good (or service). If one person reads a book or listens to a song, that action does not prevent another person from enjoying it—as the wave of music file-sharing has shown, sharing music is now almost costless. The classic example of a public good in the standard economics text is the provision of national defense. Once a nuclear arsenal is created to protect persons in a nation, everyone in that nation benefits from it; in addition, once national defense is established, more people can be protected by the arsenal with few to no additional costs (within the same geographic area). For this reason, the government provides national defense because it would not likely be produced in a completely free market. Similarly, intellectual property law solves the free rider problem by giving property rights to inventions and creative works. Patents and copyrights provide incentives for investment in research and development or creative endeavor, and unauthorized use can diminish the economic returns available to the creator by diminishing the ability of the creator to charge for access or use. Yet like other public goods, once the invention or creative work has been made, the unauthorized use of that intellectual property by others does not diminish its creator's enjoyment of its substance (e.g., the quality of the music or the function of the device).

Answer (A) is incorrect. Protection of intellectual property does not solve a monopoly problem. An economic monopoly exists when there are, practically, no available substitutes for a particular product or service, and thus the seller is able to control prices and obtain unusually high profits. It is often stated that intellectual property rights confer a legal monopoly, although whether this right to exclude is truly an economic monopoly depends on the existence of practically available and acceptable substitutes in the marketplace.

Answer (B) is incorrect. Moral hazard is an economic problem involving the likelihood that someone who is insulated from risks will change their behavior, particularly by taking greater risks than they would otherwise. A classic illustration is insurance coverage, because coverage against losses might increase the risk-taking behavior of the insured. Thus, a contract or a government action that insulates parties from risks can lead to greater risky behavior. The moral hazard problem, however, does not have any particular relevance to intellectual property.

Answer (D) is incorrect. As discussed above, moral hazard and monopoly problems are not generally solved by providing intellectual property rights.

Exam Answer 57. Answer (B) is correct. Patents offer a broad right to exclude others from making, using, selling, offering to sell, or importing the patented invention for the term of the patent. There is no defense for reverse engineering or independent development of the invention.

Answer (A) is incorrect. Copyrights do offer some exclusivity as to the rights of copyright owners, but these rights are limited by a large range of defenses including independent creation, the idea/expression distinction, and the fair use defense.

Answer (C) is incorrect. Trademark law, unless there is a famous trademark (or bad faith cybersquatting), offers only the right to prevent a likelihood of consumer confusion. There are also defenses for, among other things, descriptive fair use and limited area prior users. The rights of the owner of a federally registered trademark owner, while strong and not subject to a defense of "innocent" or "independent" development, are not absolute and are highly contextual. A competitor can even make limited, careful use of another's trademark in comparative labeling or advertising without creating trademark liability.

Answer (D) is incorrect. Trade secret protection does offer some exclusivity, but the owner of a trade secret can only exclude competitors who obtain the information by breach of confidence, improper means, or other similar conduct. Moreover, trade secret claims do not prevent reverse engineering or independent development.

Exam Answer 58. Answer (C) is correct. A feature of a product that is primarily functional, but is also simultaneously original and aesthetically pleasing, can be protected under utility patent law, which protects useful inventions. The fact that the functional feature also happens to be aesthetically pleasing or original will not disqualify it from being protected by a utility patent, nor will the fact that consumers, during the duration of the patent, might find it distinctive of source.

Answer (A) is incorrect. Copyright law does not offer protection for functional or useful features of a product. As defined in section 101 of the Copyright Act, a "'useful article' is an article having an intrinsic utilitarian function that is not merely to portray the appearance of the article or to convey information." As then explained in the definition of a "pictorial, graphic, or sculptural work,"

> the design of a useful article, as defined in this section, shall be considered a pictorial, graphic, or sculptural work [and protected] only if, and only to the extent that, such design incorporates pictorial, graphic, or sculptural features that can be identified separately from, and are capable of existing independently of, the utilitarian aspects of the article.

17 U.S.C. § 101. *See also Star Athletica, L.L.C. v. Varsity Brands, Inc.*, 137 S. Ct. 1002 (2017). So, while an original feature of a useful article can be protected if that feature is not itself functional or utilitarian, if the feature in question is itself utilitarian or functional and the original features cannot be separately identified from the utilitarian aspects, then copyright cannot protect the feature.

Answer (B) is incorrect. Trademark law cannot protect functional or useful features of product design, although product designs that are nonfunctional can be protected if they have acquired distinctiveness in the marketplace. *See TrafFix Devices, Inc. v. Marketing Displays, Inc.*, 532 U.S. 23 (2001) (providing a multi-part test for functionality of product features, or trade dress); *Wal-Mart Stores, Inc. v. Samara Bros., Inc.*, 529 U.S. 205 (2000) (acquired distinctiveness required for product design trade dress).

Answer (D) is incorrect. As discussed above, functional features can be protected by utility patents, even when the feature also happens to be original and aesthetically pleasing or has become distinctive or source-identifying. Functionality, however, is a bar to protecting a feature through copyright or trademark law.

Exam Answer 59. Answer (D) is correct. All three listed forms of intellectual property protection are potentially available for computer software—patents, copyrights, and trade secret law—as long as the requirements for those forms of protection are met by some aspect of the software. As long as the software, or some feature thereof, satisfies the applicable requirements of a utility or design patent, it can be patented. *See generally Gottschalk v. Benson*, 409 U.S. 63 (1972); *Diamond v. Diehr*, 450 U.S. 175 (1981). Software code and user interfaces can also be copyrightable subject matter, as either a literary work or an audio-visual work. Finally, software can be maintained by a firm as a trade secret. *See, e.g., Justmed, Inc. v. Byce*, 600 F. 3d 1118 (9th Cir. 2010) (discussing trade secret protection for software code under Idaho law and under the Copyright Act). As this book goes to press, the Supreme Court has granted certiorari in *Oracle Am., Inc. v. Google LLC*, 886 F.3d 1179 (Fed. Cir. 2018), cert. granted, 2019 WL 6042317 (U.S. Nov. 15, 2019)(No. 18-956). One of the issues on which the Court granted certiorari involves the scope of copyright protection for a software interface.

Answer (A) is incorrect. As discussed above, all three listed forms of intellectual property protection are available for computer software.

Answer (B) is incorrect. As discussed above, all three listed forms of intellectual property protection are available for computer software.

Answer (C) is incorrect. As discussed above, all three listed forms of intellectual property protection are available for computer software.

Exam Answer 60. Answer (C) is correct. Under both the Uniform Trade Secrets Act and the federal Defend Trade Secrets Act, a trade secret is defined with reference to its economic value to its owner or holder. The absolute amount of that value is not the question—the value may be small—but economic value is nevertheless part of the definition of a trade secret. Under the UTSA, that definition is (with emphasis added):

> information, including a formula, pattern, compilation, program, device, method, technique, or process that:
>
> *derives independent economic value, actual or potential, from not being generally known to, and not being readily ascertainable by proper means by, other persons who can obtain economic value from its disclosure or use*; and
>
> is the subject of efforts that are reasonable under the circumstances to maintain its secrecy.

Uniform Trade Secrets Act § 1(4). Under federal law, a trade secret is now defined as:

> all forms and types of financial, business, scientific, technical, economic, or engineering information, including patterns, plans, compilations, program devices, formulas, designs, prototypes, methods, techniques, processes, procedures, programs, or codes, whether tangible or intangible, and whether or how stored, compiled, or memorialized physically, electronically, graphically, photographically, or in writing if—
>
> > (A) the owner thereof has taken reasonable measures to keep such information secret; and
> >
> > (B) *the information derives independent economic value, actual or potential, from not being generally known to, and not being readily ascertainable through proper means by, another person who can obtain economic value from the disclosure or use of the information.*

18 U.S.C. § 1839(3). The Restatement of Torts, which guided states before the UTSA, also included in its six non-exclusive factors the "value of the information to the business and its competitors." *See* Restatement of Torts § 757 cmt. b. These factors may still influence both any remaining non-UTSA states, such as New York, as well as courts interpreting the UTSA, *see, e.g., Minuteman, Inc. v. Alexander*, 434 N.W.2d 773 (Wis. 1989) (continuing to use the Restatement factors as a guide in interpreting the UTSA as enacted in Wisconsin).

Answer (A) is incorrect. Nowhere in the Patent Act is the value of the invention made part of the standard of patentability. Attention to value (and whether the invention, even if made exclusive through a patent, will have market value) is made the province of the inventor and patentee.

Answer (B) is incorrect. While a trademark owner will hope that the trademark creates value for it in the marketplace, there is no actual requirement that an owner prove economic or market value of the trademark before the mark can be protected.

Answer (D) is incorrect. See the explanation to correct Answer (C) above.

Exam Answer 61. If a work is published, in order for it to be assuredly in the public domain (without knowing additional information surrounding the publication), it must have been published 96 years ago. All copyright terms expire at the end of the calendar year rather than a precise number of years after the date of publication, *see* 17 U.S.C. § 305; this means that public domain status begins on January 1 of the next year. That rule plus the maximum term of 95 years for a work published under the duration rules of the 1909 Copyright Act means that a work must have been published 96 years earlier (i.e., in the year that is equal to the current year minus 96) in order to be assuredly in the public domain. The ability to refer to a period of years rather than a specific year of publication has been two decades in waiting. (The "life plus 70 years" terms will not begin to expire, for the works governed by modern copyright terms, for several more decades.)

For the first time in 20 years, on January 1, 2019, a group of published works protected under the terms provided in the 1909 Act entered the public domain; going forward, each January 1, additional copyrighted works will enter the public domain each year based on their year of first publication. Copyrighted works published in 1923 for which renewals had been timely filed entered the public domain in the United States on January 1, 2019 after the maximum term of 28 initial years plus the 67-year renewal (for a total maximum of 95 years) expired at the end of 2018. Works published in 1924 and timely renewed will enter the public domain on January 1, 2020; works published in 1925 will expire on January 1, 2021, and so forth.

Copyrights for works published before January 1, 1978 are governed by the Copyright Act of 1909, with extensions provided by later amendments, for a maximum of 95 years from publication (28-year initial term plus 67 years in the renewal term). Works published under the 1909 Act, which provided for renewal terms, can thus still be copyrighted as long as the copyright renewal was effectuated. (If a work was originally copyrighted between January 1, 1964, and December 31, 1977, a 1992 amendment made the renewal automatic.) Works published on or after January 1, 1978 are governed by the Copyright Act of 1976.

Before 2019, under U.S. copyright law, a work must have been published before 1923 in order for it to be assuredly in the public domain. Under the terms of the 1998 Sonny Bono Copyright Term Extension Act (CTEA), all copyright terms received an additional 20 years of copyright protection. The Act's extended terms included all works whose terms were governed by either the 1976 Act or the 1909 Act, but it did not "resurrect" protection for any work whose term had already expired. The 1998 CTEA therefore added an extra 20 years to the terms of works whose terms were set to expire at the end of 1998 at the end of their then-maximum terms of 28 initial years plus a 47-year renewal term (for a total maximum of 75 years). It did not add any years to those works whose terms had expired at the end of 1997 and which had therefore entered the public domain on January 1, 1998—which were the works that were first published during 1922 (1922 + 75 = 1997; term ends December 31, 1997). The CTEA's sudden addition of 20 years to the works published in 1923 and later is what created the 20-year gap in term expirations for published works whose terms were governed by the 1909 Act.

Exam Answer 62. The four typical requirements for enforcement of a covenants not to compete in employment settings are that the covenant: (1) must promote a legitimate interest of the employer; (2) must be reasonable in duration and scope; (3) must not unduly burden the employee; and (4) must not be contrary to public policy. Public policy considerations include whether the covenant creates a monopoly or interferes with other important public policies, such as the attorney-client or physician-patient relationship. *See* GARY MYERS, PRINCIPLES OF INTELLECTUAL PROPERTY LAW 448 (3d ed. 2017). Covenants not to compete related to the sale of a business are typically viewed favorably by the courts. On the other hand, courts often note that that employment non-compete agreements are disfavored under the law and narrowly construed; those same courts nevertheless tend to enforce them. A good reference for these issues would be the most recent edition of COVENANTS NOT TO COMPETE: A STATE-BY-STATE SURVEY (B. Malsberger ed., Bloomberg Law), which is a treatise compiled and regularly updated by the ABA Labor & Employment Section.

Exam Answer 63. Answer (C) is correct. The design shown above can best be protected under trademark law. Under the Lanham Act, trademarks:

> Include[ ] any word, name, symbol, or device, or any combination thereof—(1) used by a person, or (2) which a person has a bona fide intention to use in commerce and

applies to register on the principal register established by this chapter, to identify and distinguish his or her goods, including a unique product, from those manufactured or sold by others and to indicate the source of the goods, even if that source is unknown.

15 U.S.C. §1127. The "a with design" mark shown would be capable of operating as a source-indicating symbol for its user when applied to the website and shipping boxes and labels as indicated.

Answer (A) is incorrect. Copyright law does not necessarily protect brand names or basic symbols, although it might protect more complex design logos, visual depictions, or marketing materials. This design might or might not pass muster—it is so simple as to potentially not be "original" and be close to the line. The copyright office will not register, for example, names, titles, short phrases, typefaces, fonts, or lettering. *See* https://www.copyright.gov/circs/circ33.pdf. Given the additional facts provided, which include the manner of use of the design, trademark law is the more directly relevant form of intellectual property. It will protect the owner against happenstance similarity of marks that is likely to confuse consumers (trademark's infringement standard) as well as against substantial similarity that arises from copying (copyright's infringement standard).

Answer (B) is incorrect. Design patent law can be used to protect an "ornamental design for an article of manufacture." There is no one "article of manufacture" specified for this design. Moreover, design patent law requires novelty and nonobviousness, which are significant hurdles, and the period of exclusivity is only 15 years from issuance.

Answer (D) is incorrect. See the explanations above.

Exam Answer 64. In the pre-Copyright Act of 1976 case of *International News Service v. Associated Press*, 248 U.S. 215 (1918), the Supreme Court recognized a broad claim for unfair competition when a competitor appropriates current news stories from a news wire service for use in direct competition. The elements of a "hot news" claim of misappropriation under *INS v. AP* and its progeny have been summarized in the Second Circuit's opinion *National Basketball Association v. Motorola, Inc.*, 105 F.3d 841 (2d Cir. 1997). The court rejected a misappropriation claim brought by the National Basketball Association (NBA) against the manufacturer of a hand-held pager, which transmitted NBA basketball scores during games without authorization from the NBA. The court concluded that only a very limited "hot news" misappropriation claim survived preemption by the Copyright Act of 1976, 17 U.S.C. §301. The court identified five elements that must be shown in order to prove a "hot news" misappropriation claim: (1) the plaintiff generates or gathers information at some cost; (2) the information is time sensitive; (3) the defendant's use of the information constitutes free riding upon the plaintiff's investment; (4) the defendant is in direct competition with the plaintiff; and (5) the free rider problem will so reduce incentives to produce the information that its existence or quality of the information would be substantially threatened.

An important issue in state law misappropriation cases is whether and under what circumstances the claim is preempted by federal copyright law. Thus, for example, in *Barclays Capital Inc. v. The flyonthewall.com, Inc.*, 650 F.3d 876 (2d Cir. 2011), the court held that the plaintiffs, which were financial investment firms, could not succeed on a claim for "hot news" misappropriation of their investment recommendations against a news aggregator because their claim was preempted by federal copyright law: "Based upon principles explained and applied in *National Basketball Association v. Motorola, Inc.*, 105 F.3d 841 (2d Cir.1997), we conclude that because the plaintiffs' claim falls within the 'general scope' of copyright, 17 U.S.C. § 106, and involves the type of works protected by the Copyright Act, 17 U.S.C. §§ 102 and 103, and because the defendant's acts at issue do not meet the exceptions for a 'hot news' misappropriation claim as recognized by NBA, the claim is preempted." *Id.* at 878.

Exam Answer 65. Answer (C) is correct. Mask works and vessel hull designs receive *sui generis* protection under current federal law, but databases do not. Vessel hull designs (largely, boat hulls—but not only "boats") are protected under the Vessel Hull Design Protection Act of 1998, Title 17, Chapter 13 of the United States Code, which provides *sui generis* protection for original designs of vessel hulls. Semiconductor products, also known as mask works, receive protection under the Semi-Conductor Chip Protection Act of 1984, which protects original mask works and related semiconductor products that are registered with the Copyright Office. A mask work is a two- or three-dimensional layout or topography of an integrated circuit, i.e. the arrangement on a computer "chip" of various semiconductor devices (e.g., transistors and resistors). *See* Federal Statutory Protection for Mask Works, Circular 100, at copyright.gov/circs/circ100.pdf. *See* GARY MYERS, PRINCIPLES OF INTELLECTUAL PROPERTY LAW 465 (3d ed. 2017).

> **Answer (A) is incorrect.** Databases do not currently receive *sui generis* protection under U.S. intellectual property law. Although bills that have been regularly introduced in Congress to provide *sui generis* protection to the creators of databases, they have not been enacted thus far. Factual databases are eligible for protection in some foreign countries, for example, pursuant to the European Union's Database Directive. And in *Feist Publications, Inc. v. Rural Telephone Service Co.*, 499 U.S. 340 (1991), the Supreme Court concluded that copyright law does not protect laboriously gathered and maintained factual compilations if they do not possess a minimum level of creativity in their selection or arrangement. That means in light of *Feist*, many factual databases also do not qualify for copyright protection. See the above explanation for correct Answer (C) regarding mask works.

> **Answer (B) is incorrect.** As discussed above for incorrect Answer (A), databases do not currently receive *sui generis* protection under U.S. law. See the above explanation for correct Answer (C) regarding vessel hull designs.

> **Answer (D) is incorrect.** As discussed above for incorrect Answer (A), databases do not currently receive *sui generis* protection under U.S. law.

Exam Answer 66. Cybersquatting is the practice of registering a domain name or otherwise establishing an Internet presence making use, in bad faith, of well-established trademarks owned by others. This practice became very common with the advent of widespread use of the Internet in the 1990s. In early cases, trademark owners brought suit using traditional theories of trademark infringement and dilution. These cases were generally successful, but traditional trademark remedies were not completely effective because many infringing websites were located in countries outside the reach of U.S. law, which made enforcement of judgments difficult. Congress enacted the Anticybersquatting Consumer Protection Act of 1999 (the "ACPA"), which amended the federal trademark law to provide specific remedies designed to more effectively address the problem of cybersquatting. *See Sporty's Farm, L.L.C. v. Sportsman's Market, Inc.*, 202 F.3d 489 (2d Cir. 2000).

The ACPA added a new section 43(d) to the Lanham Act, 15 U.S.C. § 1125(d), with remedies for cybersquatting. The ACPA provides remedies against the bad faith registration, trafficking, or use of a domain name when the domain name dilutes a famous mark or is confusingly similar to the mark of another. "Bad faith" is a key element of the statute. *See* 15 U.S.C. § 1125(d)(1)(B) (providing nine nonexclusive factors for a court to consider in determining whether the defendant's registration, trafficking, or use of the domain name was done in "bad faith").

The primary remedies of the Lanham Act, injunctive relief and monetary damages, are available for violations of section 43(d), *see* 15 U.S.C. §§ 1116(a), 1117 (a), and 1125(d)(3). In addition, a court may also "order the forfeiture or cancellation of the domain name or the transfer of the domain name to the owner of the mark." 15 U.S.C. § 1125(d)(1)(C). The ACPA also created an *in rem* action that allows a trademark owner to proceed against the domain name itself even if the owner cannot locate or obtain *in personam* jurisdiction over the owner of the domain name for a more typical civil action. *See* 15 U.S.C. § 1125(d)(2).

Exam Answer 67. Answer (C) is correct. Courts were split on this issue until the unanimous Supreme Court held, in *Fourth Estate Public Benefit Corp. v. Wall-Street.com, LLC*, 139 S. Ct. 881 (2018), as follows:

> Impelling prompt registration of copyright claims, 17 U.S.C. § 411(a) states that "no civil action for infringement of the copyright in any United States work shall be instituted until … registration of the copyright claim has been made in accordance with this title." The question this case presents: Has "registration … been made in accordance with [Title 17]" as soon as the claimant delivers the required application, copies of the work, and fee to the Copyright Office; or has "registration … been made" only after the Copyright Office reviews and registers the copyright? We hold, in accord with the United States Court of Appeals for the Eleventh Circuit, that registration occurs, and a copyright claimant may commence an infringement suit, when the Copyright Office registers a copyright. Upon registration of the copyright, however, a copyright owner can recover for infringement that occurred both before and after registration.

The copyright statute anticipates the situation in which the Copyright Office rejects a duly filed application for copyright registration: "In any case, however, where the deposit, application, and fee required for registration have been delivered to the Copyright Office in proper form and registration has been refused, the applicant is entitled to institute a civil action for infringement if notice thereof, with a copy of the complaint, is served on the Register of Copyrights." 17 U.S.C. § 411(a).

There are exceptions to this general rule, as the Court noted in *Fourth Estate Public Benefit Corp.*, 139 S. Ct. at 888:

> In limited circumstances, copyright owners may file an infringement suit before undertaking registration. If a copyright owner is preparing to distribute a work of a type vulnerable to predistribution infringement — notably, a movie or musical composition — the owner may apply for preregistration. § 408(f)(2); 37 CFR § 202.16(b)(1) (2018). The Copyright Office will "conduct a limited review" of the application and

notify the claimant "[u]pon completion of the preregistration." § 202.16(c)(7), (c)(10). Once "preregistration ... has been made," the copyright claimant may institute a suit for infringement. 17 U. S. C. § 411(a). Preregistration, however, serves only as "a preliminary step prior to a full registration." Preregistration of Certain Unpublished Copyright Claims, 70 Fed. Reg. 42286 (2005). An infringement suit brought in reliance on pre-registration risks dismissal unless the copyright owner applies for registration promptly after the preregistered work's publication or infringement. § 408(f)(3)–(4). A copyright owner may also sue for infringement of a live broadcast before "registration ... has been made," but faces dismissal of her suit if she fails to "make registration for the work" within three months of its first transmission. § 411(c). Even in these exceptional scenarios, then, the copyright owner must eventually pursue registration in order to maintain a suit for infringement.

Answer (A) is incorrect. It is true that copyright protection exists from the moment of creation and fixation, and registration is not required for gaining copyright—but registration is not "optional" for the owner of a U.S. work who wishes to litigate the infringement of its rights. As discussed above, the Supreme Court has held that the plaintiff can file suit as soon as it receives a decision on its application for copyright registration with the United States Copyright Office.

Answer (B) is incorrect. As discussed above, the Supreme Court has held that the plaintiff can file suit as soon as it *receives a decision* on its application for copyright registration with the United States Copyright Office—not upon the filing of the application for registration.

Answer (D) is incorrect. As discussed above, the copyright plaintiff can file suit if its application is either granted (as the Court has recently held), or if it is rejected: "In any case, however, where the deposit, application, and fee required for registration have been delivered to the Copyright Office in proper form and registration has been refused, the applicant is entitled to institute a civil action for infringement if notice thereof, with a copy of the complaint, is served on the Register of Copyrights." 17 U.S.C. § 411(a).

Exam Answer 68. The test for determining whether a mark is deceptive under the Lanham Act was set forth by the Federal Circuit in *In re Budge Manufacturing Co.*, 857 F.2d 773, 775 (Fed. Cir. 1988) as follows: "(1) Is the term misdescriptive of the character, quality, function, composition or use of the goods? (2) If so, are prospective purchasers likely to believe that the misdescription actually describes the goods? (3) If so, is the misdescription likely to affect the decision to purchase?" *See also In re Spirits Int'l, N.V.*, 563 F.3d 1347 (Fed. Cir. 2009). Deceptive marks are precluded from trademark registration. 15 U.S.C. § 1052.

The third question within the Federal Circuit's test—whether the misdescription is likely to affect the decision to purchase—is a question of materiality, and it distinguishes the "deceptive" mark (under section 2(a)) from the "deceptively misdescriptive" mark (under section 2(e)(1)). If a mark's misdescription is not material to purchasers, and the mark is only "deceptively misdescriptive" but not "deceptive," the mark is potentially registrable after a period of use. Proof of acquired distinctiveness can be used to overcome the refusal to register, using section 2(f). *See* 15 U.S.C. § 1052(f). A truly deceptive mark is never registrable, however, regardless of length of the period of use and whether consumers have come to recognize the mark.

Exam Answer 69. Answer (A) is correct. The presence of the defendant's commercial or profit-making purpose weighs against fair use but is only one of the relevant factors. In *Campbell v. Acuff-Rose Music Inc.*, 510 U.S. 569 (1994), the Supreme Court held that a commercial purpose (such as selling CDs for profit) was not determinative of fair use and did not give rise to a presumption against fair use. The presumption against fair use for commercial uses was found in dictum in the earlier decision in *Sony Corp. v. Universal City Studios*, 464 U.S. 417 (1984), but the Court in *Campbell* specifically rejected the idea that such a presumption exists.

> **Answer (B) is incorrect.** As discussed above, the Court in *Campbell* specifically rejected the idea that such a presumption should be applied.

> **Answer (C) is incorrect.** The Court in *Campbell* also rejected the idea that a commercial use should be presumed to be harmful:

> > No "presumption" or inference of market harm that might find support in *Sony* is applicable to a case involving something beyond mere duplication for commercial purposes. *Sony*'s discussion of a presumption contrasts a context of verbatim copying of the original in its entirety for commercial purposes, with the noncommercial context of *Sony* itself (home copying of television programming). In the former circumstances, what Sony said simply makes common sense: when a commercial use amounts to mere duplication of the entirety of an original, it clearly "supersede[s] the objects" of the original and serves as a market replacement for it, making it likely that cognizable market harm to the original will occur. But when, on the contrary, the second use is transformative, market substitution is at least less certain, and market harm may not be so readily inferred. Indeed, as to parody pure and simple, it is more likely that the new work will not affect the market for the original in a way cognizable under this factor, that is, by acting as a substitute for it ("supersed[ing] [its] objects"). This is so because the parody and the original usually serve different market functions.

Campbell v. Acuff-Rose Music Inc., 510 U.S. 569, 591 (1994).

> **Answer (D) is incorrect.** As discussed above, a commercial purpose is a factor weighing against fair use in the overall balancing test.

Exam Answer 70. Answer (B) is correct. The reproduction of the portrait in the additional prints without authorization is a straightforward violation of the section 106 reproduction right in this case. The DMCA violation involves removing the copyright management information—the copyright notice—from the downloaded copy of the portrait:

> Removal or Alteration of Copyright Management Information.—No person shall, without the authority of the copyright owner or the law—

> (1) intentionally remove or alter any copyright management information,

> (2) distribute or import for distribution copyright management information knowing that the copyright management information has been removed or altered without authority of the copyright owner or the law, or

(3) distribute, import for distribution, or publicly perform works, copies of works, or phonorecords, knowing that copyright management information has been removed or altered without authority of the copyright owner or the law, knowing, or, with respect to civil remedies under section 1203, having reasonable grounds to know, that it will induce, enable, facilitate, or conceal an infringement of any right under this title.

17 U.S.C. §1202(b). Removing the copyright notice can violate this provision of the DMCA. "Copyright management information" includes the information in a copyright notice. 17 U.S.C. §1202(c).

Answer (A) is incorrect. As noted above in the explanation for Answer (B), there is also a potential violation of the DMCA on this set of facts.

Answer (C) is incorrect. On these facts, there was no distribution of copies to the public or public display of the work. It is important to recall that the 17 U.S.C. §106(3) and (5) rights (distribution and display) both require a "public" element; private distribution and private display do not violate the Act. The distribution right is the right "to distribute copies or phonorecords of the copyrighted work to the public by sale or other transfer of ownership, or by rental, lease, or lending," and the display right is the right "to display the copyrighted work publicly." Giving the unlawful copies of the portrait to the family members would not be a distribution "to the public," nor would the displays described in the question be displays made "publicly."

Answer (D) is incorrect. Ownership of the copy of the portrait does not excuse reproduction of the work or the potential DMCA violation. The facts do not state that the customer purchased the copyright. Ownership of a copy does not imply any rights in the copyright; these are separate concepts. *See* 17 U.S.C. §202.

Exam Answer 71. Answer (C) is correct. Both patent claims and federal copyright claims can only be brought in federal court (i.e., there is no concurrent state court jurisdiction). *See* 28 U.S.C. §1338(a). For Lanham Act claims, on the other hand, there is concurrent state court jurisdiction. *Id.*

Answer (A) is incorrect. As noted above, federal courts have original and exclusive jurisdiction over both patent and copyright claims.

Answer (B) is incorrect. As noted above, federal courts have original and exclusive jurisdiction over both patent and copyright claims.

Answer (D) is incorrect. As noted above, federal courts have original and exclusive jurisdiction over both patent and copyright claims.

Exam Answer 72. Answer (B) is correct. A patent owner who imposes a tying arrangement on customers who purchase its patented product (requiring that they also purchase a second, unpatented product) is likely to have committed patent misuse if the patent owner has market power. This is a classic illustration of a situation in which patent misuse can be asserted. In light of amendments in the Patent Misuse Reform Act of 1988, market power must be shown to establish misuse on grounds of tying:

No patent owner otherwise entitled to relief for infringement or contributory infringe-ment of a patent shall be denied relief or deemed guilty of misuse or illegal extension of the patent right by reason of his having done one or more of the following: ... (5) conditioned the license of any rights to the patent or the sale of the patented product on the acquisition of a license to rights in another patent or purchase of a separate product, unless, in view of the circumstances, the patent owner has market power in the relevant market for the patent or patented product on which the license or sale is conditioned.

35 U.S.C. §271(d).

Answer (A) is incorrect. On these facts, there is possible misuse but not waiver.

Answer (C) is incorrect. As noted above, market power must be shown to prove misuse by tying.

Answer (D) is incorrect. This doctrine does not apply to this set of facts.

Exam Answer 73. Answer (A) is correct. If a home appliance manufacturer wished to obtain trade-mark protection for a particular shade of orange (standing alone) for use on its coffee makers, this orange color would most likely be found protectable after secondary meaning is shown, because the color orange is not inherently distinctive. The shade of orange does not appear to serve an aes-thetically functional or other (utilitarian) functional purpose as to coffee makers and thus can re-ceive trademark protection upon a showing of secondary meaning. *See Qualitex Co. v. Jacobson Products Co.*, 514 U.S. 159 (1995) (color marks are protectable if non-functional and if they develop secondary meaning).

Answer (B) is incorrect. In light of *Qualitex*, a mark consisting of a color standing alone must have secondary meaning to be protected. This is true even if there is no particular reason to choose that color for the product in question, making the color choice somewhat "arbitrary" for the product. The legal analysis of colors simply does not follow the *Abercrombie* spectrum of generic-descriptive-suggestive-arbitrary. All situations where a color standing alone is claimed to be the mark are treated as non-inherently distinctive (meaning the color of the prod-uct itself, as with the Qualitex green-gold color of dry cleaning press pads, or the Owens-Corn-ing pink color of fiberglass insulation).

Answer (C) is incorrect. As noted above, the facts do not give any indication that the shade of orange serves an aesthetic or other functional purpose as to coffee makers.

Answer (D) is incorrect. As noted above, under *Qualitex* even a single color can be a trademark in the proper circumstances.

Exam Answer 74. Answer (A) is correct. Independent creation of the accused work, meaning that the accused infringer had no access to the copyright owner's protected work, is a complete defense to a claim of copyright infringement. *See, e.g., Arnstein v. Porter*, 154 F.2d 464 (2d Cir. 1946) (ex-plaining that proof of copying, either by direct evidence or circumstantial evidence consisting of access and striking similarity, is required before the question of unlawful appropriation will be addressed).

Answer (B) is incorrect. Independent creation, invention, or development is not a defense to patent infringement, standing alone. The AIA did create a the good-faith prior user defense for "a process, or consisting of a machine, manufacture, or composition of matter used in a manufacturing or other commercial process" if (with certain other requirements) the accused infringer's good faith, commercial use began at least a year before the effective filing date of the claimed invention (or its public disclosure as set forth in section 102(b)). *See* 35 U.S.C. § 273(a). A good-faith prior use defense is not, however, the same as an independent creation defense; however, independent creation might be a factor in the defense, since an accused infringer is barred from raising the defense if "the subject matter on which the defense is based was *derived from the patentee or persons in privity with the patentee.*" 35 U.S.C. § 273(e)(2).

Answer (C) is incorrect. Independent creation could show that an accused trademark infringer acted in good faith, or without intent to confuse consumers, but the accused infringer's intent or bad faith is but one of many factors considered in the likelihood of confusion analysis. *See, e.g., Polaroid Corp. v. Polarad Electronics Corp.*, 287 F.2d 492, 495 (2d Cir. 1961). It is not determinative.

Answer (D) is incorrect. Independent creation is a defense to a claim of copyright infringement.

Exam Answer 75. Answer (D) is correct. As explained below, none of the listed options would apply on these facts.

Answer (A) is incorrect. The facts do not indicate that the designer extended any kind of offer to the game fan he could accept by word or action, and indeed it appears that the game fan provided information to the designer entirely of his own accord, without any invitation by the designer. *See, e.g., Smith v. Recrion Corp.*, 541 P.2d 663 (Nev. 1975) (explaining that even when related to the disclosure of an idea, a contract requires an exchange of promises (even if implied via conduct rather than expressly in words) and mutual intent to enter into a contract). Moreover, the designer's statement, "Sounds fun — I hope it gets made — I'll see what I can do to get you in touch with the right people," even if it were a promise of compensation specific enough for enforcement (which it is not), came *after* the game fan's disclosure and would generally be unenforceable for lack of consideration. *See id.* Another useful case to consider might be *Baer v. Chase*, 392 F.3d 609 (3d Cir. 2004) (rejecting, for lack of definiteness, a contract-based claim related to disclosure of ideas to the producer and writer of "The Sopranos," and also rejecting a misappropriation claim for lack of novelty of the ideas).

Answer (B) is incorrect. The facts do not support a claim of trade secret misappropriation. It is true that the game fan only initially disclosed his game concept to a limited number of friends, and he disclosed it to them under a promise of secrecy, which should mean that he maintained the information in secrecy with reasonable efforts up to the time of his disclosure to the designer. *See* Uniform Trade Secrets Act (UTSA) § 1(4). More important, however, on these facts, is that even if this were otherwise trade-secret information up to that time, the game fan did not reasonably maintain the information as a secret when he voluntarily provided his ideas and information to the game designer on the flight without any advance promises of confidentiality from her. *See id.* And because he freely provided the information to her, the designer's future use of the information was not misappropriation — she did not acquire the information "under circumstances giving rise to a duty to maintain its secrecy or limit its use," via a breach of confidence by another, or through improper means. *See* UTSA § 1(2).

Answer (C) is incorrect. The facts do not support a claim of unjust enrichment — even if the idea had been very detailed and "novel," the designer and company in no way requested the disclosure and had no prior relationship with the game fan. A classic case outlining the features of such a claim is *Matarese v. Moore-McCormack Lines, Inc.*, 158 F.2d 631 (2d Cir. 1946). As explained in that case, unjust enrichment, or recovery in "quasi contract," applies where courts find a party to be in possession of money or property that is "unjustly" benefiting that party at the expense of the other — and the court imposes a duty on the party in possession to deliver the money or property to the other party. In the "idea" situations, the *Matarese* court states, "The doctrine is applicable to a situation where, as here, the product of an inventor's brain is knowingly received and used by another to his own great benefit without compensating the inventor." The court goes on, however, to note that courts must be careful to differentiate between true cases of unjust enrichment and "spurious claims for compensation for the use of ideas." In *Matarese*, the court noted that the plaintiff could demonstrate unjust enrichment as a result of "the relationship between the parties before and after the disclosure, the seeking of disclosure by [an employee of the defendant company], [that employee's] promise of compensation [albeit without contractual effect], the specific character, novelty, and patentability of plaintiff's invention, the subsequent use of it made by defendants, and the lack of compensation given the plaintiff."

Index

Topic	Question